EFFECTIVE POLICE
SUPERVISION

Administration of Justice Series
   Harry W. More, Jr., Series Editor

CONTEMPORARY CRIMINAL JUSTICE
  Harry W. More, Jr. and Richard Chang
  Editors, San Jose State University

EFFECTIVE POLICE ADMINISTRATION: A Behavioral Approach
  Harry W. More, Jr., Editor
  San Jose State University

CRIMINAL JUSTICE PLANNING: A Practical Approach
  Michael E. O'Neill, Ronald F. Bykowski and Robert S. Blair

THE CHANGING POLICE ROLE: New Dimensions and New Issues
  Roy R. Roberg
  University of Nebraska

EFFECTIVE POLICE SUPERVISION: A Behavioral Approach
  George T. Felkenes
  University of Alabama in Birmingham

EFFECTIVE POLICE SUPERVISION

a behavioral approach

George T. Felkenes

JUSTICE SYSTEMS DEVELOPMENT, INC.
SAN JOSE, CALIFORNIA

© 1977, by Justice Systems Development, Inc.

All rights reserved. Published 1977

ISBN 0-914526-06-5

Library of Congress Card Number: 76-62531

Published by:
Justice Systems Development, Inc.
P.O. Box 23884
San Jose, California 95153

Printed in the United States of America

DEDICATION

To My
Mother and Father

Contents

Preface

Supervision of personnel encompasses much more than mechanical application of the classic rules by which leaders and supervisors are too often selected. While this book has a primary orientation to police supervision, the materials can be applied to any criminal justice organization. The reader will be exploring the human side of the criminal justice organization.

This is not a "have-to" presentation on the skills and techniques possessed by a supervisor. There are no dozen or so rules that guarantee success and which solve all the problems in supervision. The author has selected the articles and prepared the introduction to assist the student in gaining a greater insight and sensitivity to the needs of individuals including the supervisor himself. By this approach the supervisor's relationship to the organization will be sharpened and his ability to make effective decisions both on and off the job will be increased.

Many of those who read this book will not be looking for information that is all theoretical; many will want to read and understand the practical, real-world problems. This book is not excessively theoretical nor is it totally practical in its approach. It is not aimed at the top managers. It is not incomprehensible. I hope that it is a text-reader that stresses the behavioral aspects of human relations while still combined with the problems of the real world.

Some who read this book are not supervisors; some will be shortly; some will never be; and some now are. Whatever the situation, if you are employed or will be employed by an agency, the responsibilities you have as a subordinate of working with individuals and getting along with the people can be viewed from the eyes of the supervisor. Human relation both within and outside the work setting is everyone's responsibility. In this light the book will help the patrolman and husband, policewoman and wife, supervisor, records clerk, probation officer and all of those working in a criminal justice setting. After all, every person has an interest in becoming more sensitive to human behavior, anticipating problems, and offering solutions if they develop.

One final comment concerns the selection of the articles and their various approaches to the police supervisory problems. They are indeed diverse and were selected because they have something to say about police organizations from a humanistic supervisory viewpoint. They do not tell you how a job is to be accomplished, but they do point out the problems that one is likely to encounter and offer a solution to the problems. The articles are understandable and are not overly complex. They should not "turn off" the student. Rather they provide the student and instructor with a common ground upon which supervisory problems can be discussed in a learning situation.

The reader will also notice that each part of the book has an introduction which briefly reviews some of the more complex behavioral aspects of supervision discussed in succeeding articles. I hope it assists you by providing a theoretical basis for what follows.

Supervision and its behavioral underpinnings are fascinating. Let's begin its study.

George T. Felkenes

Acknowledgments

My research assistant, Mr. Burt Butler contributed diligently and exceptionally to the preparation of this book. His work was always prompt and professionally done. I am grateful to him. My appreciation also goes to Mrs. Sharon Vacarella who read the manuscript and offered her suggestions. Valuable contributions were also received from Dr. C. Allen Graves, Dr. Calvin Swank and Mr. Wayne Smith, University of Alabama in Birmingham. I thank them. Dean George Passey also deserves acknowledgment for his encouragement of this project. Mrs. Pat Riley and Mrs. Barbara Smith responded beyond the call of duty when typing the manuscript on short notice. Lastly, my wife, Sandra deserves a special commendation for moral support that I needed in completing this manuscript.

I am also grateful to those for whom I have worked throughout my career. I have learned much from them—whether good or bad!

George T. Felkenes
Birmingham, Alabama
December 1976

PART 1

OPERATING IN AN ORGANIZATIONAL SETTING

The Study of this Part Will Enable You to:

1. Develop a working definition and understanding of the supervisory concept in relation to the organization.

2. Examine the police organization and stresses it places on the individual.

3. Provide insights into what may be expected of the supervisor's career in a police agency.

4. Discuss certain concepts of organization structure that shape police organizational thinking.

5. Distinguish between the formal and informal aspects of organizations.

6. Introduce the effects that education may have on the supervisory job in a police department.

7. Discuss the effects that police unions have on professionalization in the police service.

8. Examine the problems that a supervisor must face because of the newly emerging militancy among the police ranks.

9. Understand the various conflicting pressures found in the supervisor's job.

10. Investigate the organizational and supervisory disciplinary problems which may result from unionization of police officers.

Introduction

Police departments are complex organizations. Even the smallest of police agencies must provide a wide range of services requiring highly specialized skills from numerous people. The larger and more complex the organization, the greater the number of functions to be performed. The sheer volume of operations then requires the services of more and more specialists in field operations as well as administration. American police agencies deal with the entire span of the population, young and old, rich and poor, black and white, and everyone in-between. The police are committed to the crime fighting concept but nevertheless respond to the ever increasing demand for more services.

As a consequence, the police organization has had to develop a correspondingly more complex set of organization patterns. The police supervisor needs to understand the nature of this change in the organization while endeavoring to identify both the supervisory position role as well as that of co-workers and staff in the larger scheme of operations in the department.

The new supervisor first needs to have an adequate working attitude toward himself if he expects to become a leader. He should never think of himself as a person who has been chosen from lower ranks, despite personal protestations, and thrust into a supervisory capacity. If he does not think of himself in this way, he will not talk to himself this way, and thus will save his critics the opportunity of listening to what they already believe. He should not feel sorry for himself; he can always resign. Neither can he precisely say he sought and loves to be a supervisor because this runs counter to the commonly accepted peer evaluation that the only good supervisors are those who were forced into the position. The new supervisor need not be forced to choose between feigned willingness and total eagerness when questioned for reasons for becoming a supervisor. He can proudly believe that he is in the job, and say that he is, simply because the job or some aspects of it, correspond to certain elements within himself. Privately he can live with the fact that there are numerous, often conflicting reasons why he wants to be a supervisor. Others can make up their own minds what the reasons are. In this way there is an accounting for the fact that jobs and suitable incumbents do come together without an unseemly forcing of an unwilling man, or an unseemly pursuit by an overwilling man.

Once the supervisor understands himself in the job, he needs an acceptable attitude toward the working of the job and his involvement in it. He needs to avoid cliches about accepting challenges and other rationalizations for wanting the position. He cannot permit himself to think that he is a facilitation "yes-man," or a "leg-man," for the department. No first-rate supervisor or potential administrator thinks of himself as one who simply translates the wishes of others into deeds. He does, however, accept such roles because he does chores and executes group decisions. At the other extreme the first line supervisor should not think of himself as essentially a big policy man, an idea man, or a man who looks at the big picture and leaves the details to others. As a matter-of-fact, a great deal of policy is made by the simple effective performance of one's duties. The supervisor's way of handling the routine matters may do more to create an attitude of acceptance by his subordinates than all of the various platitudes about the difficulty of the job. In sum, the supervisor should not act like the little man who is waiting to be told what to do or like a big man who only makes big decisions and then tells others what to do. The supervisor should be prepared for the mundane, and at the same time find in the organizational machinery within which he lives, the devices and techniques by which he gradually moves the organizational affairs in a more favorable direction. Thus his superiors and subordinates may come to discover that there are new and better ways of doing things.

The supervisor must not think of his post as one without power—indeed, he can find numerous ways to exercise it. Power is not inherently evil as some seem to suggest in philosophizing about it. It is, in reality, inherently neutral. Almost all men enjoy it. Thus the new supervisor should understand it and use it judiciously to achieve the ends in which he is interested. Frequently he can use it to adjust inequities that exist for myriad reasons. For instance the police supervisor can exercise his power by providing rewards for jobs well done—especially those jobs which to him are beneficial to the organization. One of the chief satisfactions for a supervisor is the steering of perquisites to persons who contribute to the well-being of the organization (even though these may be persons who are not particularly well-loved). The supervisor must balance the possession of power with the knowledge that power corrupts. This knowledge may however offer an exciting challenge in the supervisor's role. He may unwittingly deceive himself over the exercise of power, but the natural alertness of his superiors and subordinates will quickly help correct the situation. In this way the supervisor can count on their moral energy to keep him appraised of any abnormal deviations. In addition to peer oversight, the supervisor has an even more sound way of monitoring his exercise of power: self audit. By this he performs every act and makes his decisions as if he were going to be audited by his supervisor or a special departmental investigative committee. An attitude of this kind by the supervisor is to be commended. However, in rare instances the supervisor must act on instinct and intuition and take a calculated risk by relying on either evidence of an undetermined quality or not even in existence. He will have to bull his way through an audit if there is one, and hope that the ultimate auditor—history—will prove him to be correct.

The supervisor has to operate in an area fraught with the uncertainty of competing attitudes—the one of the superior and the other of his subordinates. On occasions the higher-ups will think of him as a disturber of their peace and the aggressive agent of his malcontented subordinates. The subordinates will think of him as the complete taskmaster who is the puppet of the higher-ups. If the supervisor antagonizes either side unbearably, he will not be able to function in a supervisory capacity, and since part of his business is to survive, he may sometimes give the appearance of duplicity. However, despite the pressures from below and above, he has a rather wide range of choices upon which he may act. For one thing the department will not fire him unless he acts completely outrageously. After all he has been selected as a supervisor by a series of competitive tests, and he was one of the top candidates. The subordinates may like to place a fire under the supervisor, but they do not wish to see him incinerated—especially since the incumbent supervisor may be better than a new one of unknown quality.

A second choice for the supervisor is to pit the superiors (i.e. department administration) against the subordinates. He may tell both that the other won't stand for it, be it an ill-advised ruling from above or an excessive privilege seized from below. Occasionally this is an appropriate tactic, but it is dangerous because it implies slight-of-hand or tricky foot-work neither of which is healthy.

The supervisor cannot always take a partisan position or he will be immobilized. On the other hand he can not play it mechanically one way now and another way later. If this occurs he becomes too mobile and will lose the trust of the administration and the subordinates.

The new supervisor is fresh from the ranks and may still be a shadow of "infallability of the working officer!" As a new supervisor he may even be surprised that the departmental administration is not as ineffective and inefficient as he previously thought.

The supervisor initially needs to consider his own attitude to the kind of direction his unit should take. Sometimes he must act as a counter-balance between his workers and his superiors. He may feel obligated to resist higher-ups who constantly infringe on his responsibilities as a supervisor, but he must tread lightly because he may be resisting legitimately sought change. He must realize that the organization is a constantly changing organism which seeks to move forward to achieve its goals. If he stands in the way of this change without good and sufficient reasons, he risks losing whatever effectiveness he has. On the other hand the supervisor needs to realize that within the unit he leads, change may be an obligation on his part. He must not be deluded by the idea that all innovation is salvation. In his particular department it may be, but that is to be decided in each case. In general, however, change is not obligatory; what is in style at one time may be neither useful nor practical at another time. Fads need to be viewed with a suspicious eye—even when some are induced by national authorities and professional organizations. The central questions before changes are made is the efficacy of the change in improving the operations of the supervisor's unit and ultimately the entire organization.

Probably the most important aspect of the supervisor's job is to discover a manageable attitude toward the human beings he must supervise. He is much better off if he is more curious than censorious. The supervisor can be surprised rather than outraged. As the supervisor, he is more exposed than anyone else, to the self-seeking aims of his colleagues. He is constantly exposed to an unsteady sense of reality, to the longing for special privileges, to the malingerer, the ill-tempered, the disruptive, the petty, and the undependable, to name just a few. He will be expected to provide a satisfactory response to complaints about patrol vehicles, office space, typewriters, work schedules, parking problems, the distance to toilets, and similar problems. Some subordinates will be at odds with each and every decision which is made, and today there are the ever-growing complaints received, based on various grounds involving personal freedom.

In this last area, the supervisor becomes deeply involved with the complex behavior of subordinates. Sometimes the supervisor will run into an honest, compassionate and open subordinate to whom he will do well to listen. This man's perceptiveness of the things affecting his job may stimulate the supervisor to a sharper awareness that he has never had before. He needs stimuli of this kind. The supervisor must realize however that when complex behaviors come into consideration, motives rather than love of justice are often at work.

Causes attract plotters. Most lovers of causes need facades behind which to operate. A cause keeps things stirred up by arousing opposition within the organization. The supervisor is faced with a difficult and trying problem when this kind of situation arises in the unit. Compared to all the other competent hardworking persons in his unit, the cause-espouser will tax his charity, ingenuity, and take most of his time. Here the supervisor may assume a posture of half-hero, half-coward. As a half-hero he will work himself up to facing difficulties and crises from which he might prefer to turn his eyes. As a half-coward he will be saved from taking on all the problems of the world. For there is much, both problems and persons, that he must live with. Unless he wants to practice a form of behavior therapy full time, the supervisor cannot do much about the nagger, the non-stop objector, nor the cause espouser. He will have to endure some things that may be irritations. Beyond this he can still effectively guide the unit in a manner to assure achievement of the unit and departmental goals.

While the difficulties of being a supervisor are many, there are numerous rewards. To describe these satisfactions let us return to the beginning of this introduction. One seldom gets into the position of being a supervisor unless it corresponds to some element of his own being, however defined, and it is satisfying to have that element fulfilled. Once again there is the satisfaction of using power, however limited, to worthwhile ends. Additionally, one should never underestimate the value of simply keeping things operating in an orderly manner. When higher-ups, such as the department chief or commanders of major police operations, complain about lower supervisors, their complaints are not over such issues as uninventiveness or lack of imagination, but concern the failure to accomplish the routine in an orderly manner. If a supervisor prevents things from moving in a rearward direction, he has cause for pleasure. If he is lucky, there may even be some forward movement. While many top administrators profess a lack of confidence in the efficacy of change it is entirely rational that the administrator and supervisor experience pleasure when it is accomplished. If the supervisor is a master of innovation let him look in its spotlight. If he can give a nudge to improving the quality of things, let him relish his accomplishment. However, the supervisor's greatest satisfaction may not be so much what he does—rather what he perceptibly is. He may be the ideal image for the unit rather than merely the image of it. His unit will tend in some degree to become what he is, and knowing this, he may grow into the part, thereby giving a sense of direction and movement to the unit. He has the opportunity to reflect his unit in its best professional and noblest light.

THE POLICEMAN'S OCCUPATIONAL PERSONALITY*

In the last few years a great deal has been written about the police mentality. If we can believe everything we read in magazines, journals, and sociology books, the typical policeman is cynical, suspicious, conservative, and thoroughly bigoted. This is not a flattering picture to be sure, but it recurs again and again in the popular and "scientific" literature on the police. Perhaps there is something about the police system itself that generates a suspicious, conservative world-view. Or perhaps certain personality types are inadvertently recruited for police work. Either explanation is plausible, and both may be correct. Unfortunately only a few writers have bothered with the most basic question of all: Is there really a model police personality? At one time most white Americans thought blacks were superstitious tap dancers who preferred watermelon to work. Could it be that we have stereotyped policemen in the same way? The following pages will examine the controversy over the police mentality and suggest a sociological alternative to current speculation about the nature of police personalities.

The Police Personality As It Appears in the Literature

Although authors vary in emphasis, there is remarkable agreement on the characteristics believed to make up the police mentality. The

*SOURCE: Robert W. Balch, "The Police Personality: Fact or Fiction," *The Journal of Criminal Law, Criminology and Police Science*, Vol. 63, No. 1, March 1972, 106-119. Reprinted with permission of the publisher.

cluster of traits that consistently emerges includes suspicion, conventionality, cynicism, prejudice, and distrust of the unusual. The traits are poorly defined and the names vary, but the syndrome is always the same.

Policemen are supposed to be very suspicious characters. A good policeman is always on the lookout for the unusual: persons visibly rattled in the presence of policemen, people wearing coats on hot days, cars with mismatched hubcaps, and so on.[1] A good policeman presumably suspects evil wherever he goes. As Buckner put it, "Once the commonplace is suspect, no aspect of interaction is safe, on or off duty."[2]

According to Colin MacInness, suspicion is simply a manifestation of deep-seated political and emotional conservatism.

> The true copper's dominant characteristic, if the truth be known, is neither those daring nor vicious qualities that are sometimes attributed to him by friend or enemy, but an ingrained conservatism, an almost desperate love of the conventional. It is untidiness, disorder, the unusual, that a copper disapproves of most of all: far more, even than of crime which is merely a professional matter. Hence his profound dislike of people loitering in streets, dressing extravagantly, speaking with exotic accents, being strange, weak, eccentric, or simply any rare minority—of their doing, in fact, anything that cannot be safely predicted.[3]

Furthermore, policemen supposedly have no faith in their fellow man. Most are firmly convinced that only the police stand between a tenuous social order and utter chaos.

> The people I see in the streets and in trouble are the same people who just a little while before that were in their nice homes and not involved in trouble. You can't fool me. I see people in the raw, the way they really are. Underneath their fine, civilized manners and clothes they're animals.[4]

If people in general are no good, then "coons" and "spics" are worse. All they like to do is drink, make love, and collect their welfare checks: "These scum aren't people; they're animals in a jungle . . . Hitler had the right idea."[5] Even many black officers share this outlook:

> There have always been jobs for Negroes, but the f------- people are too stupid to go out and get an education. They all want the easy way out. Civil Rights has gotten them nothin' they didn't have before.[6]

Several other traits are frequently but less consistently used to describe the typical policeman. Police officers supposedly distrust ivory-tower intellectuals and bleeding-heart humanitarians. A good policeman is a realist who learns by experience and not by reading books. He respects authority and knows how to take orders. He likes to give orders too, and he demands respect from juveniles, criminals, and minorities. If necessary he will use force to see that he gets it. Brutality is perhaps the most infamous feature of the policeman's reputation:

> A common thread of inhumanity runs through policemen in every city across the land. The potential for brutality is always there. Some psychologists say that this is the character trait that draws them to police work in the first place. . . . In too many cops the beast still slumbers, ready to enjoy another bout of sadism. . . .[7]

Interestingly enough, the cluster of traits that apparently make up the police personality also defines authoritarianism.[8] Consider the parallels between the so-called police mentality and the following dimensions of the F-Scale:

1. Conventionalism: rigid adherence to conventional, middle-class values.
2. Authoritarian Submission: submissive, uncritical attitude toward idealized moral authorities of the ingroup.
3. Authoritarian Aggression: tendency to be on the lookout for, and to condemn, reject, and punish people who violate conventional values.
4. Anti-intraception: opposition to the subjective, the imaginative, the tender-minded.
5. Superstition and Stereotypy: the belief in mystical determinants of the individual's fate; the disposition to think in rigid categories.
6. Power and "toughness": preoccupation with the dominance-submission, strong-weak, leader-follower dimension; identification with power figures; overemphasis upon the conventionalized attributes of the ego; exaggerated assertion of strength and toughness.
7. Destructiveness and Cynicism: generalized hostility, vilification of the human.
8. Projectivity: The disposition to believe that wild and dangerous things go on in the world; the projection outwards of unconscious emotional impulses.
9. Sex: Exaggerated concern with sexual "goings-on."

Only superstition, apparently, has never been used to describe policemen. Otherwise the dimensions of authoritarianism seem to describe police officers very well. In fact, the typical policeman, as he is portrayed in the literature, is almost a classic example of the authoritarian personality.

Is There Really a Police Personality?

While many writers assume as a matter of course that there is a police personality, the empirical evidence is less than convincing. Unfortunately good data are hard to come by. In one study the authors compared the authoritarianism of policemen with a partially matched sample of nonpolice students.[9] Both police and nonpolice subjects were attending the John Jay College of Criminal Justice at the time. Using Rokeach and Piven scales, they found the policemen were considerably *less* authoritarian than the other students. At a glance these results cast doubt on the so-called police personality, but in fact they cannot be interpreted so easily. In the first place, the nonpolice students cannot be equated with the general population because as many as 25 percent of them said they were "completely committed" to a career in police work. Second, the non-police students were still less authoritarian than a sample of noncollege policemen in a previous study by the same authors.[10]

The preliminary results of a recent study[11] using the Edwards Personal Preference Schedule indicate there are significant differences between police recruits and nonpolice college students, but the differences are not necessarily consistent with the authoritarian stereotype of policemen. The recruits were more likely to believe in the value of punishment, and they received significantly higher scores on the dimensions of deference and orderliness. They also appeared to be far less independent than the college students, and they were less likely to prefer new experiences. On the other hand, the recruits did not differ from the college students on three dimensions which are closely related to authoritarianism: aggression, nurturance, and intraception. The recruits also scored lower on the dimension of heterosexuality which belies Niederhoffer's claim that policemen are preoccupied with sexual matters.[12]

Another study undertook extensive psychiatric assessment of 116 applicants for the Portland Police Department.[13] All the applicants had passed their mental and physical exams, so, before the program of psychological testing began, they would have become officers as vacancies occurred. The authors administered a variety of psychological tests including the Edwards Personal Preference Schedule, Strong Vocational Interest Blank, and the Minnesota Multiphasic Personality Inventory. They concluded that the typical police applicant was very similar to the average male college student. Of course it is entirely possible that a unique police personality develops *after* recruits have spent some time on the job. Unfortunately there has been no follow-up study of the Portland recruits.

There are studies of experienced policemen in other cities, but they have not used the same personality scales. Bayley and Mendelsohn,[14] for example, administered an extensive questionnaire to a sample of Denver policemen. The questionnaire included items designed to measure anomie, authoritarianism, prejudice, and social distance. Using Srole's five-item F-Scale as their measure of authoritarianism, they found that Denver policemen scored lower than control populations sampled in previous studies. Their conclusion is worth repeating. Since their sample consisted of experienced policemen, the evidence also does not support the belief that a particular personality develops after joining the force.

In a study of the New York Police Department, McNamara used the original F-Scale to measure the authoritarianism of recruits in the police academy.[15] The recruits' mean F-score was virtually the same as the mean for working-class males found by Adorno and his colleagues. If we define "working class" as skilled, semi-skilled, and service work, then between 60 and 70 percent of the recruits in the New York Police Department come from working-class homes.[16] Therefore, McNamara's findings suggests that police recruits are typical of the class from which they are drawn. But since socio-economic status is inversely related to authoritarianism,[17] it is also ʾrue that working-class men, and therefore policemen, are more authoritarian than most. The McNamara study has to be taken with a grain of salt, however, because McNamara did not compare his recruits with a contemporary sample of working-class men in New York. Not only had many years elapsed since Adorno and his colleagues completed their study, but their working-class sample was selected on the West Coast.

McNamara also found evidence of increasing authoritarianism over a period of time. He re-tested the recruits at the end of their first year and discovered a slight increase in their mean F-score. He also compared the recruits with men who had served on the force for two years. The more experienced policemen had the highest authoritarianism scores of all. A very liberal interpretation of McNamara's data suggests the following conclusion: Police departments do not attract particular personalities, but instead tend to recruit members from a relatively authoritarian class of people. Furthermore, the police experience itself intensifies authoritarianism. It must be emphasized, however, that this conclusion is tenuous, and certainly is not consistent with Bayley and Mendelsohn's findings.

Although not concerned with personality *per se*, a study by Toch and Schulte suggests that policemen may perceive violence more readily than others.[18] They compared a group of advanced police administration students with two control groups—one consisting of introductory psychology students and the other of first year police administration students. All subjects were shown nine stereograms for a half second each. One figure in each stereogram depicted an act of violence or crime, while the other, matched in size and outline, showed some nonviolent "neutral" activity. The average number of violent percepts was the same for the two control groups, but the advanced police administration students perceived roughly twice as many violent scenes. Because the first year police administration students did not differ significantly from the psychology students, the authors concluded that police training increases one's readiness to perceive violence.

It is widely believed that policemen are prejudiced against minority groups. For example, Black and Reiss concluded[19] that 72 percent of the policemen they observed in Boston, Chicago, and Washington, D.C., were prejudiced against Negroes. Observers rode or walked with officers for eight hours a day, six days a week, for seven weeks in 1966. Officers were classified as "highly prejudiced" when they "referred to Negroes as subhuman, suggested an extreme solution to the 'Negro problem,' expressed dislike to the point of hatred, or used very pejorative nicknames when speaking of Negroes."[20] Officers were classified as "prejudiced" if they "simply showed general dislike for Negroes as a group." On the other hand, Black and Reiss did not find that verbal expressions of prejudice were translated into discriminatory behavior. Police behavior was "obviously prejudiced" in only 2 percent of the cases and showed "some signs" of prejudice in only 6 percent. Moreover, whites were targets of police discrimination more often than blacks. Apparently, aggressive discriminatory police behavior was a response to the citizen's demeanor rather than his race. Skolnick[21] came to a similar conclusion when he observed the behavior of warrant officers on the Oakland police force.

The Black and Reiss data are not easy to interpret, however. Their "highly prejudiced" category could have been inflated by including officers who used "pejorative nicknames." As Skolnick points out, many officers use derogatory nicknames even when they are not extremely prejudiced:

The policeman's culture is that of the masculine workingman. It is of the docks, the barracks, the ballfield—Joe Di Maggio was a helluva good 'wop" centerfielder, not an athlete of 'Italian extraction,' and similarly, the black man is a 'nigger," not a member of an 'under-privileged minority.'[22]

Black and Reiss also failed to employ a control group, so there is no way of assessing what their percentages mean. Skolnick, for instance, admits that policemen are prejudiced, but he does not believe they are any more so than the average white workingman.

In their study of the Denver Police Department, Bayley and Mendelsohn[23] also concluded that policemen simply share the prejudices of the community as a whole. Responses to simple prejudice and social distance scales were not greatly different from those given by a sample of white Denver citizens. In fact, neither the police nor the citizens scored highly on either scale. Similarly, Preiss and Ehrlich[24] found that 71 percent of their respondents in a Midwestern state police department were un-prejudiced and tolerant on Srole's "anti-minorities" scale. However, there was no control group in their study.

The picture that emerges from these studies is not easy to interpret. Portland police applicants are like ordinary college males. Recruits in New York are somewhat authoritarian, but not as much as experienced policemen. Denver police are less authoritarian than the general public. In Boston, Chicago, and Washington police are prejudiced against Negroes, but their prejudice is not reflected in their behavior. In Denver and a Midwestern department, the police do not even appear to be prejudiced.

The picture is further complicated by methodological problems. The studies have been conducted in different cities in different parts of the country. What is true of Portland need not be true of New York, and what holds for a big-city force like Chicago's, need not hold for a state or rural department. Even within departments there can be a tremendous amount of variation. Preiss and Ehrlich, for example, found that policies, standards, and procedures varied considerably from one post to the next in the state department they studied.

Only a few studies used adequate control groups and some did not use a control group at all. While it is very impressive to learn that 72 percent of the policemen in one study were prejudiced—or that 71 percent were unprejudiced in another—these figures are meaningless until we know how they compare to some nonpolice control group.

In addition, the methods of study and measuring instruments may not be comparable. In the studies mentioned above, three different measures of authoritarianism were employed. Prejudice has been "measured" by the subjective accounts of participant observers as well as by paper-and-pencil tests. These divergent methods may account for some of the apparently inconsistent results.

Finally, most of the results are subject to a "social desirability" interpretation. Niederhoffer[25] has commented on the policeman's transition "from station house to glass house." In other words, policemen are being watched and studied as never before. Liberals, minorities, and intellectuals are clamoring for greater civilian control over the police. The public has been sensitized to police brutality and prejudice, and police administrators are desperately trying to upgrade the quality of men in their departments. Furthermore, many policemen have a smattering of social sciences somewhere along the line, so it is not surprising that they should know how to respond to an "anti-minorities" or authoritarianism scale in order to present themselves in the most favorable light.

In short, the evidence—by its very inconsistency, if nothing else—does not indicate the existence of a police personality, authoritarian or otherwise. With approximately 40,000 police departments in the United States, the chances of finding a single dominant personality type appear to be slim, to put it mildly. Obviously, however, none of the evidence so far is good enough to draw any firm conclusions. Writers who believe in a police mentality may not have a strong case, but they have yet to be disproved. Therefore it may be worthwhile to review some of the current hypotheses about the origin of police authoritarianism. Popular explanations generally fall into two broad categories. Some writers believe that police work itself develops an authoritarian world-view, while others believe that authoritarian personalities are selected for police work in the first place.

The Consequences of Police Work

According to the first point of view, authortarianism is an unavoidable by-product of police work, *i.e.*, the formal responsibilities, informal expectations, and everyday experiences of police patrolmen. The word "patrolmen" is used deliberately. The police mentality, as described in the literature, does not develop at the top of the police hierarchy and filter down to the underlings. Instead it develops at the bottom of the ladder as men patrol their beats and is carried to the top as they work their way up. Since virtually all police administrators begin their careers as patrolmen, it would not be surprising to find symptoms of the police mentality throughout the organization.[26] Most writers only deal with patrolmen, however, and so will this writer.

Suspiciousness. Danger is a recurrent theme in police work. Stories are told of policemen shot and killed while trying to settle a family dispute or write a simple speeding ticket. Danger is part of the folklore to be sure, but even the most bizarre legends may have some basis in fact. Statistically speaking, police work is one of the most dangerous jobs in the country,[27] and policemen are aware of that fact. Sterling[28] found that policemen were more likely to perceive danger in 20 different situations the longer they had served on the force. No one can deny the widespread and often violent hostility policemen encounter in minority-group neighborhoods. At Christmas time the Black Panthers even sell greeting cards featuring uniformed pigs with knives in their bellies. Skolnick coined the term "symbolic assailant" to describe the policeman's psychological response to the continual threat of violence.

> The policeman, because his work requires him to be occupied continually with potential violence, develops a perceptual shorthand to identify certain kinds of people as symbolic assailants, that is, as persons who use gesture, language, and attire that the policeman has come to recognize as a prelude to violence.[29]

Although many policemen try to minimize the dangerous aspects of their work, Skolnick believes their "strategies of denial" are defense mechanisms that enable them to perform their job effectively. He concludes that the "unambiguous" consequence of danger in police work is a suspicious outlook on life.

Policemen are also *trained* to be suspicious. According to Skolnick, a good policeman has an intuitive ability to sense the unusual. He pays close attention to normal everyday routines so he can spot anything out of the ordinary. He notices when stores open and close, which houses are vacant, which lights are left on. He has to be suspicious or he will overlook tell-tale signs of criminal activity. Toch and Schulte's[30] study of the perception of violence indicates that police training has a very significant effect on one's perceptual processes. Suspicion, therefore, may be an occupational requirement. Unsuspecting cops do not make "good pinches."

Unfortunately most writers have not distinguished between suspiciousness as a specific or generic trait. While many of them imply that suspiciousness pervades all aspects of the policeman's life, it may well be confined to his working hours, and even then to only certain aspects of his job. Because black ghettos are high-risk areas where crime and delinquency are commonplace, the men who patrol the ghettos are understandably suspicious of the local residents. But will their suspiciousness carry over during their off-duty hours? Will they be equally suspicious when they patrol "respectable" middle-class neighborhoods? If not, we ought to be cautious about treating suspiciousness as if it were a pervasive feature of the policeman's personality. In all fairness it should be added that Skolnick may have coined the term "working personality" to avoid treating suspiciousness as a generic trait. Nevertheless, other writers have not been so careful, and even Skolnick refuses to rule out the possibility that policemen are authoritarian personalities in the generic sense of the term.

Cynicism. One of the outstanding features of the police mentality is supposed to be cynicism—a deep-seated distrust of basic human goodness. The policeman's subjective world is full of savagery and hypocrisy: police officers are assaulted every day; respectable housewives try to fix their traffic tickets; and businessmen uphold the law only when it is in their interest to do so. Everyone, it seems, is "on the take" in one way or another.

One of the most common explanations for police cynicism is public antipathy toward the police. Westley found that 73 percent of the policemen he interviewed believed the average citizen dislikes police officers.[31] As Westley points out, the policeman's image of the public is shaped by the people he deals with every day on the job. To many, perhaps most of these people, the policeman is an intruder. Nowhere is the policeman's status as an outsider better illustrated than in the case of the family quarrel. The police officer is most apt to be called to settle a family dispute in a low-income neighborhood, the very place he is most likely to be defined as an outsider. Even if he has been called by one of the parties to the dispute, there is a good chance that everyone will turn on him before he leaves. The following comment by a police officer illustrates the policeman's predicament:

> Her husband was drunk and ugly when we got there . . . I started to grab him and struggled with him and the first thing I know I felt an aluminum pan pounding on my head and there is the little woman who ten seconds ago was standing there trembling at what the husband would do when we left, beating me on the head with an aluminum pan and saying, 'You are not supposed to hurt him. Let him alone.'[32]

The policeman's social identity as a law enforcement officer, and therefore as an intruder, is a "master status." It overrides all other aspects of his public identity. Whatever else the policeman may be, he is still a cop who can arrest you if he sees fit. The exclamation, "Better watch out, he's a cop," underscores the policeman's marginal identity. Presumably the policeman withdraws into his own circle of friends and defines the public in deviant terms just as he is so defined by them.

Public hostility toward the police takes many forms, some direct, others not. One kind of hostility is the abuse the policeman absorbs day after day as he patrols his beat. Another takes the form of biased reporting and editorial attacks in the newspapers. Niederhoffer found that 72 percent of a large sample of New York police officers believed that newspapers "seem to enjoy giving an unfavorable slant to the news concerning the police . . . "[33] In a less direct way, public hostility is reflected in the low prestige of his police work generally. The police officer's pariah feelings are intensified by his low occupational status. McNamara found[34] that 75 percent of the experienced policemen he studied in the New York Police Department believed that police work should be ranked as high as medicine and law. Yet he and Reiss have found that policemen believe their prestige has actually been declining in recent years.[35] Skolnick discovered that 70 percent of the officers in a large Western city ranked the prestige of police work as "only fair or poor," while Westley found that 70 percent of the policemen he interviewed in an Eastern department said they would not want their sons to become police officers.

> [I]t appears that many of these officers exhibit characteristics similar to those shown by a persecuted minority. They are very sensitive about criticism. They seem to fear that everyone is against them including their own commanding officers. They are hypersensitive and touchy about their status and their prerogatives.[36]

As usual, however, the evidence is not completely consistent. Bayley and Mendelsohn found that Denver policemen believed they had higher-than-average respect in the eyes of the public.[37] Preiss and Ehrlich found that the state police department they studied also enjoyed relatively high prestige.[38] In a nationwide survey of police opinions,[39] only 50 percent of the experienced officers believed that "public support for the police seems to be growing." But surprisingly the more experience an officer had, the more likely he was to endorse this statement. Furthermore, only three percent of the officers said the "gradual drifting away of nonpolice friends" was the most important personal problem they faced as policemen.[40] The Denver police also displayed little evidence of social isolation. Only 12 percent said they had difficulty making friends with nonpolice families, and less than 25 percent complained of difficulties in their social relationships because of their job. As many as 68 percent even said they associated primarily with nonpolice people. Banton has also criticized the assumption that American policemen are isolated from the public.[41] He contends that American policemen, unlike their British counterparts, are able to segregate police work from the rest of their lives. In fact many of his American respondents ridiculed those who played the policeman's role in their off-duty hours. Banton found that 67 percent of his Scottish respondents said their job affected their private lives. This is considerably higher than the 40 percent found in three Illinois cities by Clark who asked the very same question.[42] Yet 40 percent is still a sizeable figure and is difficult to interpret—fully 40 percent or only 40 percent? Banton himself adds in passing that relative to other *American* occupations, policemen in this country really can be considered socially isolated.

Of course police isolation may be a myth created by policemen themselves in order to make their job easier. Ronald Tauber agrees with Banton that American policemen are not as isolated as many have claimed.[43] However, he says that policemen *need* a sense of isolation if they are going to function effectively. The greater the social distance between the policeman and the public, the less cognitive strain there is in enforcing the law. According to Niederhoffer, the most successful policemen are the most cynical.[44]

Another commonly mentioned source of police cynicism is the judicial system. Policemen believe they have been hamstrung by the courts. The police officer is not just paid to enforce the law—the public *demands* that he do so. The blame for rising crime rates invariably falls on the police department, yet policemen are frustrated at every turn in their efforts to win convictions.

> Because of the defense attorney's interrogations, [the police officer] often feels that he is being tried rather than the culprit. He is made to play the part of the fool. He is often frustrated in his attempt to make a pinch stick by the political machinations of the courts and the existence of the fix. He tends to lose faith in the course of justice and in obtaining the support of the courts for his judgments. He may feel that the only way in which the guilty are going to be punished is by the police. He has anxieties about the results of court action, for if the prisoner is declared innocent, he, the policeman, may be subject to a suit for false arrest.[45]

As this quotation illustrates, police officers are not just frustrated by fast-talking attorneys and bleeding-hearts on the bench. They are frustrated by the "fix," the back-stage deals against which they are helpless. Not even the courtroom is immune to corruption which the policeman believes pervades our society.

A persistent theme in discussions of police cynicism is the police officer's continual exposure to the very worst in life.[46] While it is true that policemen spend more time rescuing cats and giving directions than they do fighting crime, one could argue that they still have more contact with the seamy side of life than most people. The very nature of their position makes them constant targets for bribes and payoffs by "respectable" and disreputable citizens alike. Of course policemen are not the only ones who see the "dark side" of human nature. Ghetto dwellers see crime and violence every day. But the policeman sees these things from a unique point of view. As a law enforcement officer the fact of *deviance* is foremost in his mind. Not surprisingly, Niederhoffer found that cynicism in the New York Police Department was directly related to the length of time an officer spent on the force.

Bigotry. Police cynicism supposedly finds its strongest expression in racial prejudice. Prejudice, after all, is really a kind of "directed cynicism." There is some indirect evidence that anti-minority sentiment among policemen is directly related to the amount of contact with members of minority groups. Black and Reiss found that a larger proportion of officers made "highly prejudiced" statements in Negro precincts than they did in racially mixed or white areas.[47] Of course the crime rate is higher in black neighborhoods; the poverty is greater; and the values are different. According to Johnson,[48] many policemen suffer from cultural shock in the ghettos, so it would not be surprising to find a high degree of prejudice among them. Kephart found a similar relationship between the arrest rate in black neighborhoods and the negative attitudes of white policemen who patrolled there.[49] The high crime rate might have contributed to the officers' prejudice, but the causal arrow could point the other way as well. The officers could have arrested more blacks because they were prejudiced in the first place. Not only that, but Kephart failed to find any relationship between anti-Negro feelings and length of service on the police force. As Skolnick points out, it is wise to keep police prejudice in the proper perspective: "the policeman may not get on well with anybody regardless (to use the hackneyed phrase) of race, creed, or national origin."[50]

Anti-Intraception. Policemen have been accused of anti-intraception. They are supposedly opposed to tender-minded, sympathetic visionaries who insist on complicating "reality" with unworkable idealism.

> Police tend to be pragmatists, a characteristic related, no doubt, to the exigencies of their calling. Much of a policeman's work calls for action—now. He frequently handles emergencies in which time is precious. He has to make decisions in situations where facts are hard to come by and guidelines are uncertain. Small wonder, then, that he values 'common sense' more than theory, successes more than ideals.[51]

According to Watson and Sterling,[52] the policeman's hardbitten pragmatism is closely tied to his cynical outlook on life. Deterministic theories which, from the policeman's point of view, excuse the criminal from responsibility for his actions are inconsistent with a cynical, misanthropic world-view. Nevertheless, Watson and Sterling found that most officers *disagreed* with the view that social science is unrelated to the "everyday realities" of police work.

Violence. Critics also accuse the police of being overly fond of violence as a problem-solving technique. Police cynicism supposedly forms a background against which police brutality is understandable. Policemen need not have compunctions about splitting the heads of vile, degenerate men. The police officer's reaction to the sex offender is a prime example: "If I saw a guy beat up a sex criminal I'd figure the guy had a good reason for it. If the guy is no Goddam good . . . I think it's all right to rough him up."[53]

Westley[54] believes that the root of police brutality is the public's definition of the police officer as a pariah. Policemen simply spend too much time dealing with the public to escape its opinions. They are ambivalent about their status. On the one hand, they regard themselves as competent craftsmen performing a vital task; yet on the other, they are condemned and degraded by the very people they have sworn to protect. Because their status is insecure, because they are not even sure if they respect themselves, policemen feel compelled to demand respect from the public. Significantly, Westley found that disrespect for the police was the greatest single reason officers gave for "roughing a man up." Likewise Black and Reiss concluded that a "disproportionate part of 'unprofessional' or negative police conduct is oriented toward citizens who extend no deference to them."[55]

According to Banton[56] and Tauber,[57] American policemen cannot rely on the authority vested in their uniform to gain compliance. Instead they feel compelled to assert their *personal* authority. The citizen may take offense at the policeman's intimidating manner, and the stage is set for a violent confrontation in which each party is struggling to maintain his self-respect in the face of a perceived threat by the other. Westley adds that the lower the status of the citizen, the greater the threat he poses to the officer's uncertain self-esteem. In this context police brutality is indeed understandable.

Conventionalism. One of the policeman's outstanding characteristics, we are told, is his rigid adherence to middle-class values. By and large, policemen are recruited from the working class, but they are required to display middle-class values. Mustaches and long side-burns are prohibited, and hair must be trimmed in a conservative style.[58] In their study of a Midwestern police department, Preiss and Ehrlich found[59] that over a ten-year period most of the cases to come before the department's trial board were for social offenses——intoxication, sexual promiscuity, financial negligence, and so on. A police department is a paramilitary organization. Strict discipline is required at all times, and conformity to the rules can become an end in itself. When in doubt, the safest course of action is to follow the rules, even if it means ineffective law enforcement.[60] The policemen's suspiciousness could also contribute to his conventionality. Things out of the ordinary indicate criminal activity.

In addition policemen are politically conservative and seem to be heavily represented in the John Birch Society.[61] In the 1964 Presidential election, Denver policemen not only voted for Goldwater in far greater proportion than the general public, but in greater proportion than white Denver citizens with the same educational and economic backgrounds as policemen. Watson and Sterling found that respondents in a nation-wide survey of police opinions tended to "side with" a sample of "civilian conservatives" more often than a sample of "civilian liberals."[62] The conservatives included several Klansmen and members of the John Birch Society. However, the police officers were not as extreme in their views as the conservatives, and Watson and Sterling caution us against "the mistaken impression that the police are 'all of a mind'—that they are a monolithic group so far as their views, opinions, and attitudes are concerned. This is definitely not the case. . . ."

Skolnick has suggested that Festinger's theory of cognitive dissonance may explain why policemen are conservative and support the laws they enforce. Unless they were tough law-and-order conservatives when they joined the force, they are apt to experience some cognitive strain since they are required to enforce the law whether they believe in it or not. Their dissonance can be reduced in one of two ways. They can either modify their behavior—and risk losing their job—or they can decide that the laws are pretty good after all.

Policemen, then, seem to have good reason to be suspicious, cynical, conventional, and so on. There seem to be powerful forces at work in the policeman's role that could generate an authoritarian outlook on life. Recall that McNamara[63] found that more experienced policemen were more authoritarian than recruits in the police academy. However, policemen do not confront their problems alone. They are submerged in a subculture which provides a ready-made set of solutions. When police recruits leave their sheltered academies, experienced patrolmen begin to re-socialize them. Preiss and Ehrlich[64] found that the police supervisors took special delight in debunking what rookies had learned in school—in fact, they considered it an important part of their job. Authoritarianism may not be an individual reaction which, incidentally, happens to be shared by others. It may be an attitude that is conveyed from one generation of policemen to the next. Niederhoffer is quite explicit about the system's ability to create authoritarian personalities. He goes so far as to say the system is a failure if it does *not* develop authoritarianism.

The Selection of Authoritarian Personalities

An alternative explanation of police authoritarianism is that authoritarian individuals are recruited for police work in the first place. Three kinds of selection are possible: 1) self-selection, 2) the weeding-out of "liberals," and 3) recruitment from an authoritarian class of people.

Self-Selection. Authoritarian individuals may deliberately choose police work because it is compatible with their personality needs. It is easy to see how an authoritarian might be drawn to police work. The police are a paramilitary organization whose job is to uncover suspicious activities and protect conventional moral standards. McNamara[64a] found that police recruits did not object to the rigorous discipline of the police academy. He points out that this is what we should expect, given their relatively high F-scores. However, even if high F-scores are compatible with a militaristic organization, we cannot conclude that members have been self-selected. McNamara also believed that his recruits were no more authoritarian than the average working-class male. Similarly the authors of the Portland study of police applicants concluded that their subjects were very much like the typical male college students.[65] Bayley and Mendelsohn also concluded that policemen were "absolutely average people."[66]

The evidence that particular personalities are selected for different occupations is not at all clear. According to Donald Super,[67] the more narrowly and specifically defined the occupation, the better the chance certain personalities will be attracted. But the problem with police work is that it defies easy description. The average policeman is a social worker, watchman, detective, guide, and so on.

The Elimination of "Liberal" Recruits. Even if authoritarian personalities do not deliberately seek out police work, a second selective factor may be operating. Liberals simply may not apply for police work. This is a much more parsimonious explanation of police conservatism than the theory of cognitive dissonance. Bayley and Mendelsohn not only found that Denver policemen were considerably more conservative than the general public, but that age was unrelated to political beliefs. If police work really develops a conservative outlook, then the older, more experienced policemen should have been more conservative than the younger ones. Of course, police selection procedures are geared to weed out unconventional applicants if they do apply. Applicants are subjected to rigorous character investigations, and any tinge of radicalism in one's background may be grounds for disqualification.[68]

Even when liberals do become policemen, they are not apt to last on the job.[69] The police force is already a conservative organization when the liberal arrives—he will not find much social support there for his beliefs. Even if he is not ostracized by other policemen, the job itself may be antithetical to his values. The police organization is a paramilitary bureaucracy which rewards conformity and discourages innovation. The liberal will have to enforce many laws he finds personally objectionable, and law itself may be subordinated to order-maintenance. The liberal has three alternatives. He can develop an "underlife" by seeking alternative sources of support for his values and self-esteem. He might, for instance, find a compatible niche in the community relations division. He could also change his belief system, and this is what we might predict from dissonance theory. But if the change is too radical and would require a complete realignment of the self-concept, it may be easier to opt for the third alternative and drop out of the system altogether. It seems reasonable to assume, then, that liberals are unlikely to apply for police work, and, even if they do, they are unlikely to survive.

Working-Class Authoritarianism.[70] The third kind of selection has already been mentioned: The police recruit their members from a relatively authoritarian segment of the population.[71] It does not follow, however, that policemen themselves are authoritarian. The working class, the family background of many police officers, comprises a large portion of our population, and within that class there is room for a tremendous range of variation. While the mean level of authoritarianism may be very high, policemen could be selected from the lower end of the distribution. Bayley and Mendelsohn[72] found that Denver policemen were *less* authoritarian than their non-police control populations. On the other hand, McNamara's finding that police recruits scored as high on the F-Scale as Adorno's working-class sample does not support this interpretation.[73] In other respects policemen seem to be very much like the general public, which, unfortunately is never well defined. One study found substantial agreement between the police and the general public when they were asked to judge the rightness or wrongness of various actions.[74] Matrazzo, et al.,[75] and Bayley and Mendelsohn also found strong similarities between policemen and the public. Once more the same inconsistencies prevent us from drawing any firm conclusions.

Many writers believe that police work is a "natural" choice for working-class men. It offers reasonably good pay, security, and adventure for young men without a college education or any special training.[76] For many, securing a job on the force represents an advance in social status. Studies show that Denver policemen and recruits at the New York Police Academy are upwardly mobile in relation to their fathers.[77]

Although most policemen come from working-class homes, they share typical middle-class values such as "looking toward the future and getting ahead, owning a home and a new car, being on time, and assuming responsibility."[78] Many, however, feel insecure precisely because they are new to the middle class. In a sense they are marginal men and seem to have profound doubts about their social standing.[79] In the absence of tangible social rewards like high pay and prestige, they cling to the respectability to verify their middle-class status. As Chwast put it, the "police are more middle-classy than the average. . . . "[80] It may be significant that 52 percent of the police applicants in the Portland study arrived for their interviews wearing a suit and tie.[81] The researchers were also interviewing potential firemen, but only 15 percent of them wore ties to their interviews. Yet all the applicants had working-class backgrounds. Perhaps the policeman's upward mobility accounts for his authoritarian predilections.

> The police officer of lower class background may be insecure in his new status position and consequently may cling tenaciously to middle-class values while suppressing all traces of his previous class identification. To him, 'lower-classness' in others may be intolerable.[82]

The policeman's uncertainty is aggravated by his ambiguous standing in the eyes of the public. Many policemen believe they are not given the recognition or prestige they deserve. Some even believe the prestige of police work has been declining. Policemen also believe they are being "handcuffed" by the courts, civil right groups and local government. Not only is their social standing marginal, but their effectiveness as a law enforcement agency is being threatened. Studies indicate that a large proportion of police officers join the force in search of job security.[83] For these men especially, the uncertain status of police work must be very hard to bear.

Declining status and influence have been implicated in the growth of fascism.[84] The Nazi Party was supported initially and primarily by small business and property owners who were being squeezed out of existence by labor unions and big business. They felt powerless to cope with the changes occurring in Germany and seized on Nazism to restore their former social and economic security. Although the word fascism has been over-used and misused, and parallels should not be drawn too closely, a similar status-anxiety explanation might explain the policeman's apparent authoritarianism, especially his conventionality and conservatism.

In spite of the uncertainties inherent in police work, status-anxiety may characterize lower middle- and working-class people in general. There is some evidence that today's "silent majority" shares the policeman's feelings of insecurity. A recent Gallup Poll of the "forgotten man," the white middle-class American, reveals that middle-class whites are increasingly pessimistic about America's future.[85] Almost 50 percent believe that the United States has changed for the worse in the last ten years, and a majority believe things are going to get even worse in the next ten. They decry the decline of community spirit and religious and moral standards. They worry about runaway crime rates and believe the world is becoming a dangerous place. What we need, they say, is to take the handcuffs off the police: "To most people, the possibility of added police power offers no conceivable threat to anyone but wrong-doers. 'Behave yourself and there's no problem.' "[86] The forgotten Americans are also feeling the economic squeeze. Blacks are unfairly getting the biggest slice of the pie—they should have to work for what they get like everyone else.

Apparently the frustration and resentment are greatest in the working class—"families whose breadwinners have at most a high-school education, hold blue-collar jobs and bring home incomes of $5,000 to $10,000 a year."[87] They too worry about crime, racial violence, rising prices, and crumbling values, but they worry more and their opinions are more extreme. Marginal socioeconomic status becomes intolerable in an age of affluence.

What has been described is the white middle- and working-class American, but one could easily substitute the word "policeman" in all the appropriate places and still be reasonably correct. Members of the "silent majority" are certainly not fascists, any more than policemen are, but they seem to have many authoritarian characteristics: conventionalism, authoritarian aggression, stereotypy, cynicism, and projectivity. From this point of view, policemen appear to be good representatives of white middle-or working-class America.

Toward a Sociological Model of Police Behavior

Unfortunately, only one firm conclusion can be drawn from this review: The evidence is inconclusive. We began with the assumption that policemen are very unusual people, set apart from the rest of the population by virtue of their authoritarian mentality. Now it looks like policemen may be rather ordinary people, not greatly unlike other Middle-Americans. We cannot even be sure there is such a thing as a police personality, however loosely we define it.

According to Howard Becker,[88] everyone has deviant impulses and practically everyone violates social norms at one time or another. Yet only a few are publicly labeled deviant. The same reasoning may apply to the police. Authoritarianism, as a personality syndrome, is widespread in this country, and policemen may not be any more authoritarian than other people from similar socioeconomic backgrounds. Bigotry is hardly unusual in the United States. Nor is conservatism, cynicism, or any other authoritarian trait. From a sociological point of view, the important question is not, "Why are policemen authoritarian?" but "Why are they singled out for special attention?"

The police might have escaped the authoritarian label if they were not so visible. If the average workingman is bigoted, that is his business, but if a policeman is bigoted, that is everyone's business. Policemen may simply be very ordinary people who happen to be extremely visible. Police behavior is public behavior, not just because police work involves members of the public, or because it often occurs in public places, but because the police are being subjected to public scrutiny as never before—in news stories, editorial columns, scholarly journals, radical tirades, and everyday conversation.

However, not all aspects of police behavior are equally visible to the public. A great deal of police work is only peripherally related to law enforcement. Patrolmen spend most of their time giving directions, writing reports, breaking up family quarrels, and the like, but we hardly notice these activities because they do not conform to our popular cops-and-robbers stereotype of police work. On the other hand, we are outraged by police brutality and discrimination. We pay attention when innocent citizens are stopped and frisked, when blacks are harassed and demonstrators beaten. Law enforcement may be only a small part of police work, but it is certainly the part that attracts the most attention and criticism. Police behavior often *appears* to be authoritarian simply because the public only pays attention to certain aspects of the policeman's job.

Cummins[89] has drawn some interesting parallels between the study of the police and early attempts by social scientists to come to grips with the problem of criminality. At one time most American criminologists were preoccupied with the nature of the "criminal mind." Cummins suspects that these early criminologists were driven by an "ideological need" to separate criminals from noncriminals. Today the evidence indicates that the personality characteristics of criminals are not appreciably different from those of people generally. But as the attention of criminologists has shifted away from criminals to the agents of social control, the need to psychologize and dichotomize has reasserted itself.

> Even though the earlier researches on criminality had wandered unsatisfactorily through the thicket of psychological distinctiveness, the same basic elements of the old framework cropped up again when the sociologists turned to analyzing the police side of deviance. True to form, the sociological studies emphasize the importance of some distinguishing psychological trait structure of police officers, particularly some undesirable failure. Perhaps once again, the ideological need for separation underlies the analyses.[90]

As Cummins points out, discussions of the police mentality have strong moral overtones. The use of labels like "cynical" and "suspicious" is "implicitly unfavorable, for it is, after all, a long stretch of the imagination to portray suspiciousness as a virtue."[91] He adds that more positive adjectives like "realistic" or "analytical" might be equally appropriate. While none of the authors cited in this paper have been openly hostile to the police, their studies provide ammunition for those who are. One of the favorite means of discrediting an undesirable character is to pin a psychiatric label on him. Authoritarianism, like mental illness or any number of more specific terms, is one of those convenient labels that allows us to make sense of police behavior and to discredit it at the same time.

Perhaps, considering the unproductiveness of the personality model, we need an alternative approach to the study of police behavior. An undue emphasis on personality diverts our attention from a far more important issue: the structure of police work itself. In his remarks about the suspiciousness of policemen, Cummins points out that our concern with the police mentality overlooks the sociological aspects of police work.[92]

Police brutality in minority-group neighborhoods is often cited as evidence of authoritarianism, reflecting bigotry and authoritarian aggression. As we have seen, there are many explanations for police violence, but the most parsimonious comes from the police themselves. They will tell you that they have to be tough, especially in the ghettos, or they will lose control of difficult situations.[93] As James Baldwin put it, " . . . the only way to police a ghetto is to be oppressive."[94] In this sense, being tough is a matter of survival. Bayley and Mendelsohn[95] found that 98 percent of their police respondents claimed to have been physically or verbally abused. Under these circumstances policemen become alert to cues signaling criminal activity and trouble—the symbolic assailant. The greater their anxiety, the less likely they are to take chances and the quicker they are to try to forestall injury to themselves. Policemen are most anxious in minority-group neighborhoods and it is there that most police brutality is said to occur. In white middle-class neighborhoods the police are less apt to worry about their well-being, and therefore they can be more relaxed in their encounters with citizens. Force, then, is not just an expression of personal prejudice or a fondness for violence. It may simply be a way of forestalling injury to oneself. Likewise, if policemen stop Negroes for suspicious activities more often than whites, it does not necessarily mean they are prejudiced. Rather, the officers have learned that Negroes belong to a high-risk category and are more likely to have committed a crime.[96]

A great deal of significant police behavior can be explained solely in terms of the organizational characteristics of police departments. Wilson's study of the effect of professionalization on juvenile arrests is an excellent example.[97] When Wilson compared delinquency rates in two cities, he discovered that the city with the "professionalized" police force had a much higher juvenile arrest rate than the city with a nonprofessional force. Yet the rates of juvenile offenses known to the police in the two cities were remarkably similar. He attributed the differences to the organizational characteristics of the two departments. In the "professional" department precincts had been eliminated and the force had been centralized. Because the department had been plagued by scandals in the past, new regulations had been introduced, old ones had been made more stringent, and supervision had been tightened. Officers believed their behavior was constantly being monitored and their productivity measured. In order to "play it safe" they began to treat juveniles in strict accordance with the rules, without regard to personal characteristics or extenuating circumstances. On the other hand, the nonprofessional department was decentralized and run at the precinct level. Regulations were few, supervision lax, and individual officers had broad discretionary powers in juvenile matters. In cases where the "professional" officer would be likely to arrest, the officer in the nonprofessional department might simply give the juvenile a "kick in the pants" and send him home. In this case, police behavior can be explained without recourse to the psychological characteristics of individual policemen.

These remarks are not intended to deny the validity or usefulness of personality as an explanatory construct. Instead, they are meant to keep personality in the proper perspective. Personality and social structure *interact* with each other. For example, Watson and Sterling have argued persuasively that personality patterns acquired in childhood have varying degrees of influence on police behavior *depending on the nature of departmental organization.*

> If a police department is loosely organized, if the men get little in the way of training, if leadership is nonexistent, if supervision is lax, if there are few rules and regulations, which actually govern the conduct of the men, if the men don't see themselves as part of the law enforcement profession, if they think of their job as just another job, and if they don't feel a sense of dedication to their work, then the social class values of their childhood will probably come into play in their occupational role. To the contrary, if a department is well organized, if the men are thoroughly trained in all aspects of their work, if those in command of the department show strong leadership and direction, if supervision is constant and effective, if rules and regulations are both known and followed by the men, and if the men feel they are strongly dedicated to the law enforcement profession, then there will probably be little relationship between social class upbringing and adult occupational performance. For example, the patrolman from a working-class background would not be inclined to use rough language or show a gruff manner in the latter kind of department.[98]

Presumably the effects of social class background would be minimal in a highly professionalized police force.

Conclusion

The controversy over the police mentality will probably persist for some time to come. There is simply not enough good evidence to support or refute any side of the controversy. Even the existence of model personality characteristics among policemen is open to serious question. The devotion of social scientists to the personality model has obscured the important role that organizational factors play in shaping police behavior. Attracting better people to the same old job is not necessarily an improvement. In the case of police work, it may simply mean that college graduates will be "busting heads" instead of high school drop-outs.

NATURE OF THE POLICE ORGANIZATION

The police department is truly a complex bureaucracy. It is most frequently a multi-level organization, organized in the form of a pyramid with the top level administrator being the chief of police. At the bottom level of the organization, one finds the patrolman or line officer. The patrol officer is the backbone of the police department. The lowest level worker found in many, if not most, complex organizations usually performs the routine, repetitive kind of work necessary to keep the organization functioning. This is not the situation found in police agencies.

The police department by its very nature places the line officer in a position where he is a decision maker and manager of his area of responsibility from the first time he is given a "beat" to patrol. There are indeed few agencies in which the efficiency and parameters of the law enforcement functions are vested in those individuals who quite likely have the least amount of experience and expertise in the organization. By this is meant that in most police departments the line officer, "cop-on-the-beat," is frequently the new officer with only a minimal amount of experience and who is fortunate to have two to three hundred hours of training. Consequently, the police patrolman is an executive from day one. He operates with a very minimum of supervision, often seeing his supervisor only once or twice during a tour of duty. He must make instantaneous decisions, frequently while in possession of a minimal amount of information. Because of this unique position, there are a series of organizational stresses on the police officer unlike those normally found on individuals in other bureaucracies.

These stresses portend supervisional techniques which must be innovative, efficacious, and responsive to the individual needs of the patrol officer as well as the supervisor. One of the first unique stresses is the behavior resulting from the vast amount of authority vested in the officer. As will be seen, the use of his authority to a significant extent determines the operational behavior of the patrolman.

A second pressure which dictates behavior involves the very nature of police work. The police officer is dependent upon other police officers often for his very survival. Without a proper understanding of this "isolation" the supervisor is frequently in the dark when it comes to taking corrective actions for intentional or unintentional abuses of authority.

The police department is traditionally organized along military lines with strict channels of communication and command, authoritarian supervisory techniques, and strict obedience to orders made mandatory by detailed written procedures promulgated by the department hierarchy. Not infrequently do these organizational standards conflict with the officer's freedom when performing his daily work. His role concept as a "beat manager" is challenged by the necessity of obedience to what is viewed as petty bureaucratic rules.

A police department is by nature an aggressive organization made up of competitive individuals. Consequently, individual as well as group morale problems arise when officers feel they are insignificant cogs in the wheels of the department. Because of this competitiveness, the supervisor must be careful to explain fully, and with understanding, deficiencies he may observe or any other behavior which may interfere with the officer's confidence and performance.

One of the most pervasive organizational stresses is the pressures other officers in the police department place on the individual. This peer group pressure is a powerful influence upon the officer to mold his behavior to the norms of the group. Once the supervisor understands the nature and pervasiveness of this pressure, he can cope with many of the behavior patterns of his subordinates.

An in-depth understanding of the organizational stresses on officers determines supervisional competence and increases the efficiency of the police department. In the modern police agency, no supervisor can be effective without this knowledge.

SOME ORGANIZATIONAL STRESSES ON POLICEMEN*

The policeman today exercises an executive function. With minimal supervision and little opportunity for research or reflection, he is required to make extremely critical decisions, to intervene and resolve a variegated spectrum of human crises. In this capacity he operates with considerable autonomy and authority.[1] But police work is a high stress occupation which affects, shapes, and also scars the individuals and families involved.[2] Some of the typical stresses are related to environmental work factors such as danger, violence, and authority.[3]

---

*SOURCE: Martin Reiser, "Some Organizational Stresses on Policemen," *Journal of Police Science and Administration*, Vol. 2, No. 2, June 1974, 156-159. Reprinted by permission of the publisher.

Organizational and role pressures also routinely impinge on the policeman, contributing to his total stress load.[4]

Behavior related to the policeman's symbolic significance is an often overlooked but important factor that generates stress and operates at a largely unconscious level. His symbolization of authority elicits the dormant or active ambivalence that many people feel toward authority figures perceived as potentially threatening or punitive. Individuals whose conflicts are significant and largely unresolved, typically react to authority symbols with resentment, hostility and aggression.[5] Not only the individual police officer, but the organization as well, signifies and exerts symbolic influence over its own members and others in the community.[6]

The police department represents a family to the individuals working within it. The chief of police is the father figure, with all of the consonant feelings related to power, dependency and independence. The hierarchy involves a pecking order which operates on the principles of seniority and rank within the "family" organization. Traditionally, the chief is all-powered and rules with an iron, if not despotic, hand. The "brass" are usually older, more powerful "siblings" who behave in a paternal and patronizing way toward the young street policemen who occupy the role of younger siblings striving and competing for recognition, acceptance, and adulthood. This dynamic profoundly influences the organization in many significant areas such as communication, morale, discipline and professionalism.

In the traditional police organization, authoritarian management approaches predominate, with relatively little attention or concern being given to individual problems or human factors.[7] Typically, the jackass fallacy is operative.[8] This is based on the carrot and stick approach to personnel management, which assumes that without either dangling a tasty reward in front of someone's nose or beating him with a stick, he will not move. More enlightened police leadership is aware that management by participation is necessary in order to move from the stifling effect of the pecking order to the energetic involvement and commitment of employees who are actively identified with management.[9] These administrators recognize that organizations are (at bottom) only people and that without the interest and conscientious enthusiasm of the individuals comprising it, the organization can only limp along ineffectually, fighting both internal and external battles. In implementing participative management concepts, modern police managers are utilizing approaches such as decentralized team policing, territorial responsibility and an open system between policemen, the press and the community.[10]

In the past, job security was rated highest in the police applicant's need hierarchy. However, as the conditions and status of the police profession have improved, the primary motivators on the need hierarchy have advanced to that area on the spectrum related to self-actualizing and ego needs.[11] Job tenure and a livable wage are no longer enough to keep the young policeman happy. Like others in our society who are upwardly mobile, when survival and security needs have been met, he wants to be included in the organizational action. He wants to know the reasons for actions affecting him and to feel that he has some say in the decision-making process.

Even as police departments slowly move, however, toward more democratic ways of operating, numerous internal pressures and stresses still exist that affect the individual policeman. These include such issues as how he is rated. Will the old numbers game be the basis for his evaluation, or will qualitative factors such as his ability to engage in preventive work and in-service functions be considered more important? Will he be given his assignment of choice or are assignments determined in some capricious or discriminatory fashion? Is the promotion system equitable, especially when he goes before an oral board for evaluation? Can the board be objective and impartial in its assessments? These are some of the common questions usually associated with executives that frequently involve a high level of stress and anxiety.[12]

Policemen tend to be very competitive, and failure of promotion at an anticipated time may result in feelings of alienation from the group, depression and low self-esteem. This loss of group identification may seriously affect functioning ability on the street. There are usually no post-examination sessions scheduled to cope with these reactions. Properly conducted, such sessions could help ameliorate some of the negative feelings and remotivate the individuals for the next exam.[13]

Another common stress factor is related to the internal discipline structure within a police department. The officer often feels that he is in double jeopardy in that he is not only liable criminally and civilly for a misdeed, but, in addition, faces punishment within the organization. He is expected to maintain personal and moral standards at a level higher than would be demanded in the general community.[14] If an officer receives a complaint, an investigation is usually undertaken, and in serious situations which may involve criminal matters or the reputation of the department, all stops are pulled. The officer may be subject to a Polygraph examination, in addition to lengthy interrogations, and a trial board hearing. It is interesting that the feelings of policemen toward the internal investigative branch are somewhat analogous to the feelings of certain citizens toward the police department. This is the assumption of an antagonistic stance and the expectation of unfair treatment and punishment.

Although training also has some bearing on the amount of stress officers will later experience, the formal training programs are often superseded by the informal training and attitudes the officer is exposed to in the field. The police academy attempts to reduce future stress on the recruit by simulating as closely as possible those critical field situations which he is expected to encounter later. This gives him increased coping mechanisms and reduces anxiety through familiarity and experience. However, negative attitudes by training officers or older, more influential policemen in the field can effectively diminish the value of the initial training program.

One of the most profound pressures operating in police organizations is peer group influence. As with adolescents, it is a particularly strong motivator because it has shaping influence on attitudes, values, roles and operational behavior at the street level. Identification with the group as "one of the boys" is a powerful, if not irresistible, force. One of the main reasons for this is that peer group identification serves a necessary defensive function. It bolsters and supports the individual officer's esteem and confidence, which then allows him to tolerate higher levels of anger, hostility and abuse from external sources.

As long as peer group supports are functioning adequately, the feelings of camaraderie and *esprit de corps* dominate. However, when there is internal strife in the organization, with cliques and special interest groups pulling in different directions, feelings of depression, alienation, and low morale tend to emerge. The price that the individual officer pays for the enhanced support and bolstered strength that he gains in identifying with his peer group is a loss of autonomy in the areas of values and attitudes. Group values and attitudes are developed and shared, while guilt feeling resulting from any dissonance are diluted by group apportionment and rationalization. Without the peer group effect, young policemen would find it much more stressful and difficult to survive the initial acculturation process.

The young recruit is typically idealistic, intelligent and eager. One of his primary motivations in entering the police profession is a desire to help in the community. He likes action, wants recognition, and desires to assume responsibility. During his recruit training period he is relatively flexible, open and accepting. However, he very shortly begins to develop what has been called the "John Wayne Syndrome."[15]

The symptoms of this malady are cynicism, over-seriousness, emotional withdrawal and coldness, authoritarian attitudes, and the development of tunnel vision. This is a nonocular condition in which there are only good guys and the bad guys and situations and values become dichotomized into all or nothing. The syndrome appears to develop as a result of shaping influences within the organization, particularly by peer group, but is also part of a developmental process which helps protect the young officer against his own emotions as well as outside dangers while he is maturing and being welded by experience.[16] Frequently, part of this developmental picture involves distancing from his family as the new policeman strongly identifies with his peer group and feels he must choose between the two. He may become emotionally cool and lose some of his "love" for his wife. Consequently, she feels alienated and rejected and reacts in ways that significantly influence their total relationship, including communication, sex, and value systems. The John Wayne syndrome usually lasts for about the first three or four years on the job, with subsequent gradual loosening up, regaining of a sense of humor, and rediscovery of family. Concomitantly, a less bifurcated set of perceptions and values evolves.

The officer who successfully survives the multiplex influences from within himself, from the organization, and from his working environment benefits from the process. Having been tested and tempered in some of the most difficult crisis situations possible, he has coped, gained maturity, poise, judgment, and increased self-confidence. Authority has replaced authoritarianism. At this point the John Wayne syndrome is no longer predominant because he is now functioning as a professional.[17]

POLICE UNIONS—A NEW ORGANIZATIONAL FORCE

The thought evokes conflicting opinions; some often heated; some quite favorable. However, no matter what the viewpoints are, police unions are a fact which must be dealt with in today's police agency. The police agency has been ripe for unionizing efforts because of its very structure and relationships within the organization. What are some of the factors, both internal and external, which have been the focal point for the unionization impetus?

One critical factor has been the para-military organizational structure of most police departments. Communications operates all too frequently in a one-way direction—downward from the chief resulting in an oppressive type of management which is hardly conducive to an environment in which some semblance of efficiency is sought. However, over the past fifteen years there has been a noticeable change in the demands on law enforcement. This has resulted from a greater understanding of the police function, larger involvement of the public, increased demand for police responsiveness to social needs, and technical and personal improvements within the police hierarchy. It has also been found that the skills of the police officer are not solely technical; rather the job requires a whole host of human relations and problem solving skills. As a result there has developed pressure for change in the traditional police organization. The "cops and robbers" image has been successfully challenged. The trend has been to humanize the police bureaucracy so as not to alienate the community from the police.

The desire for change has given a sense of urgency to the unionism movement. The desire for an input into decisions which affect the officer himself, a movement toward participative management, and an implicit distrust of the military type organizational structure as not being well-suited to the needs of modern law enforcement, make the law enforcement agency a prime target for unionization.

In some quarters, the development of a national police union has been encouraged. In others, it has been condemned. However, polemics seldom aid in reaching an understanding of the benefits and drawbacks of a nationwide police union. Those not favoring a national union have largely been the chief administrators of police departments whether the department was large or small. The greatest fear of this group is that the national union will create internal operational and disciplinary problems. It would also remove much of the power from the chief to administer the agency as he sees fit.

All chiefs are not opposed to the idea of police unions, however. Some recognize the merits of a police union as a means of combatting the unfavorable image that the police forces have in the eyes of significant segments of the public. They believe that the benefits of police unions outweigh the detriments by being able to exert pressure on court decisions and legislation to strengthen law enforcement, and by providing a central office to attend to such topics as increasing wages, establishing salary scales and fringe benefits and developing standardized training programs.

The impetus toward increased unionism in police ranks has been most criticized for its deleterious effect on the discipline of the police. However, the extent to which unionization affects police internal discipline is unclear. The study by Ralph A. Olmos presents a new approach to collective bargaining for police unions. His article presents experiences in two cities concerning the effects of police unionism on organizational structures, behavior and internal relationships within the two police departments. He cites two main areas in which police unions are likely to become involved in police disciplinary procedures as union representatives of its members before internal trial boards and before local civil service commissions.

These areas are extremely important to the supervisor because he must have a basic knowledge of the bargaining process, the kinds of disputes likely to arise from supervisory problems, and the various procedures used by the union and department to arrive at an amiable solution. The supervisor, if he is competent in his job, must be well trained in the general area of job performance and the conditions upon which unions thrive.

EFFECTS OF POLICE UNIONS ON DISCIPLINE*

The recent surge of unionism in law enforcement has had a considerable impact on the administration of criminal justice. Societal concern for "law and order" has enabled the police, through their employee organizations, to enhance their financial status. It has also permitted concurrent development of police political power in community politics.

What effect has police unionism had on the *internal* structuring and relationships of law enforcement agencies? Have police chiefs been able to retain their autocratic posture or have the unions forced participatory management to any extent?

This paper will examine this question within the parameters of discipline, that is—the means of obtaining order, compliance, and morale within the police agency. Specifically, it will examine: (1) what effect has the imposition of union intervention had on the police chief's authority? (2) if union intervention has caused changes in

*SOURCE: Ralph A. Olmos "Some Effects of Police Unionism on Discipline," reprinted by special permission of the *Police Chief*, copyright © 1974 by International Association of Chiefs of Police, Vol. 41, No. 4, pp. 24-28.

discipline, has it been in the substantive nature of the rules or rather in the due process aspects of discipline?

Conflict is inherent in the union-management relationship. Indeed it is necessary if both the union and management are to survive.[1] Union leadership that is in constant agreement with management will not likely remain in office for long, and management which accedes to every union demand will soon find itself bankrupt.[2]

In discussing areas of labor-management conflict in the private sector, Sumner H. Slichter coined the term "industrial jurisprudence" to describe the part of collective bargaining which introduces civil rights and grievance relief into the rubric of union concern and responsibility.[3] In the police service, one of the principal facets of industrial jurisprudence or human relations is the question of discipline.

In law enforcement agencies, discipline has traditionally been imposed through negative means. The police officer who violates the rules is usually *punished,* and it is the chief of police, generally, who has the authority and responsibility for imposing the punishment. Forms of discipline can include oral or written reprimand, loss of days off, suspension from duty without pay, and, finally, dismissal.

The advent of the police employee association, with its attendant political and financial strength, has made it feasible and practical to contest disciplinary action; the employee organization assumes this obligation (the investigation and review of discipline) as part of membership benefits.[4]

What effect does, and will, this have on the chief's power to control and/or influence the behavior of his men in relation to the ability of the employee association to review effectively or contest his methods of control? Will the chief be able to continue receiving quasi-military obedience, or will he be forced to modify his posture in order to reach an accommodation with the organizations that represent his men? Simply knowing that his action may be challenged and may generate conflict with the union, a conflict in which he may eventually have to yield, might cause a chief to examine his prerogatives more closely before he acts.

By studying the general dimensions of disciplinary practices, this paper hopes to gain some insight into the overall implications of police unionism on the power of the police administrator and to generate more specific ideas for future research in this area.

The data for this paper were obtained from in-depth interviews of the administrators and union leaders of two medium-sized police departments located in an industrial, midwestern state. Two purposes in surveying these departments were to establish what types of relationships exist between the employee organization and the administration and then to examine the effects of the relationships on administrative discipline. The surveys concentrated on *perceptions* of authority rather than trying to measure, empirically, the actual changes in the chief's authority.

Background Information

CITY "A"

"A" is an industrial city of approximately 200,000 population. Its economy is largely dependent on its automotive factories. During a prolonged automotive strike which occurred in 1971, the city was so adversely affected that the police department seriously considered the possibility of layoffs. Like many urban, industrial areas, "A" is experiencing considerable racial strife, and the racial polarity of the city is reflected in the police department. Of the 368 sworn personnel, in a city that is 35 percent black, there are eleven black officers. This fact has become a political issue in the city.

The chief of "A" has almost twenty-four years of service. He was appointed nine years ago after having worked his way up through the ranks. He holds a master's degree in police administration and was quite active in the Fraternal Order of Police (FOP) prior to becoming chief.

At present, department "A" requires that an applicant must have two years of college training to be eligible for service. This has proven to be an impediment to recruiting more black policemen. The administration is attempting to hire more blacks, but neither it nor the FOP is willing to agree to a waiver of the college requirement, in spite of strong pressure from community groups and some governmental agencies. The demand for compromise has been advanced under the concept of "affirmative action." This is a very volatile issue within the police department and the FOP is strongly committed to resisting this program.

The FOP is the bargaining agent for the patrolmen and the detectives; it enjoys almost 100 percent membership. The FOP has national and state lodges which receive per capita payment from every member. However, for all practical purposes, a local lodge is autonomous with its own leadership, by-laws, and policies. The lodge in "A" was organized many years ago, but it was not until the mid-1960s that it evolved into a unionlike organization. Superior officers are still able to maintain membership (most of them do), but they are not part of the bargaining unit.[5] Although there is no written contract, all agreements between the FOP and the city have been incorporated into city ordinances.

Present agreements call for binding arbitration on all impasse matters *excluding* discipline. The FOP is currently opting for this right and the chief is strongly resisting as he feels that the issue of discipline is not negotiable nor a working condition. The FOP *does* have the prerogative of providing representation for its members who are called for a hearing before the police trial board. The trial board consists of three to four officers of superior rank who act as a quasi-legal tribunal. The chief may prefer charges against any officer for alleged misconduct or rules violation, and then direct him to appear before the trial board. Members are arbitrarily selected by the chief and they advise him as to their findings. The chief may accept or reject the recommendations of the trial board, although in practice he usually abides by its decisions.

In punishments involving dismissal and/or suspension from duty for 29 days or more, there must be an automatic appeal to the civil service commission which has the power to uphold or overturn decisions by the chief and/or trial board. After appeal to the civil service commission, the charged officer may then carry his case to the circuit court. In cases involving suspension of *less than 29 days*, the charged officer has the option of appeal to the commission. In commission hearings or in court appeals, the FOP provides legal counsel for its members although the organization's executive body may refuse to furnish counsel if it feels that the member's cause has absolutely no merit. The FOP also provides representation, in the form of an official from the association, to assist a member called in front of the police trial board.

The question was raised during the course of the interviews as to whether or not transfers were ever used as a form of discipline. There was strong disagreement between the FOP officials and the administration, with the former claiming that transfers are used for this purpose and the latter asserting they are not.

CITY "B"

"B" is a community of approximately 90,000 people, with an economy largely dependent upon its automotive plants. About 30 percent of the population is black. This city also has had its share of racial problems, largely centering around the issue of busing.

The police department has 167 sworn officers, twelve of whom are black. The bargaining group is an independent Police Officers Association (POA). For the past four years, the POA has operated as an agency shop and all detectives and patrolmen are required to pay dues (there is close to 100 percent voluntary membership, however). There is also an FOP lodge, but it serves strictly as a social and fraternal organization.

The relationship between the POA and the administration in "B" is more institutionalized than in "A," and the organization is more firmly established. The POA has a collective bargaining contract, but like "A" there is no provision for binding arbitration on disciplinary matters. There are, however, some unusual provisions in the contract. For example, detectives are not required to work evenings nor midnight shifts. If the services of a detective are required during those hours, he is "hired-back" and paid a minimum of six hours. (All "hired-back" officers receive a minimum of six hours' pay at their regular hourly rate even if their services are required for only a few minutes.) Another provision of the contract allows each officer the privilege of having a union steward present during reprimands by a superior officer. If the reprimand occurs during the steward's day off, then the steward is "hired-back" and receives a minimum of six hours' pay.

As a result of negotiations with the POA, city "B" has also instituted what is termed the "4-40" workweek. Each officer has three days off each week, selected by seniority, and works ten hours per day, four days per week.

The POA began its operations in the mid-60's as an offshoot of the FOP lodge. At present there is a power-struggle taking place within the association. The current vice-president was elected on a platform of promoting professionalism and increasing discipline. He is planning to challenge the incumbent president in the coming election. If successful, the vice-president intends to change the focus of the POA from the current trade union model to a more professionally oriented association. He claims to have popular support for this concept among the membership of the POA.

Patrolmen in "B" are not as dependent upon their association for protection in disciplinary matters as are those in "A." City "B" is obliged to provide legal assistance to any patrolman against charges which originate outside the department, i.e., citizen complaints.[6] On complaints which originate within the department (charges against a patrolman or detective by a superior officer or the chief), the association is obligated to provide legal aid for the officer.[7]

The chief of department "B," who is in his late forties, has spent his entire career of twenty-six years with this department, and has been chief for the past nine years. He has completed advanced training courses for administrators although he has no college degree.

The chief's power to discipline is restricted; serious charges are handled through a civilian trial board which has been in operation for thirty-five years. The chief is empowered to require that an officer work up to ten of his regular days off, without pay. These minor punishments are subject to review by an inquiry board of police officers. An inquiry board for a patrolman is comprised of a patrolman, a sergeant, a lieutenant, and a captain. It has an advisory role, but in practice the chief usually abides by its recommendations. For more serious offenses, the chief is obliged to refer a case to the civilian trial board. The board is appointed by the city commissioners and contains seven members. It is legally empowered to dismiss or suspend police officers and its decisions are final, subject to review by the circuit court.[8]

Citizen complaints against police officers are handled by the sergeant in charge of police-community relations. He investigates every complaint and must submit a report on his findings to both the chief and the civilian trial board. The board has the option of settling the case by negotiation, refusing to hold a hearing for lack of evidence, or conducting a full hearing into the matter and imposing a judgment. Any citizen can initiate a complaint against a police officer by filing an affidavit with the police department or the civilian trial board.

Promotions are more plentiful in "B" than in "A" with more youthful detectives, sergeants, and lieutenants in evidence. Morale in the lower ranks and the upper echelon appears to be good, but there is a noticeable morale problem in middle management. This could be partly explained by the fact that the chief enjoys a good relationship with the union and has developed his labor-management skills to a high degree, but the everyday operational problems of working within the framework of a somewhat restrictive union contract seems to have fallen on the shoulders of middle management.

Survey Questions

The following summary represents the responses of police administrators and union officials from city "A" and "B" to seven questions. In City "A," two administrators and two union officials were interviewed; in City "B," two administrators and one union official were questioned:

• *How would you describe the overall effect of police unionism on administrative authority? To what extent has the authority of the police chiefs been challenged?* The administrators in both departments felt a greater threat from the unions than the union leaders were willing to acknowledge. This misperception is evident in the following: the union official in department "A" who answered "appreciable challenge" qualified his answer by stating that the attempt to challenge the chief's authority had been great, but that the results had been only moderately successful.

● *How would you compare the task of a chief in a unionized department to one in a nonunion department insofar as to the task of imposing discipline?* In discussing the relative difficulties in managing a unionized police department *vis-a-vis* a nonunion department, the union leader and the captain of "B" surprisingly agreed that it is much easier to administer a unionized force. Respondents went on to say that the contract or agreement with the union provides definite ground rules wherein the chief can function with less misunderstanding; it is easier for the chief to operate within the framework of an institutionalized relationship.

● *It is generally agreed that police associations have the right to represent the men on matters pertaining to wages and general working conditions. However, there is some question as to whether or not disciplinary matters are working conditions or should be left up to the discretion of the chief alone. To what extent would you agree or disagree that disciplinary procedures (including punishment) should be subject to union involvement?* The administrators and union leaders in "A" both conceded the fact that theirs was an adversary relationship which made the administrative situation more difficult for the chief. In "B" the chief and the captain were somewhat more democratic in their attitudes. The fact that serious discipline is handled by an outside agency in city "B" (civilian trial board) may explain why there is less polarization of attitudes on this question.

● *If you think that association involvement in matters of discipline and punishment has caused improvement in discipline, then which part of discipline has improved, the actual rules and regulations—or the procedures (due process)?* The chief and assistant chief of "A" were unwilling to concede that the FOP has brought about any changes in discipline. However, the chief of "B" freely stated that the union has brought about the due process improvements from the standpoint of the patrolman. Chief "B" felt that it would be unrealistic to assert that an autocratic or paternal administrator would have had as much consideration for due process as an administrator whose actions are subject to review by an employee group.

● *Giving an opinion, would you say that in matters pertaining to discipline and punishment, the administration is sensitive to possible association reaction?* In department "A" both the chief and the assistant chief felt there was no administration sensitivity to union reaction on disciplinary matters ("sensitivity" here means: the sense of providing for and anticipating the actions of another). The negative replies of the administrators are in direct contradiction to those of the union officials. The overall mood of the interviews with both the chief and the FOP leaders on "A" indicate a pronounced adversary relationship with each side quite sensitive to the reactions of the other.

In "B" the union official agreed that the chief was not sensitive to union reaction, but that there were problems of "sensitivity" in middle management. The implication is that chief "B" has learned to develop a good working relationship with the POA, but perhaps somewhat at the expense of his middle management. One example of this, given by the union official, was the practice of waiting for the appearance of a union steward when a supervisor wished to reprimand a patrolman. This practice can tie up patrol cars for long periods of time, and in certain instances the supervisor may opt to ignore a situation rather than become involved in the procedural requirements. This union official (vice-president from "B") stated that he planned to delete this requirement from the contract should he be elected president.

• *What effect do you think that association involvement in disciplinary proceedings has on morale?* In responding to union effects on morale, the captain of operations of "B" qualified his negative answer by adding that the union has caused some problems with the sergeants and lieutenants in terms of morale. He also noted, in explaining his answer, that some of the procedures (such as the shop steward system) have caused a certain loss of efficiency. However, he did feel that in general terms the POA has effected an improvement in the morale of the patrolmen.

Aside from the formal answers to the above question the interviews of the principles show that the relationships between the administration and the FOP in "A" are still in flux and that the labor-management struggle may be responsible for an increased level of emotionalism on the morale issue. In "B," these relationships appear to be more stable and institutionalized, and the chief is more willing to deal with the POA on egalitarian terms. The result is that in "B" each side may feel less threatened by the other and the union, because this relative lack of threat is not the paramount factor in morale.

• *What do you think is the most important part of membership in the association, the wages and fringe benefits or the protection and help you receive when you are in trouble?* In discussing the relative values of union membership benefits, the union leaders of "A" stated that their membership felt threatened by the affirmative action movement, and that the chief did not have the political power to stand up against brutality charges—primarily those charges instituted by blacks.

In "B," the city assumes the financial responsibility for defending policemen against charges initiated by civilians. Additionally, serious disciplinary problems in "B" are handled by an outside agency (the civilian trial board), which means that the chief of "B" does not need to be as concerned about pressure from various citizen groups when brutality cases arise. The brunt of such pressure loses much of its effectiveness when it is divided seven ways between the members of the civilian trial board.

On the other hand, the chief of "A" must bear the full weight of citizen pressure when controversial cases arise. In these situations, he must be politically sensitive to the demands of the community while at the same time able to provide support and leadership for the men of his department. The FOP leaders of "A" believe that the patrolmen are sophisticated enough to comprehend the situation and thus they place a high value on the legal help the union provides.

Summary and Conclusions

The administration of department "A" does feel that the union (FOP) has challenged its authority, and the FOP officials believe that the administration of department "A" is sensitive to possible FOP reactions.

The authority problem in "B" centers around middle management rather than the chief. The supervisors appear to experience the greatest difficulty in making the department "run" on a daily basis within the framework of the union contract.

Although both associations "A" and "B" have agreements which call for arbitration as a last step in grievance proceedings, the question of discipline is presently excluded from arbitration. Both groups do, however, have other areas of intervention in discipline, and the association in "A" is attempting to obtain binding arbitration on this issue.

The two principal areas of union involvement in discipline are the representation that the employee organization (FOP) provides at police trial boards of department "A" and the similar representation by the POA for the police incident boards of department "B." The FOP also provides formal legal assistance for the men of "A" for hearings in front of the civil service commission and appeals to the circuit court. In "B," through a POA-gained benefit, the city provides legal counsel for policemen who face civilian trial board hearings. In situations where the city does not provide this aid (complaints that arise internally as opposed to external citizen complaints), the POA is obligated to furnish legal aid for its members.

In department "B," the labor-management conflict appears to be more subdued than in "A," primarily because the chief of "B" has never had the same degree of disciplinary power that the chief of "A" enjoyed prior to unionization. The more serious discipline cases are adjudicated by the civilian trial board, and this board does not have personal, daily interaction with the men of "B." It would appear then, that the advent of the union (POA) in "B" has not caused any significant alteration in the relationship between the patrolmen and the chief. This is not to imply that there has been no challenge to administrative authority. The fact that the POA has induced the city to provide legal aid for its members is a good indication that the association has had an effect on management's authority generally —if not the chief's specifically.

The union leaders from both departments feel that their unions have caused some improvement in discipline, and that this improvement has been primarily in the procedures rather than the rules. There is also a general consensus that union involvement in discipline has been beneficial for morale, although the men in "B" are not as dependent upon their association (POA) for moral support.

The in-depth interviews with the union officials point out that they are most concerned with promoting impartiality rather than attempting to change regulations. They claim that their members are prepared to live with the existing rules, provided they are administered fairly.

In examining the preceding data and the interviews, it appears that the participatory management effect of unionism has changed the administration of discipline in both departments, both procedurally and attitudinally. Attitudinally, the changes are not as pronounced in "B," but this may be explained by the fact that the civilian trial board's involvement in discipline is responsible for a much lower-keyed type of conflict between the chief and his employees' association.

One very crucial factor in the collective bargaining agreements of both departments is the legal status of discipline. The question of whether discipline is a working condition, subject to binding arbitration, or an administrative prerogative is in doubt throughout the state in which these two departments are located. It seems reasonable to predict that this issue will necessitate legal adjudication before it is resolved. At present, both the administrators and the unions are well aware of the importance of this issue and each is strongly resisting the other's efforts in this area.

In relative terms, the development of police unionism has come about rather suddenly. In this fast-moving society, it is not unusual for events to outrun skills and knowledge, and police-employee relations is a good example of this type of gap.

The contrast between chief "A" and chief "B" offers a valid argument for training in labor management skills for police administrators. Chief "B," while he has no formal college training, has acquired an accurate appraisal of current police-employee relations and has trained himself to cope with these new developments with a minimum of conflict. Chief "A," while possessing a master's degree in police administration, still adheres to traditional ground rules, and as a result, experiences a much greater degree of conflict than does chief "B."

While much more research is needed concerning the legal, economic, and social implications of police unionism, the first step toward resolving some of the conflict must lie in training and educating police administrators and police union leaders in labor-management skills. Learning by trial and error, while it may be dramatic, is costly and inefficient. In this regard, it is suggested that advantage be taken of the available training facilities offered through the resources of the federal government, the large labor unions, and many schools and universities. This would be a valuable step in helping to close this "knowledge gap."

FORMAL AND INFORMAL ORGANIZATIONS

Law enforcement personnel are trained primarily to react to a conflict situation. The vast amounts of time devoted to physical training, weapons proficiency, baton usage, and self-defense attest to this orientation. Little effort in the training of recruits or later in-service training is devoted to the solution of conflict without the use or threatened use of some kind of coercion. Too frequently this focus of police training is a direct or indirect precipitator of violence. Many police services and functions suffer from this form of violence proneness, poor community relations, increases in internal complaints of brutality, and loss of a professional image.

Managing conflict situations is extremely important if not crucial to the police officer. The training for handling these potentially explosive incidents presents a difficult problem because police officers are faced with a complex set of behavioral factors which are manifested in overt actions. The police officer must be aware of these factors, be able to recognize them, and implement the most effective means available, to solve the problem presented. In any event, the key to success, is a knowledgeable officer.

How is knowledge about the management of conflict acquired? First of all, formal classroom instruction merely sets the scene by discussing the theory behind conflict and possible solutions to various conflict-producing occurrences. However, the officer's experience is a central issue for two reasons. First, it dictates his own response and second, it provides him with an understanding of the responsible person's behavior. The police officer must understand his own set of values to act in a conflict situation. For example, many police officers are from a different generation and do not understand the behavior values, or even the spoken word used by youth. The police tend to be more concerned with their own image of what social values should be. Too frequently innocent behavior by young people is misunderstood by the officer and a conflict situation develops which could have been avoided.

A corollary to the need for managing conflict is the need for the police officer, and especially the supervisor, to develop a perceptiveness to change; that is, to recognize it and then try to ascertain how this change affects the individual officer and the mission of the department. He must analyze changing conditions in light of his own experience, and apply the new insights and knowledge to his work environment. Too often the police officer says "Let them change, not me." This attitude has a direct bearing on personal and organizational efficiency.

Look at police-community relations. Not too many years ago, policemen were not directly concerned with problems arising from what might be called community tensions, minority frustrations, and the like. The entire concept of community relations as being a law enforcement problem had not been perceived. The 1960's, however, brought drastic changes in police thinking. Police agencies suddenly found themselves immersed in tensions and various conflict situations. Riots developed because of the lack of understanding of group and social psychology. The general unrest deposited on the police door step the need to develop a response to potentially conflict producing incidents other than the use of force. The police have been meeting this challenge by supervisors instilling in their subordinates the idea that there are a vast array of ways of meeting conflict challenges other than by force.

A newly emerging supervisional problem has arisen over the past decade in the form of increased militancy of police officers: This

"Blue Power" has many ramifications as pointed out in the following article by William Kronholm. It may mean that the militant officer is seeking some ideological or political goal or he may be the kind of person who sees lawful restraints on police as unnecessary and wrong and ignores them in order to more effectively do his job. Either kind offers a supervisional problem. The militant officer is in a minority, but is nevertheless significant. He must be recognized and understood if he is to be dealt with by his supervisor.

UNDERSTANDING CONFLICT*

In a previous article in the November, 1971, issue of *The Police Chief* ("Dissent and Society"), I sought to persuade law enforcement officers that understanding the dimensions of issues was more important to their work than the use of force. The response to my efforts was gratifying; in fact, one result was an invitation to address the executive development seminar of the Royal Canadian Mounted Police. During that address, a discussion developed concerning the meaning of conflict in contemporary America. Both myself and the members of the seminar (they were all command officers with at least forty men under them) found the discussion helpful and enlightening. What follows is an attempt to share the contents of that discussion.

At the outset, it is necessary to restate the fundamental premise of my work with law enforcement agents. Understanding and knowledge are the best tools for effective police work, especially when there is a question of better police-community relations. Violence gathers to itself only more violence; and if the police wish to be viewed as professionals, they must equip themselves with the best knowledge available. In that way, persuasion replaces force, and professionalism (along with the esteem of the public) increases. Law enforcement agents are in a difficult position. They require society's cooperation but at the present moment find themselves mistrusted and mistreated by the society they serve. The key to reversing this situation lies in the direction of more knowledge and a better grasp of the dynamics of conflict.

Conflict is too often regarded as a mere clash of behavior

---

*SOURCE: Joseph Grange, "Understanding Conflict: Experience and Behavior," reprinted by special permission of the *Police Chief*, copyright © 1974 by International Association of Chiefs of Police, Vol. 41, No. 7, pp. 36-37, p. 78.

patterns. Such a simplistic view ignores the fact that beneath the surface of behavior lies a living person who not only acts but also experiences his world in a continuous and unfolding manner. It is this person, and not his outward actions, who is at the core of conflict situations. This is especially true when the conflict assumes the proportions of a cultural battle, as is the case with young people today who dissent from society's accepted standards of behavior. Law enforcement agents are in the uncomfortable position of having to enforce behavior standards without understanding the personal experiences that give rise to troublesome behavior. As such they often do not understand the consequences of their actions and repeatedly find themselves accused of brutality, ignorance, or savagery. One remedy for this unfortunate predicament is an understanding of the difference between behavior and experience.

Behave better or else! What do we mean when we say something like that? Ordinarily, we are demanding that external actions come up to a standard that we have set. In other words, behavior involves primarily outward actions that can be judged according to some pre-established performance rating system. These systems are usually derived from the values that we choose. For example, if punctuality is a paramount value, then the person who is always on time is regarded as behaving well. It is to be noted that as far as behavior is concerned, the carrying out of actions is of the utmost importance. Concern for the inner world of the person is secondary for the externals of a situation are the determining factors.

Behavior lies on the outside of a human being in much the same way as his skin. We do not regard the color of skin as an indication of the whole person except, of course, in cases of obvious racism. Judging behavior runs a risk similar to that of racism for we take a part for the whole and assume that what happens on the outside is the same as what is going on inside. That this is not the case is all too obvious. Many times, we find ourselves misjudging the actions of others because we have not understood the way in which they see a situation. Behavior can and, in many instances, does serve as an obstacle to understanding.

The problem with behavior-judgments is that they are too narrow and tend to be the outcome of our own values. Thus, if we consider punctuality as in the example given above to be important, all people who are late run the risk of being judged lazy and worthless. Such quick judgments ignore the complexity of problems and succeed only in widening the gaps between people. Also they only reinforce our own values and shut off the possibility of enriching ourselves through attempts at understanding others. To take behavior as the sum total of being human is to narrow excessively the meaning of man.

Another danger in regarding behavior as representative of the whole man lies in the fact that such a viewpoint can only *explain* things and tell us *why* something is happening. It does not tell us *the meaning* of what is happening. Let us look at a simple example. A teen-ager grows his hair long; in other words, his external appearance or behavior changes. If we take behavior as the key to his personal world, then certain judgments about his values can be made. We *assume* that he is like all the rest and that he shares all their values. But what are those values? Can we derive insight into the personal world of another from his outward appearance? All the rest have been previously judged by their behavior as well, and so the circle grows and grows. I judge you by your behavior and you judge me by my behavior, but we never enter each other's personal world. The best that a behavior-oriented view can do is merely tell us why something is happening. Thus, there are many theories about "permissiveness," inadequate education, etc., but none of these tells us the *meaning* of the long hair. They explain why it happened but they do not tell us what it means. In effect, attention paid to external actions only allows us to judge what the person has done. Behavior rarely tells us the full meaning of a person's world.

The simple word "behavior" tells us much but also conceals much more. If used in a simpleminded manner, it prevents communication and condemns whole groups of people to preformed judgments. By stressing only one side of the meaning of being human, it leads to the types of misunderstanding that play such a large role in the problems faced by law enforcement agents today. To avoid those problems, police work must include an attempt to get inside another person and feel his world and its dimensions. Reliance on behavior alone will not give entrance to that inner world. We must understand the experience of living in that world.

Experience! If behavior is a misleading word, then experience also has its problems. We say such things as: "Experience is the best teacher" or "It's experience that counts." What is experience and how does it differ from behavior? Experience issues from the awareness of a human being, and awareness means how I see my world. This indicates that I am the source of my world. In other words, I not only act (or behave) in the world; I also experience the world as mine. How do I take what is out there and bring it in here so that I can call it *mine*. The way in which I transform "out-there" into "mine" is by being conscious or awake. To be awake is to be already *in-the-world*, not as a neutral observer but as an active participant.

Another way to put this is to say that there is never a moment when I can say, *"There* is the world and *here* am I."* I am always experiencing the world as part of me, and that part of me that is the world is my understanding of the world. If I understand the world as a threatening place, then the world for me is a frightening experience. And no amount of unfrightened behavior will change my understanding of the world until my experience of the world changes. Experience stands opposed to behavior in the sense that it emphasizes the person as the irreducible source of meaning. To change my world is to change my experience of the world and not to change my behavior. In summary, behavior is not the source of the way I experience my world. Rather I behave because I experience my world in a certain way.

Now the importance of this for law enforcement agents lies in its direct application to their work with young people. Youth, and by that I mean the longhairs, the bearded, and the dissenters—those with whom the police come into contact the most—experience their world in a manner entirely different from that of other persons. In fact, so different is their experience that they form a counterculture, a way of looking at the world that differs markedly from the way law enforcement officers view their world. Of course, if one takes a behavioral approach, the response to the world of youth will be something along the lines of a rebuke to their behavior. But this approach only succeeds in aggravating the conflict because behavior change does not change the way in which we understand our world. The situation, of course, reaches extremes at the very moment when law enforcement agents are called in. It is a cultural conflict that they are required to resolve, and the only resource that they have is force, which alters behavior but not world views. Obviously, the police are in a difficult position.

What can make their task easier is an understanding of the world of youth. Let us try to sketch some of the ways youth experience their world rather than the ways in which they behave. In the first place, youth see their world as a place where they can derive meaning, and their aim in life is to derive the most intense possible meaning. Thus, they use drugs which alter consciousness so that a flood of experience is available to them rather than the common, ordinary world that is the normal state of man. Also, they want experience immediately, so they tend to reject planning and the postponement of pleasure. Finally, they refuse to be judged as performers and require instead that others participate in their world in order to find out its meaning.

These three qualities of the world of youth—intense meaning, immediate experience, and participation—stand in contrast to the way in which older persons normally view their world. Stability or security becomes a basic standard by which they judge the quality of life. Also, older persons tend to demand predictable behavior which can be rated or judged. Lastly, an atmosphere of law and order becomes more comfortable than a seeming chaos of experiences. Setting down these differences, we come out with a picture of cultural conflict that looks something like this:

- *Youth* wants meaning, experience, and participation.
- *All others* want security, predictable behavior, and adherence to law and order.

It is these contrasting worlds that concern the law enforcement officer in his work. Obviously, it is easier for the police to work with the "others" than with youth, but ease is not the sole determinant for police work. Professionalism comes from an effort to understand a complex situation, and increased respect follows when law enforcement agents are viewed as professionals. The conclusion follows that the more complex a situation, the more the police need a thorough training in the underlying issues that complicate their work.

Again, it is not a matter of professional police work to determine which world is better or more correct. Such decisions lie with individuals, and the role of the police in terms of better police-community relations lies in the direction of entering the world of youth so as to gain a feel for its dimensions. In so doing, they will gain the respect of youth for young people will no longer regard them as an enemy invading their world but as fellow human beings seeking to understand their world.

How do you enter the world of another? Since the world of another is his place in the sense of the world always being *his world,* I must be invited in. To gain an invitation requires the respect of another; he must want me to come into his world because he trusts me as a person. In terms of law enforcement, this means that reliance upon the uniform and insignia of the police is not sufficient. Such uses of authority, while necessary in some cases, will not produce an invitation to enter the world of youth. In fact, it will positively prevent such an occurrence. A person does not wish to be regarded merely as an object that performs or behaves in a certain way. Rather, every human being (and that includes the police) sees himself as one who experiences the meaning of his world and who requires that we understand his world if we are to respect him.

The meaning of this view of the person and his world has large consequences for effective police work. If better police-community relations are the desired goal, then each and every police officer should be required to gain a feel for the world of youth. This means that they must open themselves to the meaning of youth's world. That meaning was briefly sketched above; let us now attempt to fill it in more concretely by looking at the question of drugs. Again, we are after the meaning of drugs, and not arguing for their legalization.

Why do young people take drugs? The world of the Establishment emphasizes stability and security, and also sees predictability as a sign that all is well. Youth sees such a world as a "World of Ice"—frozen, settled, and finished. The temperament of youth runs counter to such a world, for it stresses change, immediate gratification, and excitement. Now drugs—especially the hallucinogenics —give youth access to a world that is precisely characterized by novelty, immediacy, and intensity, a "World of Fire." From this perspective, the taking of drugs by young people assumes an entirely different meaning than that of mere criminal behavior. Furthermore, no amount of law enforcement is, in and by itself, going to prevent drug abuse. If we wish to halt the use of drugs, we must build another world for youth, one in which the use of drugs is not required for excitement, change, or intense experience.

Of course, it is not the sole responsibility of law enforcement agents to build that world. But they do have a key role to play in its formation since police officers, more than any other segment of society, come into contact with youth at the most critical moments. It is these moments that call for the utmost in tact and patience. These virtues cannot be acquired merely by assuming a professional manner. That is the way of behavior-oriented police work. Tact and patience are acquired through knowledge of the other person's experience and that means gaining the other person's confidence. No show of force nor any threatening behavior will gain the trust of the other. What is needed is knowledge of the inner world of the person, and that is only gained through respect for the individual, no matter what his legal status.

The executive development seminar of the Royal Canadian Mounted Police is attempting to open law enforcement agents to new perspectives. In so doing, it provides renewed hope that increased professionalism in police work will lead to improved police-community relations. No better outcome could be desired for we live today on the edge of a cultural crisis; and, like it or not, police officers will share a heavy burden of responsibility insofar as the reconciliation of that conflict is concerned.

BLUE POWER: THE MILITANT POLICEMAN*

There has been much written in both the popular and scholarly press of the student activist and the black militant. Both have been defined, catalogued, explained, promoted, and condemned. But little has been written about another type of militant, one significant not because of his numbers but because of his position. He is an official of our government, one endowed with the public trust, and the one with perhaps the greatest claim on the title "public servant." He has only recently emerged, in part as a reaction to the more widely known activist. And, probably most troublesome, he is apparently widely accepted by both the public and many of his peers as the solution to acknowledged and important problems. He is the militant policeman.

In general it seems that two types of militant policemen have emerged. One is the officer who sees in his job, either consciously or unconsciously, the possibility of fulfilling or working toward the fulfillment of a political or ideological goal. The second type seems more common and more altruistically motivated, but still can cause serious problems. He is the one who sees lawful restraints on police power, whether right or wrong, as unnecessary formalities which may be ignored in order to "do his job."

The militant policeman is still a tiny minority. But he is far from insignificant, for he can cause damage far out of proportion to his numbers. For this reason, he must be recognized and understood by administrators and dealt with before he becomes a major power.

That militant policemen are "here and now" is readily evident in the formation of the Law Enforcement Group (LEG) in the New York City Police Department in 1968. It was originally organized, without sanction of the New York Police Commissioner, in the 80th Precinct in Brooklyn,[1] when officers circulated a petition demanding the removal of Criminal Court Judge John F. Furey from the bench for allegedly giving his tacit approval to the disruptive tactics in court of two Black Panther suspects.[2] Before long, however, the petition drive

*SOURCE: William C. Kronholm, "Blue Power: The Threat of the Militant Policeman," reprinted by special permission of the Journal of Criminal Law, Criminology, and Police Science, copyright © 1972 by Northwestern University School of Law, Vol. 63, No. 2, p. 294-299.

became an organizing drive. A list of seven demands were circulated through all New York precincts. The major demands were for a grand jury investigation of opposed "coddling" of criminal suspects in Furey's and other Criminal Courts, and the abolition of the department's Civilian Review Board. A LEG spokesman also said it would "contact and wholeheartedly support the United States senators who are trying to prevent another Warren Court."[3]

In appears that the LEG was a militant faction of New York's Patrolmen's Benevolent Association, and it chose to involve itself in politics. In some inspecific manner, the LEG was connected with the attack on September 4, 1968, on a group of Black Panthers on the sixth floor of Brooklyn Criminal Court. The *New York Times'* David Burnham reported that about 150 white men, swinging blackjacks, descended on the Panthers. "Many," he said, "were off-duty and out-of-uniform policemen . . . At least two . . . are on the executive board of the Law Enforcement Group."[4]

Whether the beating was a function of the new group or was a spontaneous reaction to which the LEG members were sympathetic is of little consequence. The militant action had the same results. The heads of two Panther leaders were bloodied, and another complained of being shoved down and kicked (twenty or twenty-five times) in the back. And, according to Burnham, one of the injured Panthers later grimly promised revenge while fingering his bullet-laden bandolier.

New York Police Commissioner Howard R. Leary offered an explanation for the appearance of a militant right wing, but did not hint at a solution. Mr. Leary said the emergence of the rightest groups was a reflection of a similar swing to the right in the community at large. "They are responsive to what they believe the community wants," Leary said.[5] Only three days later, New York Patrolman Michael P. Churns, a director of LEG, promised that members of the organization "would continue to mobilize the police and the public in the fight against crime despite the threat of expulsion from the Patrolmen's Benevolent Association." Churns also told reporter Burnham that LEG was not "a right-wing organization, not a radical organization. We simply are endeavoring to weld the public and police into a single New York and national organization that is anti-crime and pro law and order."[6] What Churns did not say, and perhaps does not even recognize, is that the term "pro law and order" is going to mean very different things depending on to whom he is speaking. It has become a political stance, not a statement of ideals.

LEG is not the only problem in New York. The Patrolmen's Benevolent Association, which is considered by no means as militant as LEG but which becomes involved in political matters on occasions, has issued at least one directive to its membership (about 99 percent of the force) which could be interpreted as militant. On August 12, 1968, president John Cassese instructed officers "that if a superior told them to ignore a violation of the law, they should take action notwithstanding that order."[7] On its face, the directive sounds good. However, as a task force of the National Commission on the Causes and Prevention of Violence points out, it can subvert the control of the administrator in potentially explosive situations. Under the directive, the administrator cannot order his men not to shoot looters during embryo racial disturbances and be sure of obedience. The directive could, in some situations, turn a relatively minor disturbance into open warfare.

New York is not the only city with militant police problems, as Mayor Carl Stokes of Cleveland could point out. On July 23, 1968, there was a gunfight between police officers and black militants. Stokes, a Negro, was blamed by many policemen. During the next few weeks, the police bands crackled with occasional obscene references to the mayor and his picture appeared frequently on station bulletin boards with the caption: "Wanted for Murder."[8]

Stokes' problems with the police have continued and are continuing. When the mayor ran for re-election in 1969, for example, about 40 off-duty policemen and firemen, many driving cars with stickers supporting Stokes' opponent, appeared at polling places to challenge voters who were supposedly improperly registered. The majority went to the Negro sections, where Stokes claims his greatest strength. The officers had to be ordered away from the polls by their commanders.[9] Four days before the primary elections in Cleveland, the Fraternal Order of Police took full-page ads in the city newspapers condemning the mayor for "refusing to respond" to the organization's suggestions for police improvement. Stokes and police leaders, notably then Chief Patrick Gerity, have clashed openly over administration attempts to exercise control within the police department.[10]

"I talk to a lot of mayors in my work," Stokes told one reporter of his problems with the police, "and I find that the same problem is being faced by mayors in New York, San Francisco, Boston—you name it. It is just a little hotter in Cleveland."[11]

The courthouse attack on the Black Panther duo in New York involved many officers who were wearing campaign buttons for presidential candidate George Wallace. Wallace's campaign seemed to attract most of the police militants, and many of those who, though not militant themselves, sympathize with officers who are. *New York*

Times correspondent Ben A. Franklin wrote (during the 1968 campaign) on the policemen's attraction to Wallace, and gave two minor, but significant, instances where acceptance of Wallace's beliefs led uniformed officers to take politically motivated actions.

One of these was in Hammond, Indiana, where correspondent Franklin reported a middle aged couple sat high in a gallery at a Wallace rally, away from the candidate's supporters. The couple was causing no disturbance. But they were holding a small, hand-lettered sign reading "Dick Gregory for President." Almost immediately, they were escorted from the hall by a cadre of uniformed officers. The other incident, in Louisville, Kentucky, found Mr. Wallace speaking to another political rally. His commendation of Chicago police actions at the 1968 Democratic National Convention drew overwhelming response. But one small "boo" drifted across the audience. "Policemen sprinted from every direction to the gallery section from which the jarring sound had come," Franklin reported, "but were not immediately able to pinpoint the troublemaker in the throng. 'Point him out to me,' one policeman commanded. Fingers were pointed, and three cleanly dressed teenagers, two boys and a girl, were paraded down the aisle and out of Louisville's Freedom Hall to a chorus of cheers and jeers."[12]

Such action does not necessarily portend a police state. But it is hardly reassuring. Would those officers have responded the same to quiet, orderly dissenters at rallies for candidate Eugene McCarthy? If not, the patrolmen were using their office to advance the interests of a political ideology, an action which has little place in a democracy.

Yet, the political activity of police officers has continued to grow. In Detroit, officers contributed money and off-duty time to advance the mayoral campaign of Wayne County Sheriff Roman Gribbs. White police campaigned in Los Angeles for Mayor Sam Yorty. Minneapolis police hit the campaign circuit for Charles Stenvig, a detective turned mayor. Some Pittsburgh officers had to be told to remove from their patrol cars bumper stickers supporting Eugene Coon, a former assistant superintendent of police running for county sheriff.[13]

While these incidents of police militancy are fairly recent, perhaps their roots are not. Six years ago, John H. Rousselot, the national public relations director of the John Birch Society, claimed that extremist groups had members in the police department of all principal cities in the United States.[14]

The militant officer spoken of so far is of the political or ideological bent and almost certain to be Caucasian. But there is another type of militant officer who was first reported only recently. Administrators must be equally aware of his emergence. He is the black militant officer, whose militancy is directed at the white policeman. *New York Times* reporter John Darnton puts this officer in perspective:

> In many cities the gulf has widened as blacks have withdrawn from traditional police organizations to form their own. Virtually every major city now has a black policeman's organization.
>
> 'We don't meet as policemen. We meet as members of the black community,' explained Mr. [Leonard] Weir of the Society of Afro-American Policemen. Mr. Weir's group, founded in 1965, now has chapters in Newark, Philadelphia, Chicago, and Detroit. Its headquarters is in New York.
>
> The society's younger, more militant officers are currently challenging the leadership of the Council of Police Societies, which was formed in 1960 and has 22 chapters.
>
> But Mr. Weir still scoffs at black policemen in general, even those who join black organizations. 'They're all mouth and no action,' he said. 'I don't want to hear the talk. I want to hear the thunder. I want to see the lightning.'[15]

The full impact of the black police organization cannot be assessed at present. They may become black pride groups and advance their departments through recruitment of black officers and improvement of community relations in black areas. Or they may become black militants with power no black activists have had before.

The existence of the militant policeman has been established in a few specific instances. How far has he gone, what has he done, why does he do it? The report of Jerome H. Skolnick, a professor at the University of California at Berkeley, to the National Commission of the Causes and Prevention of Violence, explores these matters in a full chapter, "The Police in Protest." For example:

> The police tend to view themselves as society's experts in the determination of guilt and apprehension of guilty persons. Because they also see themselves as an abused and misunderstood minority, they are particularly sensitive to what they perceive as challenges to 'their' system of criminal justice—whether by unruly Black Panthers or 'misguided' judges.[16]
>
> Police organizations such as the Patrolmen's Benevolent Association, conceived of originally as combining the function of a trade union and lobbying organization for police benefits, are becoming vehicles for the political sentiments and aspirations of the police rank and file, as well as a rallying point for organized opposition to higher police and civilian authority.[17]

Throughout the chapter, various conclusions are drawn by Dr. Skolnick and his staff. A summary of the implications of the Skolnick report was contained in an interpretive article by John Herbers published in the *New York Times* shortly after the report came out. Herbers' article dealt only with the one chapter on police activism:

> The politicization of the police has gone so far, the Skolnick report concludes, that in many cities and states the police lobby rivals even elected officials in influence and that the militancy of the police seems to have 'exceeded reasonable bounds.'
>
> Another factor, which some find equally disturbing, is the degree of public acceptance of the police lobby and alleged police excesses. . . .
>
> Law enforcement officers from J. Edgar Hoover down to the cop on the beat tend to equate protest with subversion, the Skolnick report asserts, and Mr. Hoover is among those blamed for spreading this view, by repeating endlessly that Communists are at the forefront of a number of mass protests that have emerged in recent years. Thus, instead of the police being a neutral force maintaining the peace without fear or favor at the discretion of civil authority, they have become, the report suggests, highly partisan militants with the narrowest conception of social deviance, however legal.[18]

> In city after city, from Boston to Los Angeles, the police are bringing pressure on the regular political institutions ranging from organized support of political candidates to lobbying in state legislatures for broadening the areas in which police may use deadly force. The report cited one survey which found the police are 'coming to see themselves as the political force by which radicalism, student demonstrations and black power can be blocked.'[19]

What motivates the militant policeman is not yet fully known for there have been few studies and none involving exhaustive research—the problem is too new. But from what little has been written on the problem, and from the papers dealing with subjects roughly analogous to police militancy, one may conclude that the alienation of police from the society they serve is held by all as a common cause. The three views following, each in a different sense, present the view that the policeman is isolated and somewhat alienated from those he is supposed to serve. This alienation leads to frustration and a common antagonism toward the public. When the officer attempts to rebuild the ego that is constantly subjected to rebuffs and indignities, his idealism can gradually degenerate into an ethnocentric view of society in general and the system of justice in particular. When that mental attitude develops, and is seen in context with the very nature of the policeman's job, militancy can be seen as a not impossible result.

Hans Toch, professor of psychology at the School of Criminal Justice at the State University of New York at Albany, treats the problem headon in an article dealing with militant blacks versus militant police. His views can be generally applied to militant policemen.

Militant police officers—like militant blacks—react with the premise that they can no longer operate within the system. They feel that, to make themselves heard and respected, they must by-pass the strictures imposed by an insensitive, or even malevolent, power structure. In a sense, this goes beyond the routine gambit of positive minorityism. It represents a super-defensive reaction, which arises when standard group defenses fail. It is found among those members of a minority —mainly the young—who sense behind the self-delusion of their fellows an unresolved, permanent impotence. What they demand is removal of social institutions that enforce impotence; these, unfortunately, may include competing minorities.[20]

It would be bad enough if militant minorities presented problems for their own kind, but the threats they pose extend to non-militants, and to the public at large. No one can speak up to a Blue Power officer without implicating the police as an institution. Anything less than assent to omnipotence becomes an affront to 'the law.' In turn, anything the officer does . . . becomes an act of 'law enforcement.' Disagreeing with a militant officer lays one open to the accusation of being motivated by perversity, prejudice and incipient anarchism. For his part, the officer feels perpetually persecuted, in that again and again, as he bumbles his way through his awkward personal encounters, the social order appears subjected to unbearable contempt. This leads to cumulative bitterness and increased militancy. When bluff and bluster achieve nothing, it follows that the blame must lie elsewhere. Personal impotence is attributed to national 'criminal coddling.' The officer feels 'handcuffed,' not by his own behavior, but by bleeding-heart judges and politically motivated civilians.[21]

Columbia University Professor Robert M. Fogelson has analyzed a related problem, police violence as a contributing factor in the riots of the 1960s. Though violence is his central concern, part of his analysis is applicable to militancy.

To begin with, the police feel profoundly isolated from a public which, in their view, is at best apathetic and at worst hostile, too solicitous of the criminal and too critical of the patrolman. They also believe that they have been given a job to do but are deprived of the power to do it. Excessive force is a way to even the score. Moreover, the police, who in America are regarded as employees of the taxpayer rather than as representatives of the law, do not receive the deference accorded them in most Western European countries. Held in such low esteem that they cannot command respect merely by virtue of their position, they must rely on a personal, as opposed to a professional claim to authority. They must be tough. This sense of isolation and absence of respect render it difficult, if not impossible, for most American policemen to maintain law and order and at the same time abide by a policy of minimal physical force.[22]

A large majority of them are convinced that it is harder to maintain public order today than ever before, that the criminals are more active, the public less cooperative, and the courts too lenient. For these reasons the police vigorously assert their authority and otherwise intensify their surveillance in high-crime neighborhoods; only by these means, they assume, can patrolmen insure due respect for the police and reduce the opportunities for crime. And though the police argue that the public should approve, and indeed trust that all law-abiding citizens will do so, they do not consider public approval essential.[23]

Sociologist William A. Westley also wrote about the problem of police violence, but almost twenty years ago. Ideas presented by Fogelson and Toch are similar to those of Westley, and suggest the frightening possibility that, since 1953, things have not changed much—at least for the better—in bringing the police to a harmonious relationship with the public. In 1953, Dr. Westley noted:

> The policeman finds his most pressing problems in his relations to the public. His is a service occupation, but of an incongruous kind, since he must discipline those whom he serves. He is regarded as corrupt and inefficient by (and meets with hostility and criticism from) the public. He regards the public as his enemy, feels his occupation to be in conflict with the community, and regards himself to be a pariah. The experience and the feeling give rise to a collective emphasis on secrecy, an attempt to coerce respect from the public, and a belief that almost any means are legitimate in completing an important arrest. These are for the policeman basic occupational values. They arise from his experience, take precedence over his legal responsibilities, are central to an understanding of his conduct, and form the occupational contexts within which violence gains its meaning.[24]
>
> The existence of such goals and patterns of conduct (independent of and taking precedence over his legal mandate) indicates the policeman has made of his occupation a preoccupation and invested in it a large aspect of his self.[25]

What can be done about the militant policeman? At the outset there is a principle expressed in a New York Times editorial that the police are entitled to all the rights and privileges of any citizen, particularly in his off-duty hours. In essence, the police can do anything anyone else can do, but no more.[26] But such principle does not solve the problem; the old political dictum that one must not only be honest, but must also appear honest, can be applied to political or ideological actions of the police. When the police take on an aura of partisanship, whether deserved or not, their value to the public is lessened.

Harried police and public officials might turn to the news media for a useful guideline. Most quality newspapers try scrupulously to keep reporters from revealing any hint of partisanship in news writing. In fact, many newspapers flatly forbid their reporters from taking part in any political campaign except where their identity as newspaper reporters can reasonably be expected to be unknown, and then only in a spectator's role, not as a participant.

It may be said that objectivity is more important to newspapers than police, since the media are the public's source of supposedly unbiased information. On the other hand, if the public does not agree with one newspaper or television station, there are usually others they may patronize. But there is only one local police force to serve the highly diverse factions of society. So the police must not be allowed to select, or appear to select, who they will or will not serve.

The concept that the *impression* as well as the *fact* of political bias must be removed from the police is only slightly more extreme than notions expressed in the conclusion of the Skolnick report:

> So, while the police may be analogous to other government employees or to members of the armed forces, they are also, and perhaps more importantly, analogous to the judiciary. Each interprets the legal order to (and imposes the legal on) the population, and thus the actions of each are expected to be neutral and non-political. In the case of the judiciary, there is a strong tradition of removing them from the partisan political arena lest their involvement impede the functioning of the system.[27]

Dr. William P. Brown, a former inspector of the New York City Police Department and now, like Dr. Toch, a Professor at the School of Criminal Justice at the State University of New York at Albany, sees the need for a re-orientation of the police to meet the ambiguous and changing situations confronting them.

> We know most of the answers in terms of attitude changes and of practical working devices which could help the police to gain . . . recognition. We know that they face situations in which, in contrast to the Western sheriff model which has always characterized their own image of their work, they are not expected to emerge immediately victorious or die trying. They must also recognize that the high standard of individual rights which the Supreme Court has enunciated is not just an impediment to their work, but actually a call for a higher standard of work which will bring with it social recognition that they are performing at a higher professional level.
>
> The need is . . . to meet a standard of performance under difficulties which we could not even have visualized a few years ago. Above all, they must develop a faith that if they do perform at this level, they· will eventually win the support that can make their future job possible.[28]

The solution is far from crystal clear. However, there are steps which should be taken. The administrator must move to break down the walls which form between the police and the public. Community relations units are one step, if they are properly staffed, directed and sanctioned. Implementing a review board or other means to objectively air citizen grievances, is another if accepted by officers as distinct from a board of inquisition. Restricting policemen from partisan political activity under conditions where they would be representing themselves as officers, is a third. But probably the most important step is instruction and the "tone" of each force. Every officer must be convinced that service is his primary function, and that society's deviants and rebels are as deserving as society's leaders. The officer on the line must be willing to serve all equally, regardless of political persuasion or personal conviction. He must be convinced that this is what his superiors sincerely want.

The police militant movement, as has been stated, involves a tiny minority. The police militant must not be allowed to recruit others, and those active now, in a negative sense, must either be reformed or removed. For if the police militant ever gains prominence, we will no longer have a police force. We will have the vanguard of a police state.

EDUCATION AND ITS EFFECT ON POLICE SUPERVISION

Much has been written over the past decade about increasing the educational standards of the police officer. One example is the publication, *Task Force Report: The Police,* by the Presidents Crime Commission in 1967. Much has been accomplished in the way of increased educational and training standards for the police. More and more states are enacting legislation setting up minimum standards for police training. Many cities provide educational incentives by increasing salaries upon the attainment of a specified number of credits from universities and colleges. Quite often, award of the bachelor's or master's degree is used as a means of assignment to more technical or planning positions within the department.

Despite the emphasis on education, criticism has frequently been leveled at the increased education of police officers. First of all, it needs to be mentioned that all of the criticism has not been directed toward increased education but at the way in which the Law Enforcement Assistance Program has provided educational incentives. Loans and outright grants have been provided to encourage in-service criminal justice personnel to return to school. Some police professionals have been critical of the way loans and grants are administered. In order to secure the maximum amount of the grant and the entire loans available, students are required to take full academic loads. In addition to his duty schedule, this often places a burden on the individual so he is unable to achieve his maximum potential in his course work.

A second criticism directly affects the supervisor. Occasionally there has been the allegation that school attendance caused an apparent decrease in the performance level of officers. The argument supporting this charge is often found to be spurious because the officer is expected to react in a traditional way to a usual police situation. However, increased education and training may very well have caused the traditional response to be changed by developing a new way to handle the situation. When this happens, the department must then reevaluate the old ways in light of newly developed knowledge and techniques. The supervisor, however, must always be aware of the case in which individual performance has deteriorated bacause of excessive pressures generated by attendance at educational programs. In summary, university attendance cannot become the primary occupation of the officer. Educational efforts may indeed become "moonlighting" which is deleterious to police efficiency.

The supervisor must also be aware of tensions and rifts that may develop between advocates of higher education achievements and those who oppose any kind of preferential treatment based on academic accomplishments. The supervisor must be especially alert to this potential problem caused by education because the conflict that is likely to result will be in the area of peer and intergroup relationships.

Many academic programs in which police officers are enrolled are in the social and behavioral sciences. Consequently, it is not difficult to understand why many of these officers suffer from a role conflict. Academic training emphasizes critical examination of "what is." When this is contrasted with the disciplined, rigid organizational structure in a police agency, the officer is caught between opposing forces—conformity and dissent. The supervisor's chief concern is to blend critical evaluation with reality by encouraging initiative and innovation but retaining control, to insure that officers are channeled into achieving the goals of the department more effectively.

Another problem of which supervisors must be aware is, in reality, a managerial concern within the whole police department. Occasionally the officer who attends a university shifts his loyalty from the agency to that new route of self-advancement in the department without any regard to the needs of the agency itself.

Opportunism of this kind bodes ill for the supervisor who must take swift, positive steps to remind the person that evaluation is still based upon performance as a police officer, not as a student.

Does shift or assignment changes in order to encourage college attendance, present a serious supervisional problem? Most problems of this nature can be solved by letting it be perfectly clear that the highly educated officer is a definite benefit to the long-term goals of the police service. However, even though the men can be informed beforehand that reasonable tolerance will be the rule to permit school attendance, it must be stressed that priority will be given to the goals and mission of the agency. In this manner all will be appraised of expectations and educational assistance policies. In the following article by James Weber, several additional supervisional concerns are addressed, such as the recruiting and retention of college trained officers.

Several positive factors also need to be mentioned at this point. The college trained officer appears to be able to adjust to complex situations, such as attacks on his masculinity, by exhibiting a greater understanding of the reasons behind such aggression. There is also less likelihood of disciplinary problems arising from the use of excessive force. As noted in the Weber article, the benefits of the college degree can have a definite positive effect in the police department.

IT CAN WORK FOR YOU*

The Multnomah County Department of Public Safety became the first non-federal law enforcement agency in the United States to require baccalaureate degrees of entrance level applicants for deputy sheriff. When the college requirement was initiated, there were 15 college graduates on the staff of 210 officers. Presently, 114 of 213 commissioned members possess a baccalaureate degree or higher.

This attainment of a college degree requirement was not accomplished without difficulty. Former Sheriff Donald E. Clark, presently a member of the Multnomah County Board of Commissioners, and Samuel G. Chapman, formerly an Undersheriff, now Professor of Law Enforcement at the University of Oklahoma, have recorded the struggle in their book, *A Forward Step–Educational Backgrounds for*

*SOURCE; James K. Weber, "It Can Work For You!," reprinted by special permission of the *Police Chief* copyright © 1973 by International Association of Police Chiefs, Vol.XL, No, 10. pp. 41-43.

Police. After the initial implementation, the program has weathered criticisms and settled into a position of acceptance. Fears of spiraling personnel attrition rate and of a too restricted recruiting base were dispelled as the program gained momentum.

At present, the Multnomah County Department of Public Safety is having no trouble in offsetting its present personnel attrition rate through the hiring of new personnel. Four hundred and twenty-nine applicants sought employment with Multnomah County in 1971. Twenty men were hired during this period reflecting a "hired" to "applied" ratio of 1 : 22. Recruiting has been limited to paid advertisements in West Coast newspapers. Our success in attracting qualified applicants has not been dependent on concentrated department effort, but is accredited to the social limelight now held by the police service, the attractive salary adjustments in the police service, and the increased number of college graduates on the job market. The baccalaureate requirement, itself, appears to have a magnetizing effect on recruiting graduates. The appeal to work for a police agency requiring four years of college as an entrance requirement has become a standard response of applicants when asked why they applied for a position with our department.

Retention of the college-trained officer has been a potential problem which has failed to materialize. Multnomah County's personnel attrition rate for baccalaureate-holding officers has averaged approximately four percent yearly. An attractive salary has served to block any large exodus of personnel, but a mandatory retirement age of fifty-five and eligibility for promotional examinations after two years of service have aided in our retention of personnel. Another retention device, recently instituted, is a system of "Senior Patrolman" designations. These senior grades are meritorious classifications with accompanying salary increases based on length of service and continued in-service and educational training. The senior patrolman concept was initiated to offset the negativism created by the small number of promotional positions inherent in a 320-member department. Personnel attrition for college-educated officers actually differs little from normal police personnel attrition. Family responsibilities and regional ties serve to prevent excessive mobility, thus creating career officers. Probably the greatest retention device available to our department is the nature of the police service itself. The police function, with all its complexity, offers a challenging career which is satisfying to most college graduates.

Personnel attrition in a college-trained police department often has a salutatory effect. Such attrition in a department with high educational requirements has the effect of increasing the efficiency of the department. An officer not really suited for police work will often stay with his department merely out of lack of options for a vocation with comparable salary benefits. This man, ill-suited for his job, becomes a detriment to the police service and the taxpayer. The college-trained officer, who is similarly unsuited for the police service, has options in other fields and will go to an alternate vocation, leaving a better police department in his wake. Another benefit of personnel attrition in a college-trained department is the development of police goodwill ambassadors. The degree-holding officer who decides to leave the police service seldom forgets his police experience. This ex-officer will usually go to his new vocation or profession with an understanding of the police service which he can impart to fellow workers or associates.

The President's Commission on Law Enforcement and Administration of Justice in its *Task Force Report: The Police* recognized that the quality of police service in the United States will not significantly improve until higher educational requirements are established for its personnel. Although ripe for such a project, no sophisticated study has been made to check the improved performance of police personnel in Multnomah County. Generally, however, most observers have noted an increased degree of professionalization within the department, marked by a noticeable sensitivity to citizen complaints. With the higher educational requirement has come its counterpart of reduced reliance on physical aggression and improved attitudes toward minority groups.

Many advantages of putting college graduates in patrol cars are so subtle that their presence may go unrecognized. For example, how does one measure or evaluate the effect on the attitude of the officer who meets the public armed with the built-in ego boost of simply possessing a degree? The degree-holder appears to be more immune to the ego-deflating negativisms and attacks met routinely by all policemen in field assignments. Another subtle advantage of a college degree requirement is in intra-department personal relationships. Having a large proportion of degree-holding policemen allows the individual graduates to avoid becoming submerged by traditional attitudes. Further, it allows him to maintain his college modes of speech and discussion. A college man surrounded by non-college trained officers is apt very rapidly to divest himself of his "Joe College-ism" to conform to the more traditional police image. When college graduates work in an environment of college graduates, they appear to be liberated to make the most of their education.

Today, many police administrators are searching for improved procedures or equipment which will help professionalize their departments. Personnel standards are being raised by cautiously increasing educational requirements to one or two years of college. Faced with the President's Commission recommendation of a baccalaureate degree for all police officers, too many administrators become doubters and label such a recommendation as unrealistic. The Multnomah County Department of Public Safety does not have an impressive headquarters building or an elaborate system of police hardware. It does have an ever-increasing aura of professionalism. No large fiscal expenditure was necessary to develop this. A baccalaureate requirement was initiated with no guarantee of success. Multnomah County had no uniqueness which insured the availability of applicants. No federal funding was available to underwrite a trial run. Multnomah County took a bold step forward. It worked for us. It can work for you.

Topics for Discussion

1. Which person in the police agency has the responsibility of providing for capable and trained future supervisors?
2. What educational and experience backgrounds are needed to become a successful supervisor in your department? Is a college degree necessary? Is one desirable?
3. What is the general background of first line supervisors in your agency. In your estimation are they well suited for the position? Are they successful?
4. What effect will unionism have on the police organization? How will this affect the job of the supervisor when dealing with subordinates?
5. Distinguish between the formal and informal organization? In your agency, to which do the supervisors turn for information on complaints within the department? Which source of information is preferable? Discuss fully.
6. Describe the unique position of the first or bottom-level supervisor.
7. Contrast the views of the police leaders in your department with the idea that police departments should be organized in conformity with sound human relations.

Supervisory Problems

PROBLEM# 1—KNOWING VIOLATION OF POLICY—A QUESTION OF DISCRETION

Background. South City has a population of about 500,000. Its police department has a force of 620 policemen. Sergeant Mighty is a shift commander in the central (main) precinct. His immediate superior is a captain who commands the precinct. Under Sergeant Mighty's supervision are three sergeants and thirty patrolmen. Sergeant Mighty is well respected, does his work competently and is considered to be one of the bright prospects in the South City Police Department (SCPD) for future high-level assignments. Sergeant Mighty is twenty-six years of age.

Cream Park is located inside the main precinct. During the past several years the park has attracted a large criminal element marketing drugs to the hippies and young people who use the park as a meeting place. Large amounts of stolen property have been recovered as a result of several arrests in the park. Citizens have complained about the assaults, lewdness, fighting, and drunkenness. The park is small—about four acres. It is surrounded on its four sides by streets, one of which is a main thoroughfare of four lanes. No streets pass through Cream Park but there are numerous foot paths. Footpatrols are the only way to patrol the park.

About a year ago an order was given that no policeman could enter the park unless told to do so by a dispatcher to answer a complaint call. The order also stated that any major action taken inside the park had to be approved by the Chief or Assistant Chief, who was the patrol division commander. These orders resulted from strained relations between the police and the park people.

Problem. On Labor Day, Sergeant Mighty was working, from 7:00 a.m. to 3:00 p.m. The Main Precinct Commander was off sick and Mighty was the precinct commander. A parade took place earlier in the day and there were quite a few complaints of drinking and fighting in Cream Park. Mighty decided to visit the area of the park when he received numerous reports that a large crowd had gathered there. Estimates ranged from one thousand to fifteen hundred. The situation became tense as several persons started to throw fire crackers on the four lane street. Traffic started to back up and fighting and abusive language between the park people and motorists began to be reported. Patrol officers outside the park attempted to keep traffic moving while also breaking up fights. By about 12:30 p.m., the situation deteriorated to almost riot intensity. The police closed the main thoroughfare, and the opposing crowd of park people had almost taken over the street. They were openly shouting obscenities to the public and police, and were demanding the reopening of the street.

Issue. Sergeant Mighty felt the situation would shortly become a full scale riot and attempted to get in touch with the Chief and Assistant Chief to advise them of the problem. Neither could be reached. By 12:45 p.m., the situation became critical; one person had been assaulted with a chair, another had been stabbed, and an officer directing traffic was injured by a thrown firecracker. Mighty was still not able to locate the Chief or the Assistant Chief to make the decision for the police to enter the park or take any other action.

Alternatives. What alternatives were available to Sergeant Mighty? For instance, could he do nothing and hope the situation would go away?

Actions Recommended. What alternative is best suited for this situation? How would it be best implemented? Discuss the pros and cons of each alternative and why each was rejected or accepted. What other department or city personnel should be alerted or called in for assistance? What are the likely consequences of the action taken?

Should consideration be given to changing the departmental policy?

PROBLEM# 2—AN UNPOPULAR DECISION

Background. A command decision was made to eliminate one of the two precincts in Plum City, population 95,000. The closure would affect thirty officers. The closure directive emphasized there should be a minimum amount of disturbance with the operations of the Plum City Police Department (PCPD). The change would, however, cause some personnel job shifting. The command decision has received much criticism from the local Peace Officers Association (POA), the community, and local politicians.

Problem. Over the past three years, there have been rumors that the PCPD would close one precinct in order to centralize operations. The news media widely publicized the plan. Various community and business groups met with the city council to oppose the closure because they felt the quality of police protection would suffer. Because of the pressure, the plan was shelved until a new mayor, council, and police chief were installed. The same mayor and council were elected, and a new chief appointed. The closure plan was raised again. Once more community and business groups became vocal in opposition to the plan. Sergeant Thinker, who is the father of the closure plan has been told by various political pressure groups that if he continued to press for the implementation of the plan, he would be removed from his current supervision/planning position and possibly be reprimanded.

The Sergeant and the city are determined to proceed with the plan because they feel the public will be saved a considerable amount of money, and more men will be placed on the street because of a reduction of the number of station assignments. Sergeant Thinker has done his best to explain the plan, reassure that no reduction of manpower will result, and present its positive features. He has been assailed continually by the POA as being the moving force behind the plan. One basic objection is that there has not been an adequate public hearing to inform the public. The objections also prominently mention that an opportunity to voice displeasure perhaps would have changed the position of the mayor and city council.

A court order was obtained to hold additional hearings but the city still voted to implement the plan. A large amount of money has been spent to purchase lockers and modify space in the remaining precinct.

Issues. What are the issues affecting the first line supervision in this problem? What issues did Sergeant Thinker consider or neglect to consider? Is centralization desirable in face of the furor created?

Alternatives What alternatives are now available? Should these have been pursued prior to announcing the closure plan? How could the alternatives have been presented?

Actions Recommended. What course of action do you now recommend? What will be the probable consequences of the recommended actions? Should the P.O.A. have even been contacted? Why or why not? Discuss your solution.

PROBLEM# 3—SUPERVISORY RESPONSIILITY VERSUS FRIENDSHIP

Background. In the Midd City Police Department (MCPD) there is a Special Tactics Unit (STU) composed of one sergeant, three corporals, and eighteen patrolmen. Sergeant Runner is the supervisor of the unit. The unit is divided into three teams, each lead by one of the corporals. Main duties of the unit include responding to emergency situations, being trained in the use of several kinds of special weapons and equipment, and acting as a mobile strike force. Under the direct supervision of Sergeant Runner is a K-9 squad, bomb disposal group, and special operations squad.

The STU was organized during the late 1960's to handle potential riot situations. The training was largely conducted along military lines and has continued to the present, even though the active crowd control problems have passed. This kind of training was thought necessary because of the mission of the unit. The three teams work, train and act, largely independently and only on very rare occassions meet for unit training or to handle large hostile groups. The corporal in charge of each team has developed close ties with the team members. The men in each team are also closely knit. Because of the lack of interaction and communication between the three teams, the cooperation and coordination between them is poor.

Problem. Because of these problems, morale in the STU is low and has caused Sergeant Runner much concern. Several members of the unit filed grievances which they thought should have been brought to the patrol captain, who was Runner's immediate supervisor. Those members who initiated the complaints called a meeting of STU members without inviting Sergeant Runner who did have knowledge of the gathering and its purpose.

Sergeant Runner believed that the three corporals who were in charge of the three teams were not being loyal to him and were involved in instigating the filed grievances. Sergeant Runner spoke with his captain both before and after the unit's meeting. He also consulted with Corporal Mohr (the team leader most controversially involved) who appeared not to fully support the patrolmen's actions.

Sergeant Runner told Corporal Mohr that the Captain wanted to speak with both of them. The Captain asked the corporal if he knew about the grievance meeting. The corporal at first denied knowledge but when he realized that the captain knew he was present during the meeting, the corporal admitted his knowledge of the grievances and future meetings.

As a result of the unit's meeting, an informal statement of grievances and issues was signed by all but three officers and Corporal Mohr. The statement was given to the Captain at a meeting at which all of the STU members were present. The issues were based solely on personality differences between Sergeant Runner, Corporal Mohr and the team members. After a long discussion, only a few minor grievances were settled. The major grievances were to be handled by Sergeant Runner, and the three corporals with the Captain to retain the right of final decision. The Captain was most concerned with the actions to be taken by Sergeant Runner and the three corporals. The grievance did not appear to interest him. It appeared to Sergeant Runner that the three corporals had become too personally involved with their men. Personal friendships were allowed to influence their supervisory function. The Captain and Runner were of the opinion that the three had compromised their supervisory function. Consequently they believed that the entire administrative structure of the STU was in danger.

Issues. The grievances of the officers are not the main problems in this exercise. The main issue here is performance of the supervisory function by the three corporals as viewed by Sergeant Runner, and of Runner as viewed by the Captain. What are the main problem areas regarding the corporals' supervisory activities as seen by Sergeant Runner? What problems could be foreseen by the corporals in their relationships with the patrolmen? How could one say that Sergeant Runner was lax in his own supervisory responsibilities? Discuss each issue.

Alternatives. There are several ways that the captain and Sergeant Runner could attempt to correct the problems. What are they?

1. The situation could be overlooked, but it is likely that only time would be bought because of the friendship between the patrolmen and the corporals.
2. What about the Captain's authoritarian, military handling of the situation?
3. Additional alternatives? Discuss each one fully.

Actions Recommended. What alternative is the best possible in this situation? What are your reasons for selecting the particular alternative? What reasons can be given for rejection of the other alternatives before deciding on the action recommended?

A most important concern will be the consequences of the action taken on future relationships in the STU. What are the consequences of the action taken in relation to the control that the corporals have over their men? The Sergeant's supervisory control over the corporals? The Captain's control over the Sergeant and the entire STU?

ANNOTATED BIBLIOGRAPHY

Bopp, William J., *The Police Rebellion: A Quest For Blue Power,* Springfield, Illinois: Charles C. Thomas, 1971. This book consists of selected articles concerning the new police militancy which has evolved during the past decade. The first part of the book is an overview of the police rebellion with an examination of some of the ecological circumstances that have motivated police officers to effect change. Included in this section is a discussion of off-duty police organizations. The second part of the book offers perspectives on police militancy by some scholars and police watchers. The last part of the book presents a field oriented view of selected case studies in blue power.

Igleburger, Robert M. and John E. Angell, "Dealing with Police Unions," *Police Chief*, March, 1971. This article discusses approaches for the police administrator to take regarding police unions. The avenues recommended are designed to provide structure, information, and support for developing an effective police management-union relationship.

Kenney, John P., *Police Administration*, Springfield, Illinois: Charles C. Thomas, 1972. This text provides a theoretical rationale for a number of police practices and introduces the administration, organization, and management theories which have emerged in the past two decades and which have been adopted by business, industrial and numerous governmental agencies. The book is of practical value to the police supervisor who desires to gain a better understanding of the role of the police in society as well as providing definitive guidelines for more effective operation of our police departments.

Nichols, John F., "Management and Legal Aspects of Police Strikes," *Police Chief*, December, 1972, pp. 38–43. In this article the police commissioner of the Detroit Police Department retraces the major events of the 1967 police strike, the first such strike in the modern history of the country. This new organizational stress on the policeman presents new problems for the police administrator. The article focuses on what was done—both right and wrong—during this first strike. Alternatives are offered which would help alleviate some of the problems the union movement creates.

Niederhoffer, Arthur and Abraham S. Blumberg, *The Ambivalent Force: Perspectives on the Police*, Waltham, Massachusetts: Xerox Company, 1970. A book of selected readings that brings together the variegated approaches of the academic behavioral scientist, the journalist, the psychiatrist, the lawyer, the policeman, and the historian in the assessment of some major features of the police occupation and role. The section on "Police Organization and Control" deals with the organizational and institutional constraints of the police system with careful attention to the bureaucratic qualities that determine the life styles, career lines, and policy decisions of police organizations.

Richardson, James F., *Urban Police in the United States*, Port Washington, New York: Kennikat Press, 1974. This book examines the many-faceted policeman individually and as part of a community institution. It focuses on the policeman as a product of prevailing ideology, economical and psychological motivations, political manipulation, technology, and class pressures. The author also explores police duties and administrative structure as reflections of increasing urbanization. He cites the tremendous changes which have evolved from the simple, relatively autonomous order-keeping activities of early America to present law enforcement, crime detection/crime prevention responsibilities operating out of the complicated twentieth century bureaucracy.

Wilson, O. W. and Roy Clinton McLaren, *Police Administration*, 3rd Edition, New York: McGraw-Hill Book Company, 1972. First published in 1950, this book is one of the first texts written on police administration, and it has become a classic. Continually updated, it offers a great deal of insight for the police supervisor operating in an organizational setting. Using the classical concepts from traditional theory and scientific management, the book presents the classic organization structure and organization for command found in most police organizations today. Administrative and leadership functions within the police organization continue to be stressed in revisions of the book.

NOTES

PART 1 OPERATING IN AN ORGANIZATIONAL SETTING

The Policeman's Occupational Personality

1. Adams, Field Interrogation, *Police* 28 (Mar.–Apr. 1963).

2. H. T. Buckner, *The Police: The Culture of a Social Control Agency*, 1967, at 190 (unpublished Ph.D. dissertation, University of California, Berkeley).

3. Quoted in J. Skolnick, *Justice Without Trial: Law Enforcement in a Democratic Society* 48 (1967).

4. A. Black, *The People and the Police* 6–7 (1968).

5. Black & Reiss, Patterns of Behavior in Police and Citizen Transactions," 2 *Studies of Crime and Law Enforcement in Major Metropolitan Areas* 113 (1967).

6. *Id.* 137.

7. J. W. Sterling, *Changes in Role Concepts of Police Officers During Recruit Training: A Progress Report.* 1969, 31 (mimeographed), quoting Harriet Van Horne.

8. J. Adorno, E. Frenkel-Brunswich, D. Levenson & R. Sanford, *The Authoritarian Personality* 255–57 (1955).

9. Smith, Locke, & Walker, "Authoritarianism in Police College Students and Non-Police College Students," *J. Crim. L.C. & P.S.* 440 (1968).

10. Smith, Locke, & Walker, "Authoritarianism in College and Non-College Oriented Students," 58 *J. Crim. L.C. & P.S.* 128 (1967).

11. Sterling, *supra* note 7.

12. A. Niederhoffer, *Behind The Shield: The Police In Urban Society* (1967).

13. Matarazzo, Allen, Saslow & Wiens, "Characteristics of Successful Policemen and Firemen Applicants," 48 *J. Applied Psychology* 123 (1964).

14. D. Bayley & H. Mendelsohn, *Minorities And The Police* (1969).

15. McNamara, "Uncertainties in Police Work: The Relevance of Police Recruits' Backgrounds and Training," in *The Police: Six Sociological Essays* 163 (D. Bordua ed. 1967).

16. *Id.;* Niederhoffer, *supra* note 12.

17. R. Brown, *Social Psychology* (1965).

18. Toch & Schulte, "Readiness to Perceive Violence as a Result of Police Training," 52 *Br. J. Psychology* 389 (1961).

19. Black & Reiss, *supra* note 5.

20. *Id*, at 133.

21. Skolnick, *supra* note 3.

22. *Id*, 82.

23. Bayley & Mendelsohn, *supra* note 14.

24. J. Preiss & H. Ehrlich, *An Examination of Role Theory: The Case Of The State Police* (1966).

25. Niederhoffer, *supra* note 12.

26. Significantly, the President's Commission on Law Enforcement and the Administration of Justice recommends increasing the amount of lateral entry into police administrative positions. President's Comission On Law Enforcement And The Administration Of Justice, *Task Force Report: The Police* (1967).

27. W. Wirtz, quoted in "Copsules," *The Police Chief* (January 1969).

28. Sterling, *supra* note 7.

29. Skolnick, *supra* note 3.

30. Toch & Schulte, *supra* note 18.

31. W. Westley, *Violence And The Police* (1970).

32. *Id.,* 61.

33. Niederhoffer, *supra* note 12 at 234.

34. McNamara, *supra* note 15.

35. Reiss, "Career Orientations, Job Satisfaction, and the Assessment of Law Enforcement Problems by Police Officers," in 2 *Studies of Crime and Law Enforcement In Major Metropolitan Areas* (1967).

36. N. Watson & J. Sterling, *Police And Their Opinions,* 9 (1969).

37. Bayley & Mendelsohn, *supra* note 14.

38. Preiss & Ehrlich, *supra* note 24.

39. Watson & Sterling, *supra* note 36, at 55.

40. *Id.,* 101.

41. M. Banton, *The Policeman In The Community* (1964).

42. Clark, "Isolation of the Police: A Comparison of the British and American Situations," 56 *J. Crim. L.C. & P.S.* 307 (1965).

43. Tauber, "Danger and the Police: A Theoretical Analysis," in 3 *Issues In Criminology* 69 (1967).

44. Niederhoffer, *supra* note 12, at 76.

45. Westley, *supra* note 31, at 82.

46. Black, *supra* note 4; Niederhoffer, *supra* note 12; Westley, *supra* note 31.

47. Black & Reiss, *supra* note 5.

48. Johnson, "Police Community Relations: Attitudes and Defense Mechanisms," in 4 *Issues In Criminology* 69 (1968).

49. W. Kephart, *Racial Factors And Urban Law Enforcement* (1957).

50. Skolnick, *supra* note 3 at 49–50.

51. Watson & Sterling, *supra* note 36, at 6.

52. *Id.*

53. Quoted in Westley, *supra* note 31, at 135.

54. *Id.*

55. Black & Reiss, *supra* note 5, at 37.

56. Banton, *supra* note 41.

57. Tauber, *supra* note 43.

58. Niederhoffer, *supra* note 12.

59. Preiss & Ehrlich, *supra* note 24.

60. McNamara, *supra* note 15.

61. Niederhoffer, *supra* note 12.

62. Watson & Sterling, *supra* note 36.

63. McNamara, *supra* note 15.

64. Preiss & Ehrlich *supra* note 24.

64a. McNamara, *supra* note 15.

65. Matarazzo, et al., *supra* note 13.

66. Bayley & Mendelsohn, *supra* note 14.

67. D. Super, *The Psychology Of Careers* (1957).

68. Niederhoffer, *supra* note 12.

69. Vego, "The Liberal Policeman: A Contradiction in Terms?," in 4 *Issues In Criminology* 15 (1968).

70. Watson & Sterling, *supra* note 36, have challenged the assumption that most policemen come from lower middle—and working-class families. However, their data seem to support the very assumption they wish to challenge: [T]oday's police officers have come from the families of craftsmen and foremen, and service workers (including police) in larger proportion than is true for the general adult work force. Conversely, the data shows [sic] that proportionately fewer police officers than other adults are children of professional, technical and managerial workers; clerical and sales workers; operatives; farmers; and laborers. (119).

71. J. Wilson, *Varieties of Police Behavior: The Management Of Law And Order In Eight Communities* (1970).

72. Bayley & Mendelsohn, *supra* note 14.

73. McNamara, *supra* note 15.

74. Clark, *supra* note 42.

75. Matarazzo, et al., *supra* note 13.

76. Although the President's Commission on Law Enforcement and the Administration of Justice has recommended that police officers have at least two years of college, very few departments require any amount of college preparation. See note 26 *supra*.

77. Bayley & Mendelsohn, *supra* note 14; McNamara, *supra* note 15.

78. Chwast, "Value Conflicts in Law Enforcement," in *Crime And Delinquency* 151, 154 (1965).

79. Bayley & Mendelsohn, *supra* note 14.

80. Chwast, *supra* note 78, at 154.

81. Matarazzo, et al., *supra* note 13.

82. Watson & Sterling, *supra* note 36, at 121.

83. Niederhoffer, *supra* note 12; Preiss & Ehrlich, *supra* note 24; Reiss, *supra* note 35.

84. S. Lipset, *Political Man: The Social Bases of Politics* (1960).

85. *Newsweek* 46 (Oct. 6, 1969).

86. *Id.*

87. *Id.*

88. H. Becker, *Outsiders: Studies In The Sociology Deviance* (1968).

89. M. J. Cummins, *The Problem of Police Minds,* undated (unpublished).

90. *Id.,* 3.

91. *Id.,* 7.

92. *Id.,* 9.

93. Niederhoffer, *supra* note 12; Skolnick, *supra* note 3; McNamara, *supra* note 15.

94. J. Baldwin, *Nobody Knows My Name,* 61 (1962).

95. Bayley & Mendelsohn, *supra* note 14.

96. Wilson, "The Police and Their Problems: A Theory," 12 *Pub Policy* 189 (1963).

97. Wilson, "The Police and the Delinquent in Two Cities," in *Controling Delinquents,* 9 (S. Wheeler ed. 1968).

98. Watson & Sterling, *supra* note 6, at 109.

Some Organizational Stresses On Policemen

1. Skolnick J., *Justice Without Trial* (1966).

2. Reiser, M., *Practical Psychology for Police Officers* (1973).

3. Wilson, J. Q., *Varieties of Police Behavior* (1968).

4. Neff, W., *Work and Human Behavior* (1968); *Task Force Report: The Police* The President's Commission on Law Enforcement and the Administration of Justice. U.S. Government Printing Office (1967).

5. Reiser, M., "A Psychologist's View of the Badge," *The Police Chief,* Sept. 1970, pp. 24–26.

6. Sterling, J., *Changes in Role Concepts of Police Officers During Recruit Training.* International Association of Chiefs of Police, June, 1969.

7. Likert, R., *Human Organization* (1967); McGregor, D., *The Human Side of Enterprise* (1960).

8. Levinson, H., *The Great Jackass Fallacy* (1973).

9. Jacobs, T. O., *Leadership and Exchange in Formal Organizations* (1971).

·10. Davis, E. M., "Basic Radio Car Plan," *Yearbook* (1971), pp. 38–43, International Association of Chiefs of Police.

11. Maslow, A., *The Farther Reaches of Human Nature* (1971).

12. Levinson, H., *Executive Stress* (1964).

13. Reiser, M., *The Police Department Psychologist* (1972).

14. Niederhoffer, A., *Behind the Shield: The Police in Urban Society* (1967).

15. *supra* at 2.

16. Niederhoffer, A. and Blumberg, A. S., *The Ambivalent Force: Perspectives on the Police* (1970).

17. Steadman, R. F., *The Police and the Community* (1972).

Effects Of Police Unions On Discipline

1. Clark Kerr, "Management of Industrial Conflict in Society," *The Pacific Spectator*, Vol. VIII, No. 4 (Autumn, 1954), p. 22. Kerr maintains that without conflict, *management* will also lose its institutional identity.

2. Even though public bargaining does not have the same marketplace constraints that exist in the private sector, the leadership of public employee associations has the mission of winning benefits for their membership while the government officialdom is charged with providing services to the public at reasonable rates of taxation. And although police unions may have some unique features, the labor-management conflict phenomenon generally holds true.

3. Harold W. Davey, *Contemporary Collective Bargaining* (Englewood Cliffs, N.J.: Prentice Hall, Inc. 1959), p. 7.

4. Hervey A. Juris, "Implications of Police Unionism," *Law and Society Review* (November, 1971), p. 28.

5. Sergeants, lieutenants, and captains maintain their own bargaining unit which is a subdivision of the same FOP lodge to which the patrolmen and detectives belong.

6. This lack of dependency on the association for legal aid is ironic to a certain extent as it was the association which gained the legal representation benefit for its members.

7. Unlike the FOP lodge of department "A," the POA is obligated to defend its members regardless of how little merit the individual case may have.

8. There is a difference of opinion on what grounds a case may be appealed to the circuit court. The administration claims that the civilian trial board's decisions can only be appealed on technical grounds (legal error, etc.), while the POA claims an appeal can be on any grounds. Evidently the ordinance is worded ambiguously and the situation has not yet been fully tested in the courts.

Blue Power: The Militant Policeman

1. Fox, "Leary Says Police Reflect Community in a Swing to Right," *N.Y. Times*, Sept. 11, 1968, p. 1.

2. Zion, "Rights Groups Assail Demands of New Police Unit," *N.Y. Times*, Aug. 9, 1968, p. 16.

3. *Id.*

4. Burnham, "Off-Duty Police Here Join in Beating Black Panthers," N.Y. Times, Sept. 5, 1968, p. 1.

5. Fox, *supra* note p. 1.

6. Burnham, "New Police Group Maintains Stand," *N.Y. Times*, Sept. 4, 1968, p. 61.

7. J. Skolnick, *The Politics of Protest: A Staff Report To The National Commission On The Causes And Prevention Of Violence*, p. 207 (1969).

8. *Id.* p. 206–207.

9. King, "Stokes Defeats Cleveland Rival," *N.Y. Times*, Nov. 5, 1969, p. 36.

10. Hess, "Stokes Challenger: Police Unit," *Christian Sci. Monitor*, Oct. 30, 1969, p. 12.

11. Mayor Carl Stokes speaking to D.J.R. Bruckner of Los Angeles Times, as quoted by Cray, "The Politics of Blue Power," *Nation*, April 21, 1969, p. 493.

12. Franklin, "Wallace Hailed by Police on Tour," *N.Y. Times*, Sept. 8, 1968, p. 78.

13. Glickman, "Police in Many Cities Shed Nonpartisan Role for Active Politicking," *Wall Street Journal*. Oct. 30, 1969, p. 1.

14. Weart, "Bircher Defends Enlisting Police," *N.Y. Times*, Nov. 17, 1964, p. 21.

15. Darnton, "Color Line a Key Police Problem," *N.Y. Times*, Sept. 28, 1969, p. 1.

16. Skolnick, *supra* note 7, p. 212.

17. *Id*. p. 210.

18. Herbers, "A Charge That Police Are Now Too 'Political,' " *N.Y. Times* June 15, 1969, 4, p.2.

19. *Id*. The inner quote is from the original study, not from the Skolnick report. see Skolnick, *supra* note 7, p. 210.

20. Toch, "Cops and Blacks: Warring Minorities," *Nation*, April 21, 1969, p. 491.

21. *Id*. p. 492.

22. Fogelson, "From Resentment to Confrontation: The Police, the Negroes, and the Outbreak of the 1960's Riots," *Poli. Sci. Q*. p. 224-225. (June 1968).

23. *Id*. p. 230.

24. Westley, Violence and the Police, 59 *American Journal of Sociology*, 35 (1953).

25. *Id*. p. 41.

26. "One Law For All" (editorial), *N.Y. Times*, Sept. 7, 1968, p. 28.

27. Skolnick, *supra* note 7, p. 214.

28. Brown, Mirrors of Prejudice, *Nation*, April 21, 1969, p. 499-500.

PART 2

BEHAVIOR
PATTERNS
OF THE
SUPERVISOR

The Study of this Part Will Enable You to:

1. Discuss selected organizational theories (that remain the corner-stone of modern organizational concepts) and police organiza-tional structures as compared with these theories.

2. Investigate the role that individual performance plays in organi-zational effectiveness within the criminal justice agency.

3. Present selected theories of leadership behavior and combine them into a coherent scheme.

4. Discuss the increasingly important topic of leadership/supervisory effectiveness.

5. Investigate job performance in relation to job satisfaction and other personal variables.

6. Introduce the interpersonal communication process and illustrate its importance as a vital link in a police department.

7. Investigate the role of the police in the community as a perfor-mance indicator.

8. Introduce the concept of supervisory planning as a stimulus for change in a police department.

9. Discuss the personality characteristics frequently found in the successful supervisor.

10. Present an analysis of self-evaluation, job analysis, and job performance.

11. Investigate the difficulty of determining organizational effectiveness.

Introduction

What does the police department want in a supervisor? When considering this question one must, of necessity, ignore the real and imagined functions allotted to the supervisor by formal job descriptions as well as the implicit expectations of those in higher administrative positions. Below, the author has attempted to arrange a series of behaviors that are frequently expected from the supervisor. In short, what he ought to be.

The range of images and behavior patterns suggested by administrators regarding the duties of a supervisor, varies from the notion of being a well trained police dog who acts immediately in obedience to commands, to that of the cattle range-rider who protects the herd from the depredations of rustlers and wild animals. No attempt is being made here to categorize the various patterns. Rather, the common thread is the idea that the supervisor is somewhere on the periphery of events while the center somehow takes care of itself. This may disturb the illusions of some, but it will certainly be accepted by many who observe the behavior of the supervisor.

Business and industrial managers, who face the problem of managerial training as a function of the profit motive, have long recognized the necessity for inquiry into the matter of supervisory placement. Those supervisory personnel in top leadership positions in police departments have failed to pay due attention to the importance of the definition of the supervisory job itself. They have too often made the improper assumption that any person who has proven capabilities in one position are indeed supervisors, wherever and whenever they may be. This is totally erroneous as an approach to the problem of selection of supervisors whether it be with or without the assistance of various promotion tests.

When one fills a position which necessitates the possession of supervisory skills, too much emphasis is frequently placed on the person rather than the job. There needs to be a far greater emphasis placed upon the training of the person, and still greater emphasis on the training of the top level chiefs and deputy chiefs to carefully identify the job they want the supervisor to perform. At the same time these police leaders need to place greater emphasis on the subordinates definition of the role of the supervisor. A supervisor is appointed, selected, hired; it makes no difference how he secured the job, the point is that he holds the position. What is frequently neglected is that he is not told what to do when he gets there.

For years, many of the largest police departments in America have struggled with the problem of selection, placement and training of supervisors. Study of the problem frequently revealed that the customary approach of "getting the best man" to do the best job was a disaster. One cannot say that the best man is in fact the best man unless he identifies very clearly the position and the particular skills required to fill it. In reality the current pressing problem of supervisor selection is not with the supervisor, it is rather with the chiefs, deputy chiefs, and high level administrators, and frequently the local personnel boards who must identify and select the supervisor. These leaders do not tell the supervisor what he is expected to do or to be.

One can freely admit that the supervisor's role is changing and consequently his behavior is also being altered. This often occurs as a result of internal and external pressures. However the departmental leadership must perfect the job identification and its requirements and then seek to develop a system to select and train the person in the supervisor capacity rather than permit the job to shape itself from the self images of the incumbent.

There is a philosophy in many departments that the able and most skillful will naturally rise to the top—the cream of the crop expectation. Still other departments adhere to the philosophy that honor and professional recognition symbols, such as marksmanship badges and letters of commendation for bravery, demonstrate leadership in and of itself, thereby guaranteeing the honor and integrity of the person who becomes a supervisor. Even an approach used in some agencies wherein a man is promoted because he has the right combination of facial and body characteristics has been a prerequisite for the supervisor's roles. In short if the man looks the part he gets the job.

Sometimes other "scientific" selection procedures are utilized in appointing supervisors. The common mistake is the promotion to a supervisory position simply because the person is at hand—he is willing and he is available. Sometimes the calendar age is a factor, although it has never been equated with supervisory maturity or even professional disciplinary maturity. What has not been recognized is the absolute necessity of explicit understanding of the function that the position's incumbent is to perform in a local sense and the specific psycho-sociological qualities which are imperative to be a success in the position. Knowing both the climate in which the individual will function, as well as those individual characteristics deemed crucial for effective job performance, the person or group choosing the new supervisor must then concern themselves with identifying the combination of leadership attitudes and values along with those personality characteristics which best match the man for the job. A phrase long used by management selection people states "If it takes a bastard to do the job, go find a bastard." When this approach is used, one finds that the supervisory position to be filled requires no special distinction in any area, no special training or education requirements, nor a high degree of intellectual activity in dealing with people. On the other hand, one may find a high degree of activity in routine clerical matters are better handled by a secretary than a professional supervisor. One often finds many things of interest when the position to be filled is critically examined.

In selecting and training for success as a supervisor, much greater emphasis must be placed on the identification of his role than upon the selection process centering around individual candidates who have reached eligibility for becoming a supervisor by spending the required number of years as a patrolman or other beginning job. Concentration upon the definition of the role that the supervisor is to play in the department will reap profits far greater than attempting to select the best man for what is often an unknown or only partially understood job. When one attempts to assess the role of the supervisor, he finds himself groping for unit and supervisory objectives, departmental goals, departmental management and administrative styles, and a whole variety of factors with which the new supervisor must cope. One must look very carefully at the question of who is determining objectives for the supervisor, the unit, the immediate superior of the supervisor, the department, or even the city council. When this is accomplished, one notes that the process leads to an assessment of the consistency with which decision-makers perform their function. The process is similar to a self-appraisal, where one must admit that the supervisor is often placed in a difficult and perhaps impossible function in the department. When this happens the department leaders have absolutely no one to blame but themselves. A supervisor sits in the hot seat. The supervisor must not be left to Dante's philosophy. "The hottest places in hell are reserved for those who, in a period of moral crisis, maintain their neutrality." The supervisor must be given the advantage of being properly chosen for his role and clearly oriented to his responsibilities, limitations and authorities.

The supervisor is in a position of leadership. In a police agency and for that matter, all criminal justice agencies, the tendency is to remain at the status quo. As a consequence, the supervisor's behavior patterns may or may not need alteration if he is to operate successfully in such a setting. To increase the effectiveness of the organization should be the primary goal of the supervisor. In a leadership capacity he can seek to change the departmental image as well as its functioning by being a member of the team. However the road may be rough and narrow. Reforms are necessary. The supervisor needs to recognize needed reforms and seek to have them implemented. A few of the necessary reforms often directly affect the supervisor by contributing to his success as a supervisor and as a change agent in the agency.

The supervisory function needs to be more adequately rewarded. Many claim that supervision of personnel is often inadequate in an agency, however, this is frequently an ill-formed statement. Too often the critics have precious little basis for comparison. Supervision of the first line supervisor is bad; compared to what? Certainly it cannot be compared to the 1940s and 1950s. Today's supervisors are frequently better prepared than supervisors of thirty years ago. They usually have vastly improved facilities available to them. Equipment and supplies are also likely to be much more plentiful. Even with these improvements, conditions are not as good as they should be. The top administrators in a criminal justice agency frequently know enough about human relations, psychology, and personnel development to do a vastly better job of providing the leadership to improve the quality of supervision. Training, job analysis and selection processes of supervisors still stand in need of improvement. Most criminal justice leaders share this belief.

The status of the supervisor as compared with many other technical and administrative jobs must be increased. Higher level administrators in police agencies in particular often will agree, at least within their closed circles, that the rewards for being a good supervisor are too frequently inadequate although the status of being a leader may be somewhat greater. The fact remains, however, that almost no one is doing anything about increasing the rewards for the bright, aggressive, intelligent supervisor who is able to consistently accomplish his objectives with a minimum of difficulty under confused conditions.

Some signs are coming into focus that various professional management groups are trying to do something about. Police leaders, management groups, and various criminal justice professional agencies are moving toward increased monetary and status rewards for outstanding supervision talents. Too often, however, high level administrators (when facing criticism from inside and outside the agency) wax defensive and do not insist that the supervisory function of their personnel is absolutely crucial to the organization's mission. The leaders must recognize that major changes in rewarding the supervisory function are called for and are of supreme importance.

In a criminal justice agency, especially the police, the acceptability of change must be increased. Police departments are relatively inflexible, resulting, more than anything else, from the great status quo behavior exhibited by top and middle level managers as well as many old line supervisors. This is not to say that these are evil men and women who resist change. It is to emphasize that they are in fact men and women. They hold enormous power in their hands—brain power and the power of not making waves to cause the ship to rock. Human resources are the key to future growth of the police. They wield tremendous power—and powerful men and women resist change when it threatens the power they already possess. However, one long-range potentially effective force for change in criminal justice agencies is the supervisor. But, to be effective, he must perceive his role as possessing important developmental and leadership responsibilities. He must face the fact, however, that in effecting change he will often be placed in controversy, primarily with his older colleagues and higher-ups. Nevertheless, as the new supervisor increases his influence, the acceptability of change (and its probability) will grow.

GROUP IMPORTANCE TO THE SUPERVISOR

During the past decade, many of the traditional police practices have been challenged, many have been discarded, and many more refined. None of the changes would have been possible without an interest in innovation by patrolmen, supervisors, and managerial personnel. The changes that have occurred in the field of police supervision are striking. One finds more and more reliance upon putting into practice contemporary supervisorial techniques.

One very significant new concern of the supervisor is in the area of his relations with the group. This matter has been prevalent in the police department only for the past decade for several reasons: lack of supervisorial and management knowledge of the operating problems involved, inadequate training of supervisors in understanding the importance of the group as well as the individual, and confusion about the effect of the group on the mission of the department. In addition, all too often the supervisor has not been convinced of the importance of the group as long as each individual could be made to understand his obligation to the supervisor and the department.

The challenge which the supervisor faces today is unique. Recruitment efforts have resulted in the selection of persons from groups in our society that a few years ago were leading demonstrations and confrontations with the police. Many of those recruited are challenging the authoritarian discipline found in police departments. Their attitude is directly related to the manner in which they enforce the laws. This type of individual initially accepts the authority within the police department while subsequently challenging the regulations under which he operates. The new recruit is constantly criticizing those laws and regulations that restrict, or even appear to restrict, individual freedom.

The supervisor's role is thus made more diverse and innovative. There are many factors of which he must be cognizant. He must have adequate knowledge of group behavior. There are also pitfalls which he must avoid. For instance, he must evade biases for or against individuals who become part of the group. In order for the supervisor to perform his function of directing a group, he must therefore find alternate approaches to his traditional supervisory task.

There are some techniques that he must understand. His handling of the group must be based on an understanding of the needs and aspirations of the individuals within the group. He must devote time to their individual as well as collective problems and appreciate the competing personal values of his subordinates. It therefore appears that training and understanding are prerequisites to successful performance of the group supervisorial aspects of the job.

Reducing the incidence of hostility or confusion over seemingly contradictory orders in dealing with group problems is one technique that every supervisor must bear in mind. The supervisor will know important details of plans which all of his subordinates do not need to know to perform their jobs. The supervisor must make it very clear that instructions given to one individual in a group may be quite different from those given to another. In most situations, a simple explanation of what appears to be contradictory orders to a single person is all that is necessary.

The supervisor should also consider developing a kind of leadership not too frequently found in police departments—consultative leadership. In the area of supervision it is a positive behavioral approach to a difficult problem. Under this kind of leadership the supervisor does not immediately make a decision on a problem until having presented it to members of the group and sought their advice and suggestions. The decision on what to do is still his, but it is not made until the group members know the problem and understand their individual roles in the situation. The democratic character of this kind of group leadership process is usually well received by group members.

The supervisor is faced with difficult times and decisions. In handling these he is required to be a person of some breadth who is psychologically attuned to the demands of the modern world. Recent tests of successful police sergeant candidates have indicated they are well suited for their leadership and disciplinary roles. The supervisor must be well-informed of the nature of police organization and its effect on his leadership style with his subordinates. He must be able to perceive his role in the organization and how it leads to the promotion of organizational effectiveness. The two articles which follow lead to a discussion of the latter as well as the psychological makeup of successful sergeants.

PERCEPTIONS OF ROLE PERFORMANCE
AND ORGANIZATIONAL EFFECTIVENESS*

There is little research on management in the public sector and even less on the management of police departments. As employment in the public sector continues to represent an increasing proportion of the nation's labor force, and as the demand for an expansion of police department services places an increasing burden on already over-strained public budgets, there is a growing need for better management of public resources. This need gave rise to a recent study of selected parts of the management process within the Seattle Police Department (SPD).

The study included all of the supervisors in the SPD from the rank of sergeant and above. The purpose was to identify the respondents' perceptions of their own role performance and of the effectiveness of the organization. A corollary purpose was to determine how these perceptions would occur in a bureaucratic setting.

Two hundred and twelve questionnaires were distributed and 171 were returned for an 80 percent response. The responses included a representative cross section of all supervisory levels in the SPD.

The average respondent had held his present rank in the SPD for three years. He had two years of college, and had been in the SPD for sixteen years. On the average, he had a total of twenty subordinates.

Indicators of Bureaucratization

Numerous research studies have shown that there are several indicators of bureaucratization in a given organization.[1] For example:

1. Bureaucracies rely excessively on rules and regulations;
2. In a bureaucracy, formal examinations provide a basis for promotion;
3 Duties and responsibilities tend to be spelled out clearly, usually in writing, in a bureaucratic organization;
4. There is usually a high degree of formality between superiors and subordinates in a bureaucracy;

*Source: Frank Harrison, "Perceptions of Role Performance and Organization Effectiveness," reprinted by special permission of the *Police Chief*, copyright © 1974 by International Association of Chiefs of Police, Vol. XLI, No. 4, pp. 56-58.

5. Bureaucracies are characterized by a highly structured network of superior-subordinate relationships;
6. On the technical side, the incumbents in a bureaucratic structure tend, as a rule, to be very competent;
7. Most of the task assignments, work activities, and problem situations in a bureaucracy are covered by procedures;
8. Formal authority in bureaucratic organizations tends to be well defined;
9. Because of a broad division of labor, bureaucracies reflect high specialization of activities, duties, and functions; and
10. Finally, in a bureaucracy, decision making tends to be centralized in the upper levels of management.

Bureaucratization in the Seattle Police Department

Altogether there were eleven indicators of bureaucratization contained in the study's questionnaire. In total, the SPD was rated "bureaucratic" by its supervisors on seven indicators and something less than bureaucratic on the remaining four. On the bureaucratic side:

1. Eighty-seven percent of the respondents stated that rules and regulations were important in the SPD;
2. Sixty-five percent believed that formal examinations were important as a basis for promotion;
3. Seventy-two percent thought that the chain of command was structured;
4. Two-thirds of the respondents rated their fellow officers as competent in their respective specialties;
5. Similarly, two-thirds also thought that most situations encountered were covered rather completely by procedures;
6. Over one-half felt that their formal authority was defined rather clearly, and
7. One-half also believed that decision making in the SPD was centralized in the upper levels of supervision.

On the nonbureaucratic side:

1. Three-fourths of the respondents stated that their specific duties and responsibilities were not defined clearly;
2. And, interestingly enough, 84 percent disclaimed any formality with their organizational superior; while 92 percent felt the same way about their relationships with their subordinates.

The conclusion to be drawn is that the SPD is a very bureaucratic organization with a good deal of team spirit and relationships characterized by considerable informality, at least on a day-to-day basis.

Indicators of Perceived Role Performance

Perceived role performance describes the way the individual sees his performance on the job. It is the way that he views the positive aspects of his effort expended in behalf of the organization. To the extent that the individual perceives himself as making solid accomplishments, he is more likely to be motivated to perform above some minimally acceptable level.

Maslow stated that management can motivate its employees by appealing to the psychogenic needs—i.e., the esteem of peers and self-actualization.[2] Herzberg's study showed that management must first lay a foundation for motivation by providing the proper work environment, enlightened and competent supervision, and, of course, equitable salary and related benefits.[3] Once these items are present in sufficient quantity, management can begin to employ the motivators which, according to Maslow, fill the individual's psychogenic needs. Herzberg said that the motivators include: (1) recognition, (2) achievement, (3) advancement, (4) responsibility, and (5) work that is challenging and fulfilling. But, again, the basic or biogenic needs must, as Herzberg's study showed, be satisfied before the individual will respond to the motivators to seek fulfillment of his psychogenic needs.

The study by Porter and Lawler showed that performance must precede satisfaction which, in turn, tends to reinforce the expectation that subsequent effort will bring rewards perceived as equitable by the individual.[4] It is significant to note that the rewards received by the individual must be somewhat equal to his expectations. If the rewards are viewed by him as inadequate, satisfaction will not result and, in fact, performance will begin to decline. Performance must be matched by equitable rewards to realize satisfaction which, to repeat, is essential for subsequent performance. Again, the basic assumption here is, that to the extent that the individual perceives himself at a high level of role performance, he is either motivated or capable of being motivated.

Perceived Role Performance in the Seattle Police Department

In total, there were eleven indicators of perceived role performance contained in the study's questionnaire. There were five indicators rated highly by the respondents and six indicators rated at a less than high level. On the high side:

1. Slightly over one-half of the respondents evidenced a high feeling of personal achievement as career police officers;
2. About the same proportion reflected a sense of job satisfaction as career police officers;
3. Almost two-thirds of the respondents indicated a feeling of personal contribution to the objectives of the SPD;
4. Slightly less than nine out of ten evidenced a strong feeling of responsibility to the SPD; and
5. Finally, just over one-half of the respondents stated that the results achieved in the course of their regular duties were commensurate with the effect expended to obtain these results.

The six indicators of role performance rated less than high were, perhaps, even more significant:

1. For example, two out of every three respondents felt that they received less than frequent recognition for a job well done;
2. The same proportion of respondents felt that their peers held them in less than high esteem;
3. Again, almost two out of every three felt that it was less than frequent for rewards to be commensurate with performance;
4. Slightly over one-half indicated that it was not too common for rewards to be equal to expectations;
5. Slightly less than two out of three respondents felt that they worked in assignments utilizing their education, training, and experience only part of the time; and
6. Only one-half believed that their careers as police officers provided them with a feeling of personal self-fulfillment.

The responses to the questions related to perceived role performance presented a mixed picture. On the one hand, over one-half of the respondents evidenced feelings of personal achievement and job satisfaction. Moreover, six out of ten felt that they were making a high contribution to the objectives of the SPD, while nine out of ten exhibited a high sense of responsibility to the SPD.

Still, on the other hand, the areas for improvement seem fairly obvious. For example, theory tells us that individuals normally respond positively when the rewards for their efforts are equal to their performance as well as their expectations. If rewards fall below the individual's perception of equity, he will not attain satisfaction and subsequent performance is bound to suffer. In this regard, recall that two out of every three respondents indicated that rewards were not commensurate with performance and over one-half felt that rewards often fell below their expectations. To the extent that the system of rewards in the SPD can be improved, it is reasonable to expect an increase in the number of individuals feeling job satisfaction. In turn, this feeling is certain to improve performance which, after all, is the desired end result.

Further, only one-half of the respondents indicated a feeling of personal self-fulfillment in their work. This proportion can certainly be raised by: (1) greater recognition from superiors for a job well done (two out of three felt this was not the case); (2) assignment of individuals to responsibilities utilizing their education, training, and experience (two out of three felt this was not the case); and (3) a system of rewards commensurate with performance and personal expectations (many also felt this was not the case).

The conclusion is that although perceived role performance and concomitant motivation is high in some key areas in the SPD, there is still ample opportunity for improvement by concentrating on other areas deserving of immediate attention by management.

Finally, it is interesting, if not actually significant, to note that although the SPD is obviously a very bureaucratic organization, the tried and tested theories of motivation still apply with all the force that one would expect in an organization offering more obvious and compelling incentives to improved performance.

Indicators of Organizational Effectiveness

Organizational effectiveness refers to the way in which management employs the resources entrusted to it in pursuit of objectives and fulfillment of the needs of the many constituencies that confer legitimacy upon management. One, and possibly the most meaningful, way in which to assess the effectiveness of a given organization is through a set of criteria which indicates the performance of management in carrying out its many responsibilities.[5]

For example:

1. It is reasonable to expect that an effective organization will have a high level of *productive output;*
2. Further, the *quality* of service provided or goods produced will normally be high in an effective organization;
3. In an effective organization, moreover, the way in which inputs are converted into outputs will involve a minimum of wasted time, energy, and materials, which is to say there will be a high level of *efficiency;*
4. Problems are bound to occur in any organization and *the early identification and timely resolution of these problems* is surely another criterion of an effective organization;
5. As the store of knowledge expands, new techniques emerge to assist organizations in fulfilling their missions. Another measure of organizational effectiveness, therefore, is *the degree to which an organization keeps up with and adopts new technology to improve its output;*
6. Change is endemic to all human life, and organizations should be prepared to accept and adapt to inevitable change. *The rapidity with which the organization accepts change and the number of personnel who readily adapt to such change* is also a measure of organizational effectiveness; and
7. Finally, in the course of daily operations, emergencies are bound to arise that require changes in schedules, work loads, and assigned duties. An effective organization is sufficiently flexible to *cope with emergency situations* without detracting from its ability to handle its regular responsibilities.

Organizational Effectiveness in the Seattle Police Department

There were eight indicators of organizational effectiveness contained in the questionnaire used in the study. The respondents rated the organization as "effective" on three indicators and something less than effective on the remaining five.

Indicators of high organizational effectivenss included the following items:

1. Seven out of every ten respondents felt that the productive output of the SPD was high;

2. Over three-fourths believed that the quality of services provided was high; and
3. Two out of every three respondents felt that the SPD coped effectively with emergency situations to a high degree.

On the less than effective side:

1. Slightly over one-half of the respondents indicated that efficiency within the organization was in need of improvement;
2. An astronomical nine out of ten felt that the ability of the SPD to identify and resolve problems was questionable;
3. Three out of every four believed that the organization could do more to keep up with the new technology; and
4. Over 80 percent of the respondents felt that the SPD should adapt more rapidly to change; and two-thirds indicated that, most of the time, the majority of personnel in the organization did not readily accept such change.

With regard to the quantity and quality of output, the SPD was seen as highly effective by the respondents in the study. Moreover, the respondents also rated the organization as effective in terms of coping with emergency situations. Given the highly bureaucratic nature of the SPD, however, with its strong reliance upon procedures, structure, and centralization, it was reasonable to expect that the traditional and measureable indicators of organizational effectiveness would be rated highly by its supervisors.

Still these same patent bureaucratic tendencies also operated to produce less than high ratings in other key areas. For example, research has shown that bureaucracies tend to be rather inflexible and resistant to change, including the adoption of new technology; and the ratings of the respondents certainly confirmed this relationship in the SPD. Moreover, because of their emphasis on the status quo and a strong procedural orientation, bureaucracies suffer from a kind of organizational myopia that makes it difficult to identify problems, especially ones that have not been encountered previously, and makes it even more difficult to develop and implement timely and cost-effective solutions to such problems once identified. Ninety percent of the respondents confirmed this situation in the SPD. Finally, again because of a slavish adherence to rules, regulations, and procedures, as well as a kind of organizational rigidity born of adherence to tradition, bureaucracies tend to utilize their resources in inefficient ways. Over one-half of the respondents identified this characteristic in the SPD.

A high rating for only three out of eight criteria of organizational effectiveness is certainly not inspirational to management. On balance, the SPD is caught up in the bureaucratic syndrome of action and reaction in a way that: (1) militates against efficiency, (2) obscures problems until they become crises, (3) relies excessively upon established rather than new technology, and, largely because of organizational rigidity, (4) renders the organization rather unadaptive to inevitable change.

Summary and Conclusions

This study has provided some insight into the management of one kind of organization in the public sector that is becoming increasingly significant in community affairs. Police departments throughout the nation are being subjected to demands for new services and an expansion of existing services to the community. Budgetary pressures and other limitations on resource availabilities impose a growing burden on the management of police departments operating, for the most part, in a bureaucratic setting to increase the satisfaction of the individual with a view toward obtaining greater productivity while, at the same time, posturing the organization for greater effectiveness.

The Seattle Police Department is, by most criteria, a high bureaucratic organization yet recognizing, at the same time, this condition, in and of itself, need not detract from its effectiveness. Moreover, the lack of formality in relationships within the SPD does not detract from its essentially bureaucratic orientation; but rather suggests that a strong team spirit exists among the members of the organization.

Additionally, many of the incumbents in supervisory positions within the SPD have strong feelings of personal achievement and job satisfaction as career police officers, as well as a highly developed sense of loyalty and responsibility to the organization. Still there was also abundant evidence that more of the incumbents would experience a stronger sense of personal self-fulfillment, not to mention an increase in the esteem accorded them by their peers, if the prevailing system of rewards were oriented toward the performance and expectations of the individual. In other words, it is most unlikely that the psychogenic needs of the individual will be fulfilled until the biogenic needs, related to tangible rewards, are met for the most part. To the extent that management can modify the system of rewards to provide for incentives that meet the individual's perception of equity, performance within the SPD will give rise to satisfaction which, in turn, will reinforce the expectation that subsequent performance will result in additional satisfaction. By this means the performance of all individuals in the organization will increase, and overall effectiveness will almost certainly rise. This is a worthy objective for the management of the SPD and, for that matter, any other police department or organization.

With specific regard to organizational effectiveness, this study has delimited, rather sharply, areas for improvement in the SPD. In essence, management should concentrate on upgrading organizational visibility which relates principally to: (1) the early identification and timely resolution of problems, (2) the continuing surveillance and assimilation of new technology, and, perhaps, most important of all, (3) the development of sensitivity, responsiveness, and adaptiveness to the myriad forces of inevitable change. One way in which the improvement can be accomplished is by placing greater emphasis on planning which tends to extend the visibility of the organization. Any organization operating without good long-range planning soon finds itself in a highly reactive mode moving from one crisis to another. The net effect is a loss of efficiency, a reduction in motivation, and an accelerating diminution of organizational effectiveness. The avoidance of this situation is the responsibility of management. It is the reason why management exists in the first place. The need is apparent; the challenge is there; the means for corrective action are available. All that remains is for management to assume the initiative. If the benefits of positive action appear unclear, then certainly the negative aspects of continued inaction are all too apparent.

PERSONALITY CHARACTERISTICS OF THE SUPERVISOR*

These are confusing and difficult times for law enforcement agencies. On the one hand, there are increasingly strident pleas for "law and order," and on the other hand, the competency and in some instances

*SOURCE: J. F. Hooke and H. H. Kraus, "Personality Characteristics of Successful Police Sergeant Candidates", reprinted by special permission of the *Journal of Criminal Law, Criminology, and Police Science,* copyright © 1971, by the Northwestern University School of Law Vol. 62, No. 1. pp. 104-6.

the basic humanity of the police is questioned (*e.g.* Misner, 1969). In the face of such irrational subjectivity, the need to obtain information about the effectiveness of local police forces has become imperative.

Basic to the appraisal of police force is an assessment of its selection and promotional procedures. In spite of the growing realization that personality assessment techniques have an important role to play in selection and promotion of personnel for many types of work, Naroll and Levitt (1963) report that few of the police forces of the major cities use personality tests as part of their assessment procedures. Yet the presence of such terms as "police mentality" in everyday speech provides evidence that personality factors may be quite important in the selection of police personnel.

The data presented here was collected as part of what was intended to be an extended study of the usefulness of objective personality inventories in the selection and promotion of police officers. Studied first were those who had passed both written and oral examinations for sergeant and, therefore, were eligible for promotion to that rank. This group was selected because, as sergeants they will play a crucial leadership and disciplinary role on the force (*e.g.* Wilson, 1950).

Method

Subjects. Thirty-seven officers of the Kansas City, Missouri Police Department were studied. All of these men had passed the written aptitude and oral examination for sergeant and were, thus eligible for promotion to that rank within the biennium. These men were from 26 to 46 years old (mean age was 33.3 years) and had 4 to 20 years experience on the force (mean service 8.7 years). Participation in this investigation was voluntary and "for the good of the department." All participants knew that the department had no access whatsoever to the test data, and, thus, it would have no bearing on their promotion.

Procedure. The following tests were administered to the successful candidates:

1. Minnesota Multiphasic Personality Inventory (Hathaway & McKinley, 1951), a widely used personality test designed to assess the presence of severe psychopathology.
2. Allport-Vernon-Lindzey Study of Values (Allport, *et al.*, 1960), intended to measure basic value orientation.
3. Gough Adjective Check List (Gough, 1952), a list of adjectives considered useful in determining self concept. In addi-

tion, on the assumption that the man who occupies a position would be a good judge of how another might perform in that position, all of the sergeants on the force were asked to anonymously rate the successful candidates. They were to assign each candidate a score from 1 (very poor) to 10 (excellent) on each of two scales: (1) "How good a policeman is this man?" (2) "How good a sergeant do you think he will be?"

An effort was made to obtain comparable data for unsuccessful sergeant candidates. These men were uniformly unwilling to cooperate. However, since most of the force had taken the Minnesota Multiphasic Personality Inventory (MMPI), it was possible to draw from this MMPI data pool a group of men who matched the primary subjects in age and length of service.

Results

The mean MMPI profiles of both the group of successful candidates and the comparison patrolmen peaked on scales 4 and 9. However, none of the MMPI scale scores were greater than one standard deviation above the mean of the general population. Overall, so far as the MMPI is adequate to reflect psychopathology, both groups of police officers are a normal lot, exhibiting high energy and little neurotic inhibition.

Statistically significant differences ($p < .05$) between the mean profiles of the two groups occurred on only three scales. The successful candidates were higher on scales K and 6 and lower on scale 0 than the patrolmen with whom they were matched. These differences suggest that as a group the successful sergeant candidates tend to depend more upon themselves, appear more self confident, are more sensitive in interpersonal relationships, and are more outgoing and genial than the patrolmen.

On the Study of Value Scales, the scores of the successful candidates did not differ significantly from those of normal males.

The Adjective Check List items endorsed by the majority of the successful candidates were both conventional and socially desirable. All but one saw himself as capable, cooperative, dependable, and practical. All but two also checked honest and responsible. Interestingly enough, despite the high pejorative nature of some of the items (*e.g.* greedy, cruel) there was no item which did not receive at least one endorsement.

TABLE 1 MMPI SUBSCALE SCORES (k CORRECTED)

MMPI Scale	Successful Candidates	Matched Patrolmen
L	2.67	3.24
F	2.97	3.51
K	17.19	14.76*
1	11.92	13.24
2	17.08	18.00
3	19.89	19.43
4	22.65	22.38
5	22.40	22.65
6	8.59	7.38*
7	23.65	23.84
8	23.68	22.59
9	19.73	20.22
0	20.43	25.03*

*Groups differ significantly ($p < .05$).

The correlation was .87 (*rho*) between the sergeant's opinion of "How good a policeman is this man?" and "How good a sergeant do you think he will be?" This indicates that those who were seen as good policemen were also regarded as potentially good sergeants.

The candidates were divided into two groups; one was made up of the 13 highest rated and the other 13 lowest rated. The MMPI and Study of Value Scores for the two groups were compared. No significant differences between the two groups emerged. However, it is of interest to note the differences between the two groups in frequency of abnormal MMPI scales. Of the 13 high-rated subjects, one had one scale above T-score 70, while among the low-rated candidates, three had one scale above T-score 70, and another had more than two scales in the abnormal range.

Conclusions

The following conclusions are suggested by the data:

1. The test material indicates that the successful candidates and their matched controls are psychologically normal.

behavior patterns of the supervisor **103**

2. The group of successful candidates, however, seems better suited for leadership and disciplinary roles than their matched controls.

3. Within the group of successful candidates for sergeant, men who were rated by established sergeants as good police officers were also rated as potentially good sergeants. Conversely, those who were rated as relatively poorer officers were also seen as poorer sergeant material.

4. The psychological tests did not differentiate between the candidates rated as good sergeant material and the group rated as relatively poorer candidates. Many explanations for this seem reasonable. For example, the two groups might be so similar that the psychological tests are insufficiently sensitive to differentiate between them.

LEADERSHIP VERSUS ADMINISTRATIVE ABILITY

Little empirical data is available concerning the relationship between supervisory and administrative skills pertaining to the role of the police supervisor. However, slowly but surely more administrative responsibilities are being given to first-level police supervisors. What personality characteristics does the supervisor possess, that can be used to reasonably assess his administrative ability? The article which follows (by Owens and Sindberg) addresses this issue.

Competence as a supervisor does not imply competence as an administrator, although there is much cross-over. Administrative ability requires attention to details, but so does good supervision. Both must demonstrate technical competence. However, the ability to handle such matters as budgeting, long-range planning, and developing personnel systems is the mark of a good administrator. While it may be desirable for supervisors to also possess this skill, it is not absolutely necessary that it be required of this person who has the day-to-day responsibility of leading, organizing, developing and urging his subordinates to perform well.

The police supervisor is quite obviously interested in the administrative matters in the police department. Primarily, he has a vital interest in the selection and training process because the new personnel eventually come to him as rookies. As a supervisor, he is constantly looking for highly intelligent, honest, and stable officers. The supervisor should constantly make suggestions on hiring processes which have failed to weed out the tempermentally, intellectually, or physically unqualified.

The supervisor is also extremely interested in the administrative processes for promotion and assignments. If either is defective, his ability to supervise efficiently is placed in jeopardy. A supervisor cannot divorce himself from many administrative matters in the department. Such pressing concerns as the affirmative action program, human relations training, minority recruit programs, and new budgetary procedures directly affect him.

Concerning the general administration of the department, the supervisor has an increasingly greater responsibility for the administrative tone of the department. The first line supervisor can help share the administrative and operational policies by recommending ways for improving the administrative demands placed upon him. He can show that various departmental regulations hinder his performance and derogate from the efficiency of the department. Often the supervisor is in the position to suggest additional administrative regulations that will ease his job (for example, the development of a simple form for responding to calls which turn out to be negative).

Rather than completing the usually required formal report, a simplified administrative procedure may be in order. The supervisor in many of these situations becomes a quasi-administrator.

The supervisor's attention is not always centered on operations which relate only to his performance. For instance, structural changes in the department or the development of new patrol, investigative or personnel procedures may appear to be feasible to him. He has the responsibility of bringing such matters to the attention of appropriate departmental administrators.

The supervisor cannot avoid administration. It is inherent in his job. They go hand in hand.

PERSONALITY TRAITS VERSUS ADMINISTRATIVE JUDGMENT*

The events of recent years have focused a great deal of attention on the skills, abilities, and personality traits of law enforcement officers. The increasing complexity of their duties and the demands made

*SOURCE: Robert G. Owens and Ronald M. Sindberg, "Personality Traits of Supervisors and Their Administrative Judgment," reprinted by special permission of the *Police Chief*, ©1973, by International Association of Chiefs of Police, Vol. 40. No. 5. pp. 70-73.

upon them have made these skills and personal characteristics increasingly important in the public eye. Psychological testing for such factors has been used to good advantage by American industry and some governmental agencies in the selection, assignment, and training of personnel at all levels for many years, but only recently has this approach been applied to policemen. So far, those studies which have been reported are almost entirely concerned with the front-line personnel of law enforcement: the patrolmen. This emphasis is not surprising, since it is primarily the patrolman who has to deal on the spot with an even greater variety of crisis situations. Still, industrial psychology tells us that the abilities and traits of the supervisory and administrative personnel of an organization are at least equally as important, even though they may be very different from those of the front-line worker. At this time, relatively little solid information is available regarding these qualities in supervisory and administrative law enforcement personnel. The present study looks at two of these factors, personality traits and administrative judgment, in a group of such law enforcement supervisors.

Selection of Measures

Since relatively little is known about the personality characteristics of this group, it is obviously desirable to use a measuring instrument which will assess a wide range of such characteristics. It should have a good national standardization for comparison purposes, and, if possible, should have been used in other police studies for further cross comparisons. Such an instrument is the Edwards Personal Preference Schedule (EPPS).[1] It not only has a suitable national standardization, but also was used in a major LEAA-supported study of Chicago policemen.[2]

Since the present study was concerned with supervisory and administrative police personnel, it was also desirable to try to evaluate at least some aspects of their administrative skills and abilities. The Adminstrative Judgment Test (AJT)[3] was selected for this purpose, largely because it had proven very useful in a previous study by the senior author with a group of high level government administrators.[4] This instrument measures one's understanding of administrative problems in large organizations, whether government or private. It is directed toward the common elements in the administrative process. It includes problems in the relationships between the headquarters and field officers in an organization and between staff and operating personnel, the timing of programs, and the organization of the office of the administrator. It does not attempt to measure technical knowledge in such fields as personnel, budgeting. or accounting. It requires some familiarity with the principles and practices of administration and also the ability to apply them.

The previous study,[5] as noted above, found that certain factors within the personality structure of public administrators were related to the effectiveness of their administrative judgment. Thus, an additional purpose of this study was to determine if the same relationships could be repeated with a group of law enforcement supervisors.

Present Study

Both the Administrative Judgment Test and the Edwards Personal Preference Schedule were administered to twenty-two law enforcement supervisors, sergeant rank and higher, from the Green Bay, Wisconsin, area, who were enrolled in a special University of Wisconsin course in administration. Some were supervisory level officers in a medium-sized city, while others were higher ranking personnel from smaller communities and rural areas.

Personality Traits

Looking first at the measured personality traits of these officers, a number of interesting comparisons can be made. It should be noted that the EPPS is designed to measure fifteen *personality variables*, plus giving a measure of *consistency*. These include:

1. **Achievement** (to accomplish something difficult; to rival and surpass others).
2. **Deference** (to admire and support a superior; to yield to the influence of another).
3. **Order** (to achieve organization, tidiness and precision).
4. **Exhibition** (to make an impression; to entertain or shock others).
5. **Autonomy** (to resist coercion and restriction; to be independent and free to act according to impulse).
6. **Affiliation** (to cooperate; to be friendly; to please; to remain loyal).
7. **Intraception** (to analyze and understand the feeling and behavior of others; to put oneself in the place of others).
8. **Succorance** (to be nursed, supported, protected, guided and consoled).

9. **Dominance** (to influence or direct the behavior of others by suggestion, persuasion or command).
10. **Abasement** (to submit to external force; to admit error or defeat; to seek punishment or misfortune).
11. **Nurturance** (to gratify the needs of the inexperienced, defeated, lonely or sick; to support, protect or heal).
12. **Change** (to seek new places, people or ideas; to be flexible, open-minded and progressive).
13. **Endurance** (to be able to withstand pain or hardships; to persist in an action despite opposition or setbacks).
14. **Heterosexuality** (to form and futher relationships with members of the opposite sex).
15. **Aggression** (to overcome opposition forcefully; to take revenge and injure others).
16. **Consistency** (the extent to which one answers the test items in the same way upon repetition).

It is possible simply to compare the traits shown by these law enforcement supervisors and administrators with those of the average male citizen. In addition, however, it is possible to hypothesize about the ways in which a police supervisor should be different from the general public in order to do his job well. The authors, based on their experiences in working with law enforcement personnel as well as utilizing general public knowledge and stereotypes, made an educated guess regarding the probable differences on each EPPS scale. The rationale for our independently arrived at assumptions was as follows:

• Policemen would show higher achievement scores than the average male because their work involves competing against other individuals who have broken society's laws.
• *Deference* would be lower because the policeman does not operate from a submissive posture.
• *Order* would be higher because of the regimentation and the mission of maintaining "law and order."
• *Exhibition* would be higher because the job, the uniform, and squad car do put him in the center of attention.
• *Autonomy* would be lower because he is generally conforming to conventionality and maintaining the status quo.
• *Affiliation* would be lower because he doesn't maintain a wide variety of friends outside of colleagues. He has to be a loner, to a considerable extent, and cannot be expected to please everyone. To do so would render him less objective.

- *Intraception* would be lower than average because he is not interested in understanding human behavior as much as he is in regulating it.
- *Succorance* would be lower because policemen should be strong enough in their functioning not to need emotional support from others.
- *Dominance* would be higher because directing the behavior of other people is the essence of his job.
- *Abasement* would be lower because they often must behave in a confident, superior manner, to a near self-righteous degree.
- *Nurturance* would be lower because even though they help people to some extent, it is not in a social work sense but rather an enforcer sense.
- *Change* would be lower because they are the guardians of the establishment and as such must resist change.
- *Endurance* would be higher because they must stick to assignments in a thorough, pursuing manner.
- *Heterosexuality* would be higher due to the ultramasculinity of the work and the typical disregard for effeminate males.
- *Aggression* would be higher because the work involves confrontation and aggressive behavior.

Since the Chicago study noted earlier[6] provided average scores for various groups of patrolmen on all EPPS scales, it also is possible to directly compare them with the scores made by the present group of police supervisors.

Table I shows the mean scores for men in general in the United States,[7] for the LEAA study[8] of Chicago patrolmen, and our own hypotheses of expectation in terms of higher or lower than average.

From Table I it can readily be seen that the law enforcement supervisors in our sample were less deferential and less affiliative, but more exhibitionistic, more dominant, and more heterosexual than the national averages for males to a statistically significant degree.

A very clear-cut similarity can be seen between the Chicago patrolmen and their near counterparts in the relatively rural Green Bay area when their scores are compared to the national average. Both law enforcement groups are in the same direction away from the national means on every scale except *Intraception* and *Consistency*. This would suggest a possible "law enforcement profile" on this particular testing instrument. The authors' hypotheses regarding direction of differences turned out to be correct except that both the Chicago and Green Bay groups were lower than average in order, higher than average in change, and lower than average in endurance. All of the differences which proved to be statistically significant were in the predicted direction.

The only differences between the scores of the two law enforcement groups which were significant at the .05 level of confidence or better were the Supervisory-Administrative group's lower scores on *Affiliation* and *Endurance* and higher scores on *Dominance* and *Consistency*. These differences may well reflect important considerations in the selection of supervisors from the patrol ranks, since it would seem that such supervisors would probably have to be more aloof from affiliation and more dominant or commanding, while psychological endurance may be a more important characteristic for a patrolman than for a supervisor. The large difference in *Consistency* is puzzling, and may well reflect other than just the patrolman vs. supervisor dichotomy.

The consistency scale tests whether the subject responds in a consistent manner in the identical situation upon repetition of that situation. The supervisory group was extremely close to the national average, but the Chicago study mean score of 4.23 tells us that, on the average, the policemen tested answered only 4.23 of 15 tests items consistently under duplicate circumstances. It would appear that this factor could have serious ramifications if this trait should prove to be synonymous with "consistently applying discretionary judgment" in enforcing the law. Inconsistency in justice can adversely affect the public's respect and confidence in law enforcement.

Administrative Judgment

With some individual exceptions, the AJT scores of this group of law enforcement supervisors and administrators tended to be considerably lower than those of the high level government administrators on whom the test was standardized. Their distribution of scores was most like those of lower to middle level government supervisory groups, although not identical with them. It should be remembered that most of these law enforcement supervisors have to function in many roles other than purely administrative ones, which may account for at least some of these observed differences.

In the previous Owens Study[9] involving 45 high level state government administrators, it was found that high *Achievement*, high *Dominance* and low *Deference* scores correlated to a statistically significant degree with administrative judgment, i.e., the higher the score on *Achievement* and *Dominance* and the lower the score in *Deference*, the higher the score in administrative judgment.

TABLE I

Personality Variables	National Means	Authors' Hyphotheses	Chicago Patrol-men Means	Green Bay Means
Achievement	14.79	Higher	16.21	15.29
Deference	14.19	Lower	13.26	12.76*
Order	14.69	Higher	12.90	13.52
Exhibition	12.75	Higher	14.69	14.52*
Autonomy	14.02	Lower	13.10	13.57
Affiliation	14.51	Lower	12.65	10.33**
Intraception	14.18	Lower	15.34	14.00
Succorance	10.78	Lower	9.40	9.67
Dominance	14.50	Higher	16.24	18.38**
Abasement	14.59	Lower	12.12	13.62
Nurturance	15.67	Lower	13.30	13.76
Change	13.87	Lower	15.28	14.09
Endurance	16.97	Higher	16.53	14.33
Heterosexuality	11.21	Higher	15.81	17.62**
Aggression	13.06	Higher	13.18	14.38
Consistency	11.35	Higher	4.23	11.81

*Significantly different from National means at .05 level of confidence.
**Different at .01 level of confidence.

It was hoped that if these results could be repeated with law enforcement supervisors they could contribute to a promotion selection guide for officers with administrative "personality structure potential." Interestingly, although the supervisory group did score higher on *Dominance* and lower on *Deference* than both the national averages and the Chicago study group, none of the correlations between individual scores on the AJT and the EPPS was significant. It is quite possible that there may not have been a large enough number of supervisors included in the present study to give a true picture of the degree of correlation. It is also important to note that the majority of this sample were in lower levels of supervision than the state administrators, and it is possible that the relationships between personality and administrative judgment are not maintained below a certain level of administration. Further and more extensive research with higher level law enforcement administrators is necessary and is planned for the future.

Summary

A group of supervisory and administrative law enforcement personnel were tested with the Edwards Personal Preference Schedule
(EPPS) and the Administrative Judgment Test (AJT), and their performance compared with national norms. Personality trait scores on
the EPPS were also compared with the published results of a large
study of patrolmen. The law enforcement supervisors were significantly higher than the national averages on the traits of *Dominance*,
Exhibition, and *Heterosexuality*, and significantly lower on *Deference*
and *Affiliation*. They were lower on *Affiliation* and *Endurance*, but
higher on *Dominance* and *Consistency* when compared with patrolmen.
They were most similar to the norms for lower to middle level
government administrators on the AJT. Further research is needed to
correlate these identified variables with measures of effectiveness to
determine if they can help serve as guides in the selection of supervisors suitable to today's task of enforcing the law in contemporary
society.

SELF EVALUATION, PERSONALITY AND
JOB PERFORMANCE*

The term "self-disclosure" was adopted by Jourard to describe the act
of revealing personal information to another. Ability and willingness
to make one's self known reflects "healthy" personality, whereas
"maladjustment" implies inability or reluctance to self-disclose.
Studies have shown positive relationships between self-disclosure and self-concept, liking, academic competence, and personal
adjustment.[1]

Not only has self-disclosure been considered an index of personal adjustment, but also a "Facilitative Condition" in various types
of helping relationships.[2] In a review of self-disclosing behavior, and
its application to policework, Parker suggested that officers may be
less hostile and defensive in their relations with citizens if they are
able to self-disclose to at least one significant person.[3]

Lasakow found that compared with male college students,

---

*SOURCE: L. Craig Parker, Jr. and Marvin C. Roth, "The Relationship Between
Self-Disclosure, Personality, and a Dimension of Job Performance of Policemen,"
Journal of Police Science and Administration, Vol. 1, No. 3, September 1973, pp. 282-286.
Reprinted by permission of the publisher.

police officers were significantly lower self-disclosers. His sample, which included primarily officers above the rank of patrolman, also was very small (N=10), so that his results must be interpreted cautiously. A number of questions may be raised concerning Lasakow's results. If police officers are low self-disclosers, do they also have significantly different personalities as compared to the general population? Does police work attract certain personalities? Does police experience shape personalities? The present study attempts to examine the relationship of self-disclosure to personal adjustment in a group of municipal police officers.[4]

Many writers and investigators have attempted to confirm the existence of a police personality which sets policemen apart from the rest of the population. Recent research has characterized the typical police officer as cynical, conservative, independent, orderly, punishment-oriented, and authoritarian.[5] However, other studies have revealed that policemen appear to be similar to the social class from which they were drawn, the general population, or even comparable to a college sample.[6]

Part of the difficulty in assessing the existence of characteristic personality traits of police has been related to defining a suitable control group. Control groups have ranged from working class males to college students. Investigators who have found differences between police and controls have suggested the existence of a police personality. While police may not possess totally different personality profiles or orientations from other individuals, they may differ on certain specified characteristics. Smith, Locke, Walker, and McNamara have found increased authoritarianism in the same officers tested over a period of time. Also, Parker, Reese, and Murray have found an increase in dogmatism in police officers over time.[7]

Another method which has been employed to study the effect of experience on personality involves comparing less experienced with more experienced officers. McNamara found that men who served on the force for two years scored significantly higher on authoritarianism. Therefore, if dogmatism or authoritarianism does not exist through occupational selection, police experience may shape personality in terms of these particular constructs.[8]

Neiderhoffer has attributed low self-disclosure to constant fear of being reported to the commissioner.[9] Therefore, some policemen, when off duty, tend to conceal their occupation and avoid conflicts of any nature. Tauber suggests that policemen need a sense of isolation from the public to reduce cognitive strain in enforcing the law. The value then of openness or self-disclosure in police work is still open to speculation.[10]

The present study is focused on self-disclosure and its relationship to general personality adjustment, along with self-disclosure and its relationship to peer ratings of police effectiveness. The specific hypotheses of the present study are:

1. Police officers become less self-disclosing as a result of experience in police work.
2. Police officers who are high self-disclosers demonstrate better personal adjustment than low self-disclosers.
3. Police officers who are high self-disclosers are perceived as more effective by their peers for work as crowd control specialists.

Method

SUBJECTS

Forty-one police officers from a Canadian city were randomly selected from a group of volunteers for crowd control training.

MEASURES

The sixty-item self-disclosure questionnaire was administered to the officers as compiled by Jourard from a list of 100 personal questions representing "the kind of thing one person asks another if one wishes to know him personally." The items were classified in groups of 10 within each of 6 more general categories of information about the self. The answer sheet consisted of a check list on which the extent of disclosure on each topic was indicated. A rating of "0" indicated no disclosure, a "1" represented disclosure of a general nature, a "2" indicated full detailed disclosure, and an "X" stood for misrepresentation of self. "Target Persons" for disclosure were "Wife" and "Male Friend." In addition to obtaining separate scores for "Wife" and "Male Friend" a total score was obtained by combining the two scales.

The California Personality Inventory was administered for the purpose of obtaining an overall assessment of personality. It provided a number of advantages:

1. the inventory was designed primarily for use with "normals";
2. each scale is intended to cover one important personal characteristic for social living and interaction;

3. the CPI has been employed extensively in prior research studies and;
4. in the absence of a control group, the officer's scores may be compared to the standardization sample.

Overall CPI adjustment assessments were made by two psychologists, with a 1 to 5 rating for varying degrees of adjustments. Both psychologists had employed the CPI frequently in their professional psychological work. Ratings were combined and the average score employed.

A peer-rating scale was devised by the investigators primarily for the purpose of selection of candidates for crowd control training. The ratings were based on peer assessments of ability to remain calm in the face of verbal attack, as well as the ability to follow instructions under emotional stress. Each police officer candidate was asked to rank up to fifteen other officers, starting by listing the most qualified officer first. Candidates were asked to rate only officers whom they knew rather intimately.

Testing Procedure

The subjects were tested in groups of approximately 20 over a period of 7 days. The testing was administered in conjunction with selection of candidates for a crowd control training program.

Results

Pearson Product-moment correlations (r) between self-disclosure, years of police experience, peer ratings of effectiveness in crowd control, and clinical assessments of personal adjustment yielded a significant correlation between years of experience and total self-disclosure. The results offered supported the hypothesis (1) which indicated that self-disclosure tends to decrease with police experience.

No significant r's were found to offer support for the second (2) and third (3) hypotheses suggesting no significant relationship between self-disclosure and overall personal adjustment or between self-disclosure and ratings of peers on effectiveness in dealing with crowds.

A group mean for each scale was plotted to yield a CPI profile for the entire sample which was highly similar to the CPI standardization sample of more than 6,000 cases. This total includes a wide range of ages, socio-economic groups, and geographic areas.[11]

Further research in this area incorporating a larger sample of police would seem to be helpful in examining the overall adjustment of police in comparison with other citizens.

Discussion

The results indicated that as experience in police work increases, self-disclosure decreases. This finding is supported by investigators and theorists who hold that there are elements within police work that encourage individuals to be closed-mouthed and cautious in their relation with others.

Figures 1 and 2 show the specific areas, or "aspects" of self-disclosure. The trends suggest that more experienced officers (with more than the mean of nine years experience) self-disclose relatively less than less experienced officers, particularly in regard to work and feelings about one's self (personality). This trend was especially pronounced in disclosure to wife. Black and Reiss found a prevalent tendency for police officers' wives to worry about their husbands' safety. Possibly officers prefer to minimize such worrying by avoiding discussion about work and areas of personal concern.[12]

Low self-disclosure to a male friend may be reflective of a general pattern of low self-disclosure, which may be learned for occupationally or personally adjustive reasons, as suggested earlier. However, reasons for low self-disclosure to wife and male friend remain speculative.

TABLE I

CORRELATIONS OF SELF-DISCLOSURES, EXPERIENCE, PEER RATING
AND CPI ADJUSTMENT RATINGS

Measures	SD Total	SD Wife	SD Male F	Yrs. Ex.	Peer R	CPI Adj.
SD Total	—	.32	.68	*−.34	.09	.07
SD Wife		—	−.02	−.22	.18	−.07
SD Male Friend			—	.22	.06	.09
Years Experience				—	.19	.23
Peer Rating					—	.15
CPI Adjustment Rating						—

* p < .05

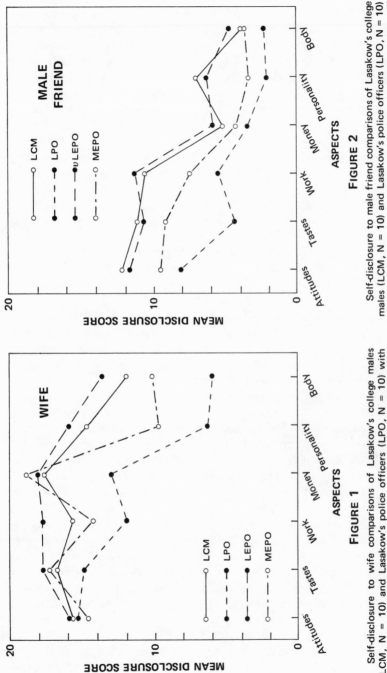

FIGURE 2

Self-disclosure to male friend comparisons of Lasakow's college males (LCM, N = 10) and Lasakow's police officers (LPO, N = 10) with "less experienced" (LEPO, N = 24) and "more experienced" (MEPO, N = 15) officers of the present study.

FIGURE 1

Self-disclosure to wife comparisons of Lasakow's college males (LCM, N = 10) and Lasakow's police officers (LPO, N = 10) with "less experienced" (LEPO, N = 24) and more experienced (MEPO, N = 15) officers of the present study.

Lasakow's conclusion that policemen as a whole are low self-disclosers was not verified by the results shown in Figures 1 and 2. The less experienced officers of the present study disclosed as much or more than Lasakow's college males. Also, the graphs suggest Lasakow's officers disclosed less than both the less experienced and more experienced officers. However, Lasakow's officers averaged 7.2 years older than the more experienced officers of the present study. The evidence has been regarded as supportive of the experience hypothesis, since age has been shown to have little effect on self-disclosure. While the U.S. and Canadian cultures resemble each other in many respects, there may be subtle differences that affect levels of self-disclosure.[13]

No significant correlations occurred between total self-disclosure and either the clinician ratings for overall adjustment or any of the individual CPI scales. Therefore, no support was offered for using total self-disclosure as a criterion for personal adjustment. Slight positive correlations occurred between self-disclosure to wife and all the scales. Also, self-disclosure of male friend correlated negatively with 14 of the 18 scales. However, no significant correlations occurred between self-disclosure to wife or male friend and overall CPI adjustment assessments. Therefore, the conclusion that self-disclosure to wife is related to personal adjustment, whereas self-disclosure to male friend is related to personal maladjustment, would require more research evidence.

No relationship was apparent between self-disclosure and peer rating of crowd control behavior. The results suggest little justification for advocating self-disclosure or personal adjustment as relevant factors for this particular dimension of law enforcement. However, more investigation is necessary to establish whether self-disclosure and personality are related to other aspects of police work.

Even though present as well as past research findings indicate that police officers tend to change with experience, the changes do not appear sufficient to justify regarding police as having a unique personality. The CPI profile for the group of officers was comparable to the "normal" population. Also, no scales correlated significantly with experience, except the self-acceptance (Sa) scale. Therefore, the police in this sample appear to be personally comparable to the general population, regardless of experience. Other changes that occur with experience may have little relationship to personality or to personal adjustment as assessed by the CPI.

The present study was limited by the possible effect motivational set of the officers. The officers were informed that the testing information would be used for selecting candidates for crowd control training and, therefore, candidates were instructed to put their names on the tests. Also, generalizations about "total" self-disclosure remain tentative. The self-disclosure answer sheet allowed for "target persons" beyond wife and male friend, including "mother," "father," "female friend," and "other." However, while 39 of the 41 officers completed both wife and male friend target persons, very few completed the other target person columns. A more global picture of self-disclosure may be attained by a careful consideration of self-disclosure to persons beyond wife and male friend.

More studies focusing on the changes which occur in police officers' personalities over-time, as well as what accounts for such changes, are necessary before determining how such changes effect personal adjustment and effectiveness in various aspects of law enforcement.

JOB SATISFACTION: A MEASUREMENT OF SUCCESS AND ATTITUDES

Job satisfaction is a term "bandied" about by academics and practitioners alike. It is quite likely that in teaching the subject of police supervision in a university or training academy, the term is used to describe morale, values, attitudes, understanding, and many, many more concepts relating to managing or supervising people.

The objective of this section is to discuss attitudes and success in the performance of police work. The article chosen introduces one aspect of this work—arrest performance in relation to job and personal satisfaction. Crucial to this discussion, however, one must consider the word "attitude" in relation to the concepts of job attitudes and values. First of all, an attitude is a predisposition of a person toward a thing or idea in a favorable or unfavorable manner. Attitudes are developed concerning how others shall and should act. Attitudes are not necessarily based on sound information or research; rather, these preconceived notions are frequently based on whim, folklore, rearing, tradition, and social conditions.

In the work environment, attitudes are often associated with sterotyping. Under this idea, certain persons and groups are fit into a specific pattern. In police organizations this is especially prevalent in some selected jobs. For example, the person who wished to enter the police community relations area is too often characterized as a "do-gooder" or someone who "can't make it on the street." Likewise the sterotypes of supervisors, middle-management persons, top-level managers, financial experts, and outside police consultants, to name just a few, are common.

The importance to the supervisor of these attitudes concerning people and jobs cannot be overemphasized because to a significant degree, they are the attitudes and beliefs of his subordinates. The concepts of job satisfaction cannot be divorced from morale. However, morale is distinguished from job satisfaction by the fact that morale refers to the collective attitudes and feelings of the group. Job satisfaction is used to describe the feeling of the individual. In short, job satisfaction is the way the individual perceives his work while morale refers to the feeling that the group has toward a collective project.

For the police supervisor, job satisfaction and morale directly affect his own efficiency plus that of his subordinates and his group because the work role of the employee can either satisfy or dissatisfy his basic needs. When workers are highly dependent upon a supervisor, as is the case in police organizations, the manner in which the supervisor exercises his power, the pressures that he exerts, and obedience he expects, determine the attitudes of the employee toward his job. The employee's job satisfaction will be low if he is placed in a situation where the job presents what appears to be a dead-end with little opportunity to participate in decisions affecting his own destiny.

One of the most important signals of which the supervisor must be aware is employee withdrawal of any pride or involvement in the goals of the unit. This comes from the conflict of roles that the employee experiences which reduces communication with the supervisor. Withdrawal is merely a means of coping with the stresses that accompany the conflict. Job satisfaction obviously suffers in such a situation. The supervisor must aggressively pursue a solution to individual withdrawal before it sets off a chain reaction and thereby jeopardizes the effectiveness of the entire unit.

In introductory material such as this, the term "job satisfaction" can be used only loosely to cover the overall favorable disposition to a job as well as the intrinsic satisfaction which is derived from the content of the work process. But the supervisor will do well to consider some of the more common items which have been indicia of favorable job satisfaction. Job satisfaction is related to challenging work. In police departments, the supervisor can help by creating a work environment that permits a reasonable degree of autonomy and freedom and not the stifling kind of leadership that discourages innovation and participation in group problems. Officers should be given credit for suggestions whether they are adopted or not.

The supervisor's desire for productivity by his subordinates is directly related to their job satisfaction. For example, if the officer sees his job as essential and he receives some satisfaction from performing it, he will likely devote the extra five or ten minutes required to successfully conclude an investigation or fully prepare an incident report. Liking the job creates the motivation to remain in the job. When this is the case, there is less of a probability that the worker will leave voluntarily. The supervisor must count on his subordinates to show up for work regularly. When he cannot, the productivity of the unit decreases. To help control this kind of situation, the supervisor must increase the job satisfaction of the individual officer, because one of the sure signs of poor job satisfaction is increased and unacceptable levels of absenteeism.

In summary, the supervisor must view the entire person when it comes to dealing with his subordinates. Attitudes and beliefs affect morale which in turn affect the job satisfaction of the officer, which in turn affects productivity. Each one has a detrimental impact on the police mission, and taken collectively, the mission cannot be accomplished. The supervisor must consider the organizational, situational, and personal methods when considering the subject of job satisfaction. Structure has its effects. Incidents themselves have an effect. Psychological and physiological restrictions have an effect. Supervision and the supervision process are central to the effective operation of a police department. If the supervisor communicates with the men so that they believe that they can have some influence on the supervisor's decision, there is a greater possibility of good job satisfaction. Open and concerned supervision is therefore mandatory. By doing his best to insure that his men like their job, the supervisor can handle group morale problems with enlightenment.

Despite the fact that there are numerous job-related matters over which the police supervisor has little or no control—salaries and fringe benefits, for example—his skill in handling assignments, decision making and fairness go a long way in assuring that the men like their jobs and are satisfied with what they are doing. The following article provides insight into one factor in the complex subject of police job satisfaction.

ARRESTS, JOB SATISFACTION AND
PERSONAL VARIABLES*

When considering the duties of a patrolman, the process of arresting law violators may be viewed as an integral part of the job. Since the arrest process has great impact on the general citizenry, an understanding of the motivations influencing the performance of the police officer is deemed valuable to law enforcement administrators.

The focus of this study is an exploration of the relationship between job satisfaction and personal characteristics among patrolmen in the Costa Mesa (California) Police Department, and their recorded arrest performance for one year. If arrests by officers differ substantially, it is valuable to identify combinations of variables influencing these differences. This information should be of great assistance in selecting the type of patrolman who would best fulfill the needs of a community as the community perceives its needs.

The general research question underlying this study may be stated thusly: *What is the relationship between arrest performance among patrolmen and various aspects of job satisfaction, political liberalism, age, time in police work, educational level, and veteran's status?*

In exploring the independent variables relating to arrest practices by policemen, there are a number of commonly held beliefs about these variables.

For example, there is a belief by the general populace that younger, as well as less experienced officers make more arrrests because of more vigor and a need to assert their authority. In other words, "rookies," after they reach a level of proficiency, make more arrests than more mature and experienced officers. The experienced officer is believed to have the capability for finding alternatives and more effective methods of arrest. The older or more experienced officers are no longer "badge happy."

Another belief holds that the student, experiencing the educational process, generates wisdom and judgment that, in turn, produces a more tolerant attitude toward his fellow man. In this respect, the higher the education attainment of an officer, the fewer arrests he will make. This theory is supported by the recommendations of *The Challenge of Crime in a Free Society.* [1]

---

*SOURCE: Robert P. Green, Edward H. Glasgow and Lyle Knowles, "Arrest Performance Among Patrolman in Relation to Job Satisfaction and Personal Variables," reprinted by special permission of the *Police Chief,* copyright ©1973 by International Association of Chiefs of Police, Vol. 40, No. 4, 28 and 33-34.

Another belief is that a satisfied employee is more productive than a dissatified one. Also, money or level of wages does not have a great influence on job satisfaction. This general belief about employees does not necessarily indicate that arrests correlate with production by police officers. The goal of the policeman is the protection of life and property; and arrests, as a deterrent to violations against life and property, are a method used to obtain this goal.

The theory designated by these commonly held beliefs about arrest performance is multifaceted. A young officer who is comparatively new in his job, who has a lower level of education, who is satisfied with his working conditions and supervision, will make a greater number of arrests than an officer who is dissatisfied, well educated, more experienced, and older.

The hypotheses evolving from the foregoing theoretical framework predict that significant differences will exist between groups of patrolmen with a high-arrest record versus those with a low-arrest record for the following variables:

- Satisfaction with opportunity for promotion.
- Satisfaction with supervision.
- Satisfaction with pay.
- Satisfaction with type of work performed.
- Satisfaction with type of person with whom he works.
- Political viewpoint.
- Veteran's status.
- Educational level.
- Months of police service.
- Age.

Limitations of the Study

Because of the ex post facto nature of the current study, the ability to manipulate the independent variables was not present. In additon, generalizations to larger populations must be considered with relative caution because the selection criteria for the Costa Mesa Police Department are different from other agencies classifying employees into the patrolman category. Costa Mesa requires 60 units of college credit to be eligible to enter the testing process. Caution should also be exercised because of the small sample used.

Research Design and Methodology

The sample used in this study consisted of 20 patrolmen, assigned to the Patrol Bureau for the year 1970, who had not transferred in or out of the Bureau during this period.

The partolmen comprising the sample were ranked from high to low according to the number of arrests made during 1970. The upper 50 percent were considered to be the "High Performance" group, and the lower 50 percent the "Low Performance" group. The 20 patrolmen were then requested to complete an anonymous questionnaire and return it to one of the authors. All of the officers complied.

The instrument used to measure the various aspects of job satisfaction was the Job Description Inventory.[2] Political liberalism was measured by an instrument, previously validated by one of the researchers, consisting of five statements of a political nature. Subjects responded to the statements on a six-point scale ranging from "strongly agree" to "strongly disagree." A high score reflects a high level of political liberalism. Veteran's status was measured on a scale of from zero to five points involving a weighted combination of length of service and highest rank attained. Educational level and age were recorded in years, and length of police service in months.

A student's t ratio was used to test for a significant difference between the means of the High Performance and Low Performance groups on the variables involved.

The Data

Upon examining *Table 1*, it may be seen that the Low Performance group had a significantly higher level of job satisfaction regarding opportunity for promotion than the High Performance group. There was no significant difference between the groups regarding the other satisfaction variables.

Table 2 reflects a significant difference between the groups at the .01 level in relation to years of education. The High Performance group reported a signifcantly higher level of educational attainment than the Low Performance group. Although no significant differences occurred regarding the other personal variable, it is interesting to note the relative low and consistent scores on the political liberalism scale. This trend toward conservatism might be expected in this case, and tends to lend validity to the results of the study.

In an effort to further explore the relationship between high-arrest performance and years of education, a Pearson's r was computed for these two variables. An r of + .51 was obtained, which was significant at the .05 level. This high-positive correlation coefficient tends to support the results of the t ratio in that the more years of education attained, the higher the arrest rate.

The correlation between number of arrests and months of service as a police officer was found to be + .015, which was not significant.

TABLE 1 DIFFERENCES IN JOB SATISFACTION

Satisfaction Variable	Group				p
	High Performance (N = 10)		Low Performance (N = 10)		
	M	SD	M	SD	
Opportunity for Promotion	6.3	2.9	10.8	5.5	<.05 t = −2.25
Supervision	37.2	14.4	42.9	9.7	>.05
Pay	12.0	3.9	12.3	4.5	>.05
Type of Work	35.8	7.6	38.0	6.0	>.05
Type of Person Worked With	38.5	11.6	39.4	12.7	>.05

TABLE 2 DIFFERENCES IN PERSONAL VARIABLES

Variable	Group				p
	High Performance (N = 10)		Low Performance (N = 10)		
	M	SD	M	SD	
Political Liberalism	12.1	1.9	12.1	3.4	>.05
Veteran's Status	3.0	1.5	2.5	1.8	>.05
Years of Education	3.9	.6	2.4	1.0	<.01 t = 4.1
Months of Police Service	36.7	13.3	52.1	37.9	>.05
Age in Years	26.9	2.4	28.4	8.3	>.05

Interpretations and Conclusions

Upon examining the results of the tested hypotheses, it appears that the theory generated from commonly held beliefs about arrest performance by patrolmen was not generally supported. Significance was revealed in only three of the statistical tests. There was a significant difference between the means of the High Performance group and the Low Performance group in relation to attitude about promotional opportunity and the educational level attained. The patrolmen were not substantially different in the means of satisfaction with their pay, supervision, work performed, people worked with, and political viewpoint. There was no difference between the means of the two groups in relation to the demographic data of age, veteran's status, and length of police service.

Two interpretations are suggested regarding the difference between the groups on their attitude about opportunity for promotion. The higher performance group may have held their opinions because their college experiences trained them to analyze the situation. The lower performance group (less education) did not have this training, and were slower to analyze the situation. There is, in fact, a limited promotional opportunity in Costa Mesa due to a retarded population expansion. Another interpretation is that the officers are dissatisfied with their opportunity, which causes a negative or punitive attitude toward the public which results in an arrest where it is possible. The authors submit that the first explanation is more accurate, particularly when it is noticed that there was no significant difference between the groups in their attitude about other aspects of job satisfaction. Another interpretation of the two group's differences could be that the college-educated officer is so motivated, that even though he realizes there is not much opportunity for promotion, he still performs at a high level of efficiency.

An interpretation of the significant difference between the groups in relation to educational attainment could be that submitting to the educational process trains the student to give those in authority over him what those in authority want.

There seems to be more ability to do the policeman's job when a higher educational level is present. The arrest process is a major portion of the methods available to the policeman to assist him to attain the goals of protecting lives and property from depredations by the antisocial segment of the population. The skills and knowledge obtained in the educational process are applicable to problem-solving situations the policeman faces. Therefore, educative reasoning might be cited as a valuable tool.

The areas where there was no significant difference contribute their share of information when considering the theory established earlier from commonly held beliefs. Where there seemed no significant difference between the high and low performance group in relation to age, length of service, and job satisfaction, the theory was not supported. Younger officers with less experience did not seem to arrest more than older, more experienced officers. The younger, less experienced officers may arrest less frequently due to lack of knowledge and the appropriate self-confidence to successfully carry through the arrest process. Whether a high-arrest performance is or is not desirable from a policeman, according to agency philosophy, this study attempted to identify those variables that could have some impact upon the predicted variable: number of arrests. It is suggested that whatever an agency desires from its patrolmen can be achieved if the information generated by this study is considered.

The authors submit that the value of the current study is twofold. First, it has revealed on a preliminary basis that many of the commonly held beliefs concerning high-arrest records among patrolmen warrant further investigation, particularly regarding the attainment of higher education. Second, the research design and methodology used in this study might well serve as a viable model for the exploration of these areas on a larger scale.

THE POLICE ORGANIZATION:
EFFECTIVENESS AS A GOAL

What is the relationship between productivity, morale, and job satisfaction? For years it had been assumed that there was a positive correlation between morale and productivity. Recent research findings, however, have destroyed this assumption. An employee can be quite happy and contented with his job and contribute nothing. Conversely, it was found that he could completely dislike his work and still be productive. These conclusions are especially pertinent for the supervisor who can, by some proven techniques, insure that productivity in his unit remains high.

Pride is one key to productivity. It is one variable that has been established as showing a distinct relationship to productivitiy. High performance and high productivity are closely related. A second key for the supervisor to consider is that workers who have a higher job involvement probably set higher levels of performance and productivity for themselves. The supervisor must take care not to place unnecessary roadblocks in the paths of workers. Stated somewhat differently, job satisfaction is decreased if an adequate account of worker aspirations is not considered. A third key to increased productivity is especially important for the police supervisor. The police officer's job is multifaceted and requires a great deal of skill to perform. Various studies have established that high productivity is correlated to job satisfaction which is closely allied with the factors and required skills present in police work. The patrol officer, for example, does not have a standardized routine job. Therefore, he has the opportunity to exhibit his talents which in turns acts as a motivator. The supervisor should always strive to create a work atmosphere where the person can secure greater job and personal fulfillment through greater productivity.

It can be seen that individual job satisfaction, group morale, and high productivity go together. What is the force which is necessary to harness this highly desirable situation? The supervisor and his quality of leadership. Because the supervisor's relationship to the group is so important, various research investigations have found that the group-oriented supervisor is a high producer. Some reasons are that he spends more time on supervision than other supervisors; he develops a closeness to his workers and tends to identify with them; he exhibits more compassion toward the employees; he does not take a punitive approach to personal problems; and finally, he is available and accessible when problems arise.

In law enforcement work, it is very difficult to identify exactly what productivity is. To the individual patrolman it may mean the number of felony arrests made, traffic tickets issued, or amount of time spent patroling his beat. To the supervisor, it may mean that selected crime rates in his area have been reduced, patrolman absenteeism has dropped, or fewer serious felony arrests have occurred because of increased patrol emphasis. The same kinds of considerations are found higher up in the organization. If the supervisor is indeed concerned about increasing the productivity of his unit, he first must decide what his goals are and the ways of achieving them. When setting out benchmarks for achieving these goals, the supervisor naturally considers increasing individual productivity to reach the goal. What this means is that to improve productivity he must be able to measure it, thereby permitting comparisons. Not only does measurement allow comparison, it also helps to identify specific problems, evaluate particular activities, identify areas in need of special attention, establish new individual and group goals, and allow proper accountability to the public.

One major way of measuring police productivity, although an admittedly weak one, is to measure the increase or decrease in crime statistics. It is frequently said that reducing crime is a major police activity. Rightly or wrongly, the public expects the police to help reduce the incidence of crime. Therefore, the supervisor, when setting his goals and organizing the wherewithall to achieve them, cannot neglect to concern himself with increasing productivity to reduce the number of reported offenses. In other measurable ways such as apprehending persons responsible for crime, improving response time to criminal and non-crime related incidents, and the public's feeling of being secure, the supervisor can establish measurable goals by which to evaluate the productivity and effectiveness within his unit.

DETERMINING POLICE EFFECTIVENESS*

The motto of the Chicago Police Department is "To Serve and Protect." How well these objectives are accomplished are matters of serious concern to command personnel and, most significantly, to its superintendent.

No police department can accomplish effectively the task of service and protection to the public without the public's support, and this support is given by the public in direct proportion to its opinion of how well the police are performing their duties.

Survey Initiated

In December 1973, the Chicago Police Department Service Survey program was initiated. Each victim and complainant who received police service that resulted in the preparation of a case report was mailed a prepaid postcard asking for his comments. The survey postcard was computer produced as a by-product of an existing computerized case reporting system. The return portion of the postcard bore an identifying case report number, permitting the department to identify the incident to which the respondent referred his comments.

*SOURCE: James M. Rochford, "Determining Police Effectiveness," reprinted by special permission of FBI Law Enforcement Bulletin, Copyright © 1974, by the Federal Bureau of Investigation, Vol. 43, No. 10, pp. 16-18

Comments received thus far show that approximately 94 percent of those responding to the survey stated they were satisfied with the service received from the Chicago Police Department. Six percent of the responses, however, were from Chicago citizens who said they had not received satisfactory service. The ultimate standard in the quality of police service is, of course, 100-percent satisfaction from the people. In pursuit of this optimum goal, I directed that an investigation be made into the circumstances that prompted a person to judge the police service he received as unsatisfactory.

Findings

An intensive examination was made of 500 cases where citizens had reported receiving unacceptable police service. Some of the findings are very enlightening and may cause changes in the traditional attitudes of police administrators concerning the training and the conduct of their men.

For example, police officers who responded promptly, acted courteously, and conducted a thorough preliminary investigation often were accused of providing unsatisfactory service. Actually, some of the most efficient police officers were among those who were the objects of more than one dissatisfied complaint. A follow-up interview with the complaining citizen revealed that the police officer may have been too impersonal. The citizen interpreted this as indifference on the part of the policeman to the victim's plight.

It also was learned from the survey that police contacts with elderly victims must be especially tactful since a proportionately large number of the dissatisfied respondents were 60 years old or older, and the majority were women. A geographic plotting of the elderly complainants indicated their residences were located in areas with a high density of convalescent and old-people homes.

According to the survey, the type of incident being investigated will influence the citizen's perception of whether he received adequate police service. The investigation of crimes against property led to 64 percent of the complaints, as opposed to crimes against the person. Burglary and theft investigations gave rise to the most complaints of unsatisfactory service. Failure to retrieve stolen property was the basis for most complaints in this category. Interviews revealed citizens expect the police to do more to recover property. This expectation is interwoven with many of the other survey findings.

The preliminary investigator must be cautious so as not to give the citizen an unreasonable expectation for the recovery of his property by the follow-up investigation. This will lessen the chance of a victim becoming disappointed and resentful when recovery of his possessions is not made. Rather, the preliminary investigator should be candid with a victim when, due to a complete lack of physical evidence and a description of the offender, the possibilities for solution of the crime and recovery of any stolen property are remote.

There was some criticism regarding the response of evidence technicians who examine the crime scenes for clues. It was found that in the majority of cases, when the technician did respond for followup investigation, the victim either was not at home or was unavailable.

Perhaps because of the influence of movies and television programs, where police investigations are brought to a swift and neat conclusion, citizens expect each and every crime to be successfully concluded. In fact, the pat solution of most crimes is not possible. Further evidence of the influence entertainment programs generate was found in the vocabulary citizens chose to rate the quality of police service. Many of the returned survey cards contained such police jargon as "No Evidence Tech responded to scene," and "Beat man okay, but Patrol Sergeant discourteous," which evidently had been adapted from cinema and television productions.

Another finding was that both black and white citizens basically had identical complaints, but that the non-English-speaking persons reported unsatisfactory service at a considerably higher rate than others.

A geographical analysis showed that on the basis of population a disproportionate number of complaints emanated from 3 of 21 police districts surveyed. While these three districts are near or in the lower half of all districts by population, they ranked first, third, and fifth in the number of complaints.

Census Bureau data confirms that high concentrations of Spanish-speaking citizens live in these three districts. Followup interviews with Spanish-speaking complainants disclosed that in most cases the police response was satisfactory, but language barriers prevented complete communication and understanding. This is not a new finding, but the survey did contribute further documentation of the seriousness of the problem.

Analysis

Analysis of followup interviews and case-report examinations performed in the survey led to the finding that only 1.5 percent of the respondents did in fact receive unsatisfactory service. This figure could be very misleading. Assuming that the 1.5 percent is representative of the rate of dissatisfaction of all Chicago residents affected by police service, it would appear that the police department has come very close to the optimum standard of 100-percent satisfaction. This, of course, is perfection and a level not likely to ever be achieved by any organization having the complex and difficult responsibilities found in law enforcement. On the other hand, projecting this percentage to all calls (2,452,806) received in 1973 for police service suggests that annually an estimated 36,792 calls might not have been handled adequately. This number (approximately 100 per day) is not an acceptable level of police performance, and steps are being taken to insure a higher rate of satisfactory service.

The survey covered a 6-month period and was concluded on June 12, 1974. A total of 176,361 cards were mailed; 46,879 were returned with:

> 44,083 (94 percent) reporting satisfactory service;
> 2,534 (5.4 percent) reporting unsatisfactory service;
> 262 (0.6 percent) other.

The "other" category represents cards returned to the department with comments irrelevant to police service or which were returned by the post office as undeliverable.

There is still one area to be explored. Although the number of respondents is sufficient to make certain projections and draw certain conclusions, an attempt should be made to determine the type of service the survey's nonrespondents received and why they failed to respond. This action is deemed necessary for two reasons. First, the police department is a service agency, and a service, as opposed to many tangible products, tends to have more degrees of relative satisfaction to a recipient than, for example, a brand of beverage, the taste of which a consumer may either like or dislike. Requiring respondents, therefore, to make a selection from among "poor, fair, satisfactory, or excellent" ratings of police service may have discouraged their participation and response. Second, the Chicago Police Department lacks information on existing police department surveys of this type which could serve as a basis for comparison.

The department's Human Relations Section, in an attempt to determine why only 26.6 percent of potential respondents replied, conducted a followup of 84 persons who had been mailed a survey questionnaire. Excluding 28 unlocated persons, plus 1 who was found to have returned his card, results showed:

78.2 percent nonrespondents were satisfied with police service rendered;
1.8 percent nonrespondents were not satisfied;
20 percent refused to comment.

However, the sampling method used for nonrespondents does not meet accepted survey standards and would not provide an accurate base for projections.

With this exception, the survey methodology is valid according to consultation with professional marketing and statistical analysts. Currently, interviews are being planned with nonrespondents from as wide a sample as can be designed.

Insights

The original cost incurred for the survey (total mailing, printing, and salary costs were an estimated $75,000) was relatively expensive, but the insight gained into how the public judges police service was well worth the price. Definite steps now can be taken by the Chicago Police Department to:

1. Inform officers that, while efficiency is at all times necessary, its dispassionate appearance can be misinterpreted by overwrought victims as disinterest in the loss or injury.
2. Provide officers with preservice and inservice training in dealing with the elderly;
3. Instruct preliminary investigators not to give victims false hopes of recovering their property;
4. Accelerate the recruitment of Spanish-speaking officers and the Spanish-language training of present officers;
5. Review present methods of response and investigation of theft and burglary calls to insure timely and meaningful follow-up investigations;
6. Design public education programs to deal with some of the realities of police investigative processes as opposed to the entertainment media's romanticized versions; and
7. Provide evidence technicians with a notice of appearance form, similar to those used by public utility employers to advise customers, to notify persons not at home of their visit.

Based on the mail-back survey, this preliminary analysis and report has highlighted some helpful insights into public opinion regarding the quality of police service rendered in Chicago. These observations will facilitate modification of training programs and operational procedures to make them more responsive to citizen concepts of superior police service. While it may be a completely unobtainable goal, we must never strive for anything less than 100-percent satisfactory police service.

WEIGHTING SCORES IN PROMOTIONAL EXAMINATIONS AND THEIR EFFECTS ON PERFORMANCE*

In the typical police promotional process, both written and oral interview examinations are administered to candidates. Frequently, other information is considered such as seniority and supervisory or performance ratings. Various weights are given to these factors, the proportions being dependent upon the importance attributed to each factor. For example, the written examination may count 40 percent, the oral interview examination 30 percent, the supervisory or performance rating 20 percent, and seniority 10 percent. Raw scores are obtained on each of these factors for each candidate, multiplied by the appropriate designated weight, and then added for a total score. Finally these total scores are rank ordered from highest to lowest and promotions are made by the appointing authority from the resulting list.

The use of this procedure often creates confusion among the candidates when the results are posted. Frequently, the remark is made that although the procedures seemed fair enough, somehow the final results were "rigged" or manipulated in some way. One of the reasons why this confusion occurs is discussed in this paper. A solution is also offered. As carefully as exams may be prepared, administered, and scored, the goal of objectivity can be easily compromised by well-meaning but erroneous compilation of component scores.

---

*SOURCE: Terry Eisenberg and Roger W. Reinke, "The Weighting of Scores in Promotional Examinations, A Little Known Problem," reprinted by special permission of the *Police Chief*, copyright © 1972 by International Association of *Chiefs of Police*, Vol. 39, No. 6, pp. 46-49.

The Problem

Because of a little-known statistical artifact, the procedure described above will work, *as intended*, only if the variability[1] of candidates' raw scores on each factor is the same. However, this equivalence or similarity of variability of scores among various factors hardly ever occurs; variability almost always differs among the factors. The variability of scores may be determined in a number of ways, such as calculating the "range" (i.e., the difference between the highest and lowest raw scores on a factor) or the "standard deviation" (i.e., the variability of scores around the mean or average of all the scores on a factor). While there are other measures of variability, the standard deviation is the variability measure of choice in this situation.

Example

The city personnel department conducts a promotional exam for the police department consisting of two factors: written examination and oral board interview. It is intended to weight the scores achieved on each part 50 percent. The raw scores on the written and oral examinations for five candidates are as follows:[2]

Candidate	Written Exam Raw Score	Oral Exam Raw Score
Adams	79	85
Baker	81	91
Cox	82	73
Davis	83	79
Edwards	85	82

WRITTEN			ORAL		
Raw Score	Weight	Result	Raw Score	Weight	Result
79	.50	39.5	85	.50	42.5
81	.50	40.5	91	.50	45.5
82	.50	41.0	73	.50	36.5
83	.50	41.5	79	.50	39.5
85	.50	42.5	82	.50	41.0

Candidate	TOTAL Final Weighted Raw Score	Promotional List
Adams	82.0	(First) Baker (86.0)
Baker	86.0	(Second) Edwards (83.5)
Cox	77.5	(Third) Adams (82.0)
Davis	81.0	(Fourth) Davis (81.0)
Edwards	83.5	(Fifth) Cox (77.5)

It can be seen above that the *intended* weights of 50 percent for the written and 50 percent for the oral are really not applying to each candidate. Performance on the oral examination is contributing more than its intended share of 50 percent to the promotional list. This discrepancy between the *intended* weights of 50 percent each and the *actual* weights occurred because of the difference in raw score variability between the two factors.[3]

It is necessary to calculate the standard deviation for both the written and the oral examinations; they are 2.0 and 6.0 respectively. (The formula for the standard deviation is:

$$S.D. = \sqrt{\frac{\Sigma d^2}{N}}$$

where Σd^2 is the sum of the differences (d) squared between each raw score and the mean of all the raw scores for the factor. N is, once again, the number of scores.) The two means and the standard deviations are calculated in the following manner:

WRITTEN				ORAL			
Raw Score	Mean	Difference (d)	d^2	Raw Score	Mean	Difference (d)	d^2
79 −	82 =	−3	9	85 −	82 =	+3	9
81 −	82 =	−1	1	91 −	82 =	+9	81
82 −	82 =	0	0	73 −	82 =	−9	81
83 −	82 =	+1	1	79 −	82 =	−3	9
85 −	82 =	+3	9	82 −	82 =	0	0
410			20	410			180

The formula for transforming a raw score to a Z-score is:

$$Z = \frac{X\text{-MEAN}}{S.D.}$$

where X is each candidate's raw score.

For example, the Z-score for Adams' written exam is:

$$\frac{79\text{-}82}{2.0} = \frac{-3.0}{2.0} = -1.5$$

The Z-score for Adams' oral exam is:

$$\frac{85\text{-}82}{6.0} = \frac{3.0}{6.0} = +.5$$

By transforming each candidate's raw score to a Z-score, the following results are obtained:

	WRITTEN				ORAL		
Raw Score	Z-score	Weight	Result	Raw Score	Z-score	Weight	Result
79	−1.5	.50	−.750	85	+ .5	.50	+ .250
81	− .5	.50	−.250	91	+ 1.5	.50	+ .750
82	.0	.50	.000	73	−1.5	.50	−.750
83	+ .5	.50	+ .250	79	− .5	.50	−.250
85	+ 1.5	.50	+ .750	82	.0	.50	.000

TOTAL

Candidate	Final Weighted Z-score	Promotional List
Adams	−.500	(First) Edwards (+.750)
Baker	+ .500	(Second) Baker (+.500)
Cox	−.750	(Third) Davis (.000)
Davis	.000	(Fourth) Adams (−.500)
Edwards	+ .750	(Fifth) Cox (−.750)

The mean for the written examination is:

$$\frac{410}{5} = 82$$

The mean for the oral examination is:

$$\frac{410}{5} = 82$$

The standard deviation for the written is:

$$\sqrt{\frac{20}{5}} = \sqrt{4} = 2.0$$

The standard deviation for the oral is:

$$\sqrt{\frac{180}{5}} = \sqrt{36} = 6.0$$

If the standard deviations for the written and oral examinations were the same, the *intended* weights of 50 percent would have been identical to the *actual* weights. However, in this example, which is typical of most real-world cases, the variability differs among the various factors. The factor that has the greatest score variability will always contribute *more actual weight* than intended; and conversely, the factor that has the least score variability will always contribute *less actual weight* than intended.

This point may perhaps be better demonstrated by referring to a particular kind of situation which frequently occurs in police departments. Typically, the range of raw scores on written exams is very low. Conversely, the range of raw scores for seniority is very high. The final results are such that frequently the men with the greatest seniority, regardless of their written exam scores, end up at the top of the promotional list.[4] This occurs even though their written performance may have been relatively low and the written exam factor was given a comparatively high weight. It also occurs in the presence of a low intended weight for seniority.

Solution

The solution to this problem is not difficult. It consists of transforming all the raw scores on each promotional factor to "standard scores." The type of standard score recommended is the "Z-score." The

Z-scores are then multiplied by the intended weights and the factor-weighted standard scores are added to obtain a total standard score for all factors.[5]

Now the *intended* weights of 50 percent for the written and 50 percent for the oral are equivalent to the *actual* weights and contribute equally to the promotional list.

More importantly is the fact that the two hypothetical promotional lists differ. The one based on weighting of raw scores is incorrect and the one based on weighting of Z-scores is correct. In only Cox's case were the two promotional lists the same. Reversals in the ordering of candidates for promotion occurred in four of the five cases. The reason why Baker came out first on the incorrect promotional list, for instance, was because he did so well on the oral examination (i.e., 91) which we indicated earlier had a disproportionate effect on the promotional list because of its greater variability. Davis, on the other hand, came out lower on the incorrect promotional list than on the correct promotional list (i.e., fourth rather than third, respectively) because his relatively low oral examination score (i.e., 79) was given more weight than the intended 50 percent. When this was corrected by the use of Z-scores, he moved up one rank to his correct position.

Conclusions

Although the proposed solution to the problem described in this paper requires additional computational efforts, it is the only way of insuring that intended or prescribed weights to be applied to various promotional factors are indeed working as intended, and are contributing as understood by all competitors to the final listing of candidates. The consequences of discrepancies between intended and actual weights should be apparent.

Because the Z-score is a rather abstract statistical term which may result in confusion among candidates and appointing authorities, it is suggested that the final summed weighted Z-scores be transformed to percentiles ranging from 1 to 100. For instance, a Z-score of $+ 1.00$ is equivalent to a percentile of 84. This transformation can easily be made by employing statistical tables found in most elementary statistical textbooks which are available for this very purpose.[6] By reporting scores in percentiles, candidates are able to see how they performed in relation to the other candidates.

In any case, the accuracy and fairness of the proposed procedure far outweighs the additional effort required and the initial confusion which may exist. The problem and solution discussed is applicable to situations involving more than two factors and/or other factors than those used as examples. It essentially occurs in any situation where there is a weighting of scores on quantifiable factors for the purpose of developing a total composite score for decision making.

A Cautionary Remark

It should be appreciated that this paper has not addressed itself to the fundamental issue which relates to the selection and measurement of *relevant* factors and weights to be employed in the promotional process. In the absence of empirical evidence bearing on the relationship between test performance and job performance (i.e., differential predictive validity), it is not possible to discuss, at this time, specific factors and weights to be employed in police promotion.

In theory, those factors which demonstrate the greatest validity and reliability should receive the greatest weight. The problem and solution discussed in this paper avoid, by necessity, this fundamental issue. However, they cannot be avoided by those responsible for police promotional decisions without courting legal intervention. The preceding discussion does demonstrate a technique for insuring compliance with the promotional guidelines promulgated by the appointing authority concerning weights to be assigned. In this regard, use of the technique should reduce some apprehension and misunderstanding among candidates when the promotional list is posted, and will insure the proper rank order listing of candidates according to the established guidelines.

POLICE COMMUNICATIONS: A TWO-WAY ROAD

Communications, both upward and downward, is the vehicle by which the supervisor performs his job. He is a key person in organizational communications because he has direct contact with the working personnel as well as the department managers. The supervisor, to be successful in exercising control, must communicate effectively in all directions. Leading practitioners and researchers have often stated that the single greatest obstacle to good supervision, and for that matter management as well, is inadequate communication. For the supervisor, communication is the only way that he can know what is going on and why.

For several reasons, the supervisor's effectiveness depends on his ability to communicate. First of all he needs information regarding the direction his resources must take. He sends requests for this information to fulfill his goals and the goals of the department. Second, the supervisor is constantly making decisions. For these to be rational, they need to be based on information which supplements the goals he has been given, the plans previously formulated, and departmental rules and procedures in existence. Therefore, communications are mandatory to insure the proper information flow to proper decision points and the people who must implement them. Third, the quality of information is critical to the communication process. This process is designed to transmit the correct information to the appropriate decision point to carry out the goals of the supervisor, his unit, and the department. In the final result, it makes little difference whether the communication channels are formal or informal, automated or manual. The important thing is the accuracy and timeliness of the information.

Organizations are structured to facilitate formal communications by providing channels through which information is supposed to flow. Persons who adhere to the idea of strictly following formal communications channels are believers in the principle of unity-of-command. It must be pointed out, however, that complete adherence to formal channels can be counterproductive because it tends to stifle creativity, takes excessive time, and does not permit coverage of all the communication needs in the department.

Informal channels of communication are necessary and supportive of the formal channels. They are, in fact, recognized today in police agencies as the way to secure information that is restricted or not available in formal channels. The supervisor must be on guard for a serious problem that may arise when most of the information necessary for him to perform his job comes through informal means. When this happens, it is his obligation to report that the current formal channels do not meet the needs of the department. The supervisor must also recognize that informal channels are not bad but that the formal channels are supposed to carry the bulk of the communications in the department.

It was mentioned earlier that the supervisor communicates upward, downward, and laterally. When communication flows downward, it is from the superior to the subordinate (supervisor); and generally the superior gives him job instructions, reasons for the job, rules, practices, and procedures in the organization, data regarding the mission of the unit, and information feedback regarding the subordinate's performance.

Upward communications from the supervisor to his superior tend to center around: requests for clarifications; feedback regarding rules, practices, and procedures; information about complaints of the performance of others or himself; feedback regarding his needs in order to do a task; and finally, additional information regarding that assignment. In a police department it is the rule, not the exception, that it is more difficult to communicate upward. This is especially so with informal communications because of the bureaucratic tendency to stifle informal communications. As a result, much valuable information for upper levels is lost.

Horizontal communications as a general rule involve coordinating information on common problems and needs common to several groups. This type of communication is based on the premise that others need to know what is happening to insure that the common mission of other comparable units is accomplished.

In supervising workers, interpersonal relations is closely associated with efficiency. How well he relates to those above, below, and to the sides of him is dependent on the relationship the supervisor enjoys with them. For example, the arbitrary, unfriendly supervisor will have a difficult time communicating in all directions. Similarly, if his ability to compose his thoughts is weak, his ability to communicate is likely to be faulty. Because communicating is a complex task, training in the skills of writing messages, inquiries, memoranda, proposals, decisions, and in conducting various kinds of meetings must be learned for the supervisor to be effective. The following article addresses some of the problems of interpersonal communications.

TRAINING IN INTERPERSONAL COMMUNICATIONS*

The importance of communication to the police officer can be found in the following statement: "Effective law enforcement depends upon close, direct and continuous communication between the police and every segment of the population." Increasingly, police departments

¹*SOURCE: Richard C. Huseman, "Interpersonal Communication Training for the Police: An Evaluation," *Journal of Police Science and Administration*, Vol. 1, No. 3, September 1973, pp. 355-361. Reprinted with permission of the publisher.

across the country are realizing the need to train their personnel in the area of interpersonal communication.

Recently, the Law Enforcement Assistance Administration funded a proposal, "Developing Interpersonal Communication Abilities and Communication Systems for More Effective Law Enforcement in Situations of Conflict," (Grant #71-DF-870). The grant period was from July 1, 1971 to November 1, 1972. One of the major thrusts of the grant was to develop and test several types of interpersonal communication training aids.

The purpose of this article is (1) to describe the three major communication training methods that were developed, and (2) to present the evaulation of these three communication training methods which was made by twenty-three (23) officers from five Southeastern states who participated in a pilot training program.

THE COMMUNICATION TRAINING METHODS

One of the major considerations in developing communication training materials was to make them realistic and relevant to the police officer's duties and responsibilities. In order to achieve realism and relevancy in developing the training package, an attempt was made to depart from traditional training methods, (i.e., lecture-discussion sessions, written case studies, and written tests, etc.). Instead, the following three instructional methods were used: Video-tape Role-Playing, Communication in Conflict Group Exercises, and Communication in Conflict Film-Based Case Study. Following is a brief description of each of these methods:

Videotape Role-Playing

As the role-playing situations were developed, several important elements were built into the training approach. A consideration of those elements is appropriate at this point.

1. *Role Reversal*—Each role-playing situation required one officer in the training session to play the role of a police officer while the other participant played the role of a citizen. This procedure was followed in order to enable the officer to "see" a conflict from the standpoint of a citizen as well as to play his normal role of police officer.

2. *No Audience Participation*—Pretesting indicated that officers did their best role playing when the rest of the training group was not allowed to observe them as the role-plays were recorded on videotape. The role-playing procedure allowed the two officers involved in each role-playing situation about ten minutes to read their role and then engage in the actual role-playing. On the average, the recorded role plays lasted approximately ten minutes.

3. *Self-evaluation*—After all of the role-plays were recorded, the trainees were divided into groups of eight. In this way each participant would see his own role play and three other role plays. Before hearing the reaction of other officers, the participants of each role play would *evaluate their own performances.* This procedure capitalized on one of the real strengths of videotape, that is, the instructors did not have to point out each detail of the communication situation. Rather, the participants observed the role-play and engaged in self-evaluation.

4. *Evaluation by Others*—After each individual had a chance to react and evaluate his own performance in a role-playing situation, others in the training group were permitted to comment and evaluate; and finally, the two training instructors, who worked as a team, commented and evaluated the role-plays.

A Sample Role-Playing Situation

Fifteen role-playing situations were developed for the project. The following role-play is one that was used in the training and should provide the reader with some idea about the content of the role-playing situations:

> *Mr. Baxter:* You have been the principal at East High School for the three years since it was built. The school has been relatively free of racial tensions, vandalism, and, as far as you know, drugs.
>
> This morning you had a call from the Chief of Police who said that his department had information that drug pushers were operating just off the campus and sometimes on the campus. He was not certain whether or not students were involved as pushers, but he recommended that his force take immediate action. He suggested an appointment between you and a plain clothes officer in your office this afternoon.
>
> You have been thinking of alternatives. You don't want a lot of police officers, or police cars, or commotion of any kind, since, in your

opinion, that would serve only to create further tensions within the student body and with parents. You have decided that you do not want any police on the school grounds.

Officer Parker: You are a plainclothes officer assigned to Narcotics Bureau duty for a six-month period. Your Chief has asked you to go to East High School and speak to Mr. Baxter, the principal. It seems there have been anonymous telephone calls reporting drug traffic on and off the campus. The Chief wants to set up surveillance on the campus. He has asked you to get the approval and cooperation of Mr. Baxter. Mr. Baxter has learned of the tips from the Chief and is expecting you.

Communication in Conflict Group Exercises

This type of exercise employed a format in which participants worked in groups of five or six people. The exercise began with the presentation of a situation which possessed the potential for conflict. This explanation was followed by a series of four or five questions related to the situation. Each of the questions sought to elicit the participants' responses at some critical point in the process of handling the conflict situation. Most of the questions provided the officer with five choices of the "best" communication alternative in multiple choice form. In some cases, however, a question called for the officer to write some brief statements which he would use in handling the conflict. The responses in both types of questions were given an appropriate number of points based upon the effect the communication was most likely to have in that particular situation.

Operating in small groups, the participants first individually chose one of the responses to the questions. This selection was followed by a discussion in which the group was asked to reach a unanimous decision concerning the selection of one of the alternatives. The directions for this exercise suggested that a group decision not be made by a majority vote but through discussion and persuasion of fellow officers. This procedure promoted competition between the officers within the group as well as between the groups.

This exercise provided participants with the opportunity to apply communication principles to conflict situations in a manner which revealed the step-by-step development of conflict. The group decision-making procedure, in addition to providing participants with the opportunity to practice the art of communicating, allowed them to compare their choices with those of fellow officers. The result was that the learning in this exercise was not merely the choice of the "best" communication alternative for the exercise, but also a method through which an understanding of the reasons for such a choice was gained through the defense of an answer in the group discussion. Other officers' explanations also served to broaden participant understanding of the handling of the conflict situation.

Following is a sample conflict exercise that participants evaluated and then recommended the particular communication alternative they would have implemented.

The Conflict Situation

You are a patrol officer alone in your patrol car cruising a traffic circle which surrounds a park square in a downtown area. Because the park is small and heavily used, laws against loitering and use by large groups have been established. The city ordinance prohibits groups to reserve the park or to occupy it for group activities, but permits such things as individual and small group picnicking. Sometimes an artist will set up his easel and a crowd of passersby will stop to watch. Police discretion is required to determine when a group constitutes a nuisance to other park users.

Today the park seems to be particularly crowded. There are quite a number of shoppers and workers on lunch hour picnicking, people resting or walking dogs, and there are a few children playing. At one corner of the park there is a lady with a tamborine taking collections for the Salvation Army. You also notice a group of three long haired youths, dressed hippie style, playing guitars and singing songs. Seated and standing around them are about fifteen people, most of them singing along.

You consider that the gathering may be a violation and a nuisance to others.

Communication in Conflict Film-Based Case Study

During the grant period, a 16mm color film was secured from Universal Studios. The film depicted a riot on a college campus that involved students, townspeople, political officials, and national guardsmen. The officers saw the entire conflict on film; however, they saw it in segments. The film was stopped at predetermined places in order to allow the participants and the instructor time to discuss particular incidents and how they were handled. Much of the film story was shown through a series of flashbacks, showing incidents only as they were *remembered* by one or more persons in the conflict situation.

Before being confronted with the film case study, the police participants were provided information on the communication process, listening, perception, and nonverbal communication.

The police participant was introduced to the conflict film by viewing a three-minute preview that showed a conflict scene between the college students and the national guardsmen. At the end of the preview the police were asked a series of questions to introduce them to the system. One of the sample questions used was:

Did you see the guardsmen . . .
(a) _____ Use tear gas
(b) _____ Load their guns
(c) _____ Fix bayonets
(d) _____ Fire a warning shot

After the preview and the introduction to the system, the participants were provided the following background information:

The film preview that you have just seen describes a situation that is familiar to all of us—a conflict situation involving students, townspeople, political officials, and national guardsmen. Although the movie is fiction, you may see in it people or incidents that remind you of things that are happening today.

You will see the entire story in the film, but you will see it only in segments, as the film will be stopped from time to time in order to discuss particular incidents and how they were handled. Much of the film story is shown through a series of flashbacks (i.e., incidents are shown only as they are *remembered* by one or more persons). So that you will be able to visualize the entire sequence of events more clearly, the following background information is provided:

Ainsworth is a town of approximately 30,000 people. The mayor and most of the townspeople have lived there most of their lives. The residents of Ainsworth have very little contact with the university students—there are 10,000 students and most of them live on the campus, which is located in the northern part of town.

On *Monday,* one thousand students staged a two-hour march in protest of the Vietnam war in the town's central business district. During the demonstration, students clashed with police. A drugstore and a sporting goods store were burned, and nine students and four townspeople were injured.

On *Tuesday,* the students staged another demonstration—this time at the University Administration building. The National Guard was summoned to curb the activity, and shooting began. The demonstration was abruptly ended, with the injury of four students and the death of two.

Because there was considerable doubt as to who was to blame for the killings, the governor of the state appointed a commission of three men to investigate. Members of the commission are Mr. Arthur Beresford, Dr. Benjamin Edwards, and Senator Hayes Stone.

The rest of the story is told in the movie, through testimony before the commission. Through each person's description, the incidents are remembered differently; the viewer must make his own evaluation as to what really happened.

After the participants had read the background material they viewed the first segment of the film. Each segment was followed by a series of questions designed to test the police officer's ability to analyze the communication in the conflict situation. The police responded to such questions as:

Of all the persons you have heard testify before the commission thus far, which person do you think is most likely *not* telling the truth?
(a) _____ Chancellor
(b) _____ Mayor
(c) _____ Deputy Mayor
(d) _____ Governor
What is it about this person (checked above) that causes you not to believe his testimony?

(a) _____ I've seen his type before—all he wants to do is to make *himself* look good to the commission.

(b) _____ There were some discrepancies and inconsistencies in his testimony.

(c) _____ His story was too smooth, too polished—he seemed to have practiced it ahead of time.

(d) _____ He looked *and* acted like he was lying.

Some of the questions pertained to communication with groups of people, for example:

Senator Stone recognized that, without the testimony of student witnesses, the commission would have difficulty arriving at an objective decision. If you were in the Senator's situation, what would you do about the students' refusal to testify?

(a) _____ Send subpoenas to the students that you think should testify.

(b) _____ Try to arrange a time when you can meet with groups of students and try to convince them to testify.

(c) _____ Try to meet students who seem to be the leaders of the protest movement. See what you can do to change their minds about testifying, hoping that they will in turn influence others to come forward.

(d) _____ Assume that no amount of persuasion will alter the students' decisions, and therefore, make no effort.

Each student responded independently to each question and then the answers were analyzed by the entire group.

Evaluation

Twenty-three police officers from five Southeastern states attended a pilot training workshop which employed the three major communication training methods that have been described. There were three major sections to the evaluation and they are described below.

The first section of the evaluation asked participants to consider three questions concerning the effectiveness of different teaching instruments or methods used during the workshop. They were to rate the item on a scale of 1 to 5 (low to high—1 = no help, 2 = little help, 3 = some help, 4 = helpful, 5 = very helpful) for helpfulness and effectiveness in improving communication skills. The "N" for each item refers to the number of participants who rated that particular item. The percentage is the proportion of "N" who rated the item as 4 or 5 on the continuum.

Respondents were told that 1 was the poorest rating and 5 the highest. At least 82% of the respondents rated each teaching instrument a 4 or 5.

The second section of the evaluation sought to determine the change in the amount of a participant's knowledge or skill in a certain area before the workshop and after. Participants rated their knowledge or skill in each area, "before" and "after," a continuum of 1 to 5. The arithmetic mean for each area, "before" and "after," is shown in the first column below, while the amount and direction of change (always positive) is shown in the second. The mean change is 1.41 points—the areas of Listening and Nonverbal Communication show the greatest positive change (.22 and .18 point respectively above the average), while Communicating with Small Groups shows the least positive change (.34 point below the average). Changes in other areas fall with .16 point around the average change.

The third section of the evaluation questionnaire questioned the relevancy of each of the above-mentioned areas to the participant's job. Twenty-three respondents all rated the relevancy as 4 or 5 on the rating continuum. The areas and part of the continuum are shown below, with the percentage of ratings corresponding to "of greatest relevancy" (rate 5) included.

How helpful to you in improving your communication skills were . . .

Item	1	2	3	4	5
1. . . . the videotape role playing N = 22, 82%	0	1	3	10	8
2. . . . the communication in conflict group exercises N = 22, 95%	0	0	1	4	17
3. . . . the film-based case study N = 23, 87%	0	0	3	5	15

When asked to provide written evaluation of the training session, the following comments were among those offered by the officers:

"Very helpful in helping me to understand nonverbal communication."

"I saw myself as others see me every day."

"Seeing yourself in a conflict situation enables you to communicate better the next time."

"A good training device to study communication."

"Being able to see and hear one's mistakes in communication is a valuable learning tool."

Finally, 100 percent of the participants recommended that their fellow officers attend a similar communication training workshop.

Conclusions

1. Each training instrument was judged Helpful or Very Helpful in improving communication skills by the great majority of participants.
2. Comments on each facet of instruction emphasized that participants realized the significance that a different perspective can have on communication.

Mean Amt. Rated Before	Mean Amt. Rated After	Direction & Amt. of Change	Area	Amt. Before					Amt. After				
				1	2	3	4	5	1	2	3	4	5
3.00	4.43	+ 1.43	The Value of Problem Solving in Small Groups	0	3	16	1	1	0	0	0	12	9
2.73	4.36	+ 1.63	Listening	2	6	11	2	1	0	0	2	10	10
2.86	4.45	+ 1.59	Nonverbal Communication	2	6	7	5	1	0	0	1	9	10
2.77	4.23	+ 1.46	Planning Communication	1	7	11	2	1	0	0	2	13	7
3.09	4.45	+ 1.36	Anticipating & Perceiving Reaction to Others	0	4	13	4	1	0	0	0	12	10
3.00	4.30	+ 1.30	De-escalating Conflict	2	3	12	3	2	0	0	3	10	10
3.38	4.45	+ 1.07	Communicating with Small Groups	0	4	7	8	2	0	0	1	9	10

| | Relevancy | | | | | % of Responses |
Area	1	2	3	4	5	rated #5
Listening	0	0	0	1	22	96
Nonverbal Communication	0	0	0	4	19	83
Planning Communication	0	0	0	5	18	78
Anticipating & Perceiving Reactions of Others	0	0	0	3	20	87
De-escalating Conflict	0	0	0	2	21	91
Communicating with Small Groups	0	0	0	2	21	91

3. Each participant registered an increase in knowledge or skill in each area after completion of the workshop. The greatest increase was reported for the areas of Listening and Nonverbal Communication. The least was reported for Communicating with Small Groups.
4. At least three-fourths of the respondents found all areas very relevant to their jobs, and none rated was below a 4.
5. Twenty-one responded on an overall reaction to the workshop with 14 percent rating a 4 and 86 percent rating a 5, and commenting very favorably on the whole.
6. Every participant recommended that other police officers attend such a workshop.

In brief, the three training methods described, Videotape Role Playing, Communication in Conflict Group Exercises, and the Film-Based Case Study, appear to be useful training methods for training police in the area of interpersonal communication skills. Moreover, those police attending the pilot training session view this type of training as being very relevant to their jobs.

POLICE SUPERVISION, ORGANIZATIONAL EFFECTIVENESS, AND COMMUNITY INVOLVEMENT

Much has been accomplished during the past ten years in the area of community-police relations. "Community-police relations" is a simple concept which has frequently been misunderstood as a highly complex theory. Basically stated, it means that the police are a part of and work for the community they serve. They are not a separate entity divorced from the community. When this idea is understood properly, the police department should have a *total orientation* to the concept, not just a single unit devoted to improving the public relations of the department. This total commitment, therefore, bears directly upon the supervisor who frequently is in daily contact with the public.

Today, few police professionals take exception to the community-police relations (CPR) concept. The supervisor can assist in making the concept work. He can make CPR an integral part of his work and constantly emphasize to his personnel its importance to the goals and mission of the organization. The supervisor must, on every occasion in which the opportunity presents itself, seek the support of the community in order to accomplish his mission because in reality, the goals of the CPR efforts are the goals of the local police.

The supervisor frequently has one major obstacle to improving relationships with the community he serves—improvement of relations with minority groups. There are few, if any, cities in the United States in which rapport with these groups is satisfactory. Too often the police contend that aggressive crime suppression is the professional approach to law enforcement, and the community needs this kind of protection. However, there is every reason to believe that this type of crime suppression may very well create new and more serious tensions in the same community that the police protect and serve. The police in general, and the supervisor in particular, must look for new ways of responding to traditional police problems. It is essential that this task be accomplished in order to decrease the distrust and disorder in our society. One method is by seeking the support and encouragement of the community.

Since the CPR subject has arisen, numerous new police responses have occurred which tend to emphasize CPR. The supervisor needs to be aware of these, especially when the time is ripe to implement one or more of them in his organization. The first example is *crime control teams* in which eight officers and one sergeant comprise a team. Three of these teams cover a beat on a 24-hour basis with one team concentrating on community service and two on crime control.

A second CPR type, the *beat commander* concept, involves a team of twenty-one officers plus one sergeant who is the beat commander being assigned the total responsibility for policing a small high-crime area. Under this innovative technique, the beat commander is given the authority to distribute his men as he deems necessary.

The use of *community service officers* is yet another idea for supplementing police resources. Under this concept, local residents are appointed to salaried, unsworn positions, are given distinctive uniforms and are then assigned to work on community service problems. A sworn officer supervises a predetermined number of the community service officers. A sergeant in turn supervises the operation in a given area. One point that must be emphasized, however, is that the community service officers do not supplant the usual beat patrol operations; they supplement it.

Los Angeles, California, has adopted the *basic car* plan in an effort to integrate the police into the community to a greater degree. Under this concept, a police precinct is broken down into beats with each one having nine officers assigned on a 24-hour basis. A team coordinator is selected from among the team members. All calls in the basic beat area are handled by the basic car if at all possible. Where specialized follow-up services are required, the basic team calls upon the police specialist.

One other new community-oriented concept needs mentioning: *team policing*. A team of eight to twelve officers is coupled with a four to six community service team of officers to perform the total policing responsibilities in a compact, high-crime area. A unique characteristic of this innovative concept is that each police officer is not only a generalist, but has an additional specialization in juvenile evidence collection or detective work.

The trend in policing today is to involve citizens more. This involvement may be in the form of citizen boards which meet regularly to assist in the formulation of policy within a specified area. Some cities have volunteer citizen units (security patrols, auxiliaries) to assist the regular police. As one may surmise, there are significant dangers in this trend because the group may see themselves as becoming a "citizens review board" rather than providing positive community support.

Other programs have been developed to improve the effectiveness of patrol and staff functions against crime. Still others have aimed at restructuring the police forces to provide new career options for selected police personnel. These new concepts to aid the CPR effort are too numerous to cover in this short introduction. It suffices to say the supervisor still has the responsibility of achieving his police mission and cannot effectively and efficiently perform his responsibilities without the assistance of the community.

POLICE ROLE IN THE COMMUNITY*

Police-community relations has become an increasingly controversial topic in the last decade. It is the authors' intention to thoroughly review the massive literature generated by this subject.

Scope of Review

An understanding of the changing police role in the community is fundamental to any discussion of police-community relations. This article, representing the first chapter of a larger monograph, reviews the recent literature on the police role.

We included all relevant books and all *significant* articles published in professional journals, and selected articles from nonprofessional publications. The last require rigorous selection, as most of these articles are based on only minimal review of other recent literature or field research and are frequently more concerned with placing the blame than with finding solutions (Cray, 1967; Smith, 1965; W.W. Turner, 1968). Should comprehensiveness be an overriding concern to the reader, we refer him to the yearly Proceedings of the Institute for Police-Community Relations. There are also several important bibliographies on the subject (Becker and Felkenes, 1968; International Police Association, 1968; Harlow, 1969.)

As with many professions, some of the best information on law enforcement is found in articles written by practitioners in professional periodicals, especially *Police* and *The Police Chief*. Papers presented at various conferences on PCR constitute another source, a particularly useful one being the Institute on Police-Community Relations at Michigan State University (Proceedings of the Institute on Police-Community Relations; Fleisher, 1967). Increasingly important also are the several national and state commissions appointed in the wake of recent civil disorders (Gourley, 1966a; National Advisory Commission on Civil Disorders, 1968, President's Commission on Law Enforcement and Administration of Justice, 1967). These reports have the added advantage of a wide range of contributors, representing both professional and academic circles. There are many significant books and articles on police from academic sources. When authors (either experienced researchers or ex-policemen) have been able to move vertically within a law enforcement agency, with access to both

---

*SOURCE: "The Police Role in the Community" by Ivan R. Gabor and Christopher Low, reprinted from *Criminology*, Vol. 10, No. 4, (February 1973) pp. 383-414 by permission of the publisher, Sage Publications, Inc.

day-to-day field activity and administrative aspects of police operations, the results have been exceptionally valuable (Niederhoffer, 1967; Skolnick, 1966a; Wilson, 1968a). Some others tend to remain at a high level of sociological abstraction, and, in our opinion, miss much of the import of the organizational setting. Finally, the International Association of Chiefs of Police (1965) has become quite research-oriented and produces much worthwhile information (see also Layton, 1966).

Now let us look at the major trends regarding the police role in the community as reflected by the literature of the past decade. It is hoped that this article may be of value to those with a need to be current but with limited time to read.

The Police Role in the Community

Much of the recent writing about PCR has revolved around the proper role of the police in the community. The idea of role, as used by most social scientists, includes both actions, such as driving a squad car or breaking up fights, and expectations—for example, that the police are primarily occupied with catching dangerous criminals. American popular expectations about police have always been somewhat ambiguous, accepting the image of the lawman standing for fair play, but not accepting official interference in personal affairs (Silver, 1967). Increasing urbanization and a changing society and technology have not yet completely modified this traditional attitude. They have, however, profoundly affected both the nature of and the means to accomplish the police task.

Recent literature on the police role and PCR reflects the following areas of concern:

1. the problem of definition for the police role;
2. the relationship between social change and the police role;
3. the professionalization of the police;
4. contrasting perceptions of the police role.

DEFINITION OF THE ROLE

It is indicative of both the high degree of national social ferment and a growing tendency for critical self-evaluation by those within the law enforcement community that the very definition of the police function has been the subject of such a high volume of comment in the last decade. There is general agreement that the police find themselves "in the middle" of disputes they did not cause and are responsible for the enforcement of laws they did not make (Routh, 1966). The major controversy centers on whether the police should be essentially noninvolved enforcers of the law or if the police should expand their service functions, actively working to alleviate the conditions which cause crime and injustice in their areas. This section will summarize some of the literature on both sides.

The service orientation requires some further delineation. There is a significant difference between nonpunitive service duties and community involvement (Wilson, 1968b). With regard to the former, Charles Chamberline (1968) has pointed out that the service functions normally associated with the local police may be the single best means of maintaining strong popular support, as well as being dictated by the traditions of the town (see also Pomrenke, et al., 1967).

On the other hand, advocates of community involvement urge active police participation in all community problem-solving activities and a more emphatic *concern with justice,* as well as with law. Not surprisingly, virtually all those who have commented positively on PCR lean toward this formulation (Curry, 1962; Germaine, 1965; Mihanovich, 1965). San Jose (California) Police Chief Ray Blackmore (1964), one of the numerous articulate exponents of this view, has stated "The police cannot operate in a vacuum. We can no longer neglect the social problems that are so prevalent in our community. For many years we have just gone along with the tide of social problems. We are finally beginning to realize that the police cannot remain passive bystanders. . . . The Police must engage in service work" (see also Thompson, 1965; Watson, 1963).

Although a thorough discussion of participation in the community as a part of PCR programs will be postponed until later in this article, two aspects merit our attention now. These are: whether the police should attempt to direct the community toward certain goals, and the feasibility of expanding police functions with chronic manpower shortages.

There are some professionals who feel that the police can be of service in leading their community toward definite social goals (Earle, 1969; Jones, 1966; Curry, 1962). An example may be seen in Pennsylvania State Police Commissioner E. Wilson Purdy's (1966) assertion that:

> Understanding, through education, must come to the police family, if we are to fill that important position of "community leader" fully prepared to lead society through today's social upheaval into a better community of tomorrow, one in which we may feel confident that we may raise our families in the traditional "American Way of Life."

Others, such as Professor Herman Goldstein, consider it more fruitful to avoid any type of political directionality, while still striving for understanding of the issues at hand (Cumming et al., 1965; Goldstein, 1968b; Wilson, 1964). Patrick V. Murphy, Assistant Director of the Office of Law Enforcement Assistance, asserts that it is possible to work against the roots of crime without becoming politically committed (Murphy, 1967; Germaine, 1970).

Both aspects of the service role tend to become indistinguishable in practice—as a highly successful New York City program illustrates (Bard, 1968, 1967· Parnas, 1967). This effort directed by Dr. Morton Bard, a psychologist, was based on the fact that, as part of their service role, the police are often called upon to intervene in family disputes. More than 50% of all mentally ill persons are first contacted by the police. Police officers were frequently injured on such calls, although, for obvious reasons, complaints were seldom filed. Dr. Bard and his associates trained a group of eighteen police officers in the techniques of handling mentally or psychologically disturbed individuals and made them aware of possible referral agencies in the precinct. The officers thus became capable of handling a standard police task without injury to themselves or their clients, and at the same time became considerably more involved in their client's future welfare, even to the extent of doing follow-up work with the agencies to see what had happened to their referrals. It is particularly important to note that the officers in the Family Crisis Intervention Unit did not cease their normal duties as patrolmen.

The *enforcement orientation* to the police role is exemplified by the formulation of Chief Bernard L. Garmire (1961) of Tucson, Arizona, who defines police functions as follows: "The preservation of peace, protection of life and property, enforcement of laws, and detecting law-breakers." He, and others, suggest that police departments which maintain a high degree of expertise in these fundamental areas will render the best service to the community (Adams, 1968; Ashenhurst, 1956).

Implicit in this orientation is a detachment from the broader, environmental causes of crime (Preiss and Ehrlich, 1966; Misner and Hoffman, 1967; Wilson, 1968c). As stated in the manual for a large metropolitan police force in the West (Los Angeles—Devonshire Division): "The police are interested in maintaining order. The fact that the group would not be a crime problem tomorrow does not alter today's tactical necessities. Police deployment is concerned with effect, not cause" (Los Angeles Police Department, 1968).

Several sources feel that the police are called upon to perform too many duties unrelated to law enforcement (Lohman and Misner,

1967; National Advisory Commission, 1968; Pfiffner, 1967). Banton (1964) has noted that policemen do a good deal of complaining about "having to do work they consider to be beneath the dignity of the law, such as impounding stray dogs and putting up no parking signs" (see also Brandstatter and Radelet, 1968). This was recognized in the report of the President's Commission on Law Enforcement and the Administration of Justice, which recommended that police be relieved of all "nonpolice duties" i.e. traffic directions and maternity calls (President's Commission on Law Enforcement and the Administration of Justice, 1967). Their reasons for this summarize the published views of a great many in the law enforcement community, as well as the highly qualified members of the commission itself. They are:

1. After the policeman has been trained to fight crime, using his services for unrelated purposes is wasteful, especially in view of the acute shortage of personnel in many departments.
2. Emergency calls may go unanswered when there are too many service calls.
3. Establishing a high degree of expertise in one aspect of crime control is impractical when the policeman is required to spend a large proportion of his time on service calls.
4. Most policemen joined the force to fight crime and take most pride in this aspect of their work. Utilization for menial or trivial service functions therefore deflates departmental morale.

A striking example of the effects of increased concentration on the basic police task is demonstrated by the experiment conducted by New York City Police Commissioner Francis Adams, in which one of the precincts with the highest crime rates was given over twice as many patrolmen for a period of several months (New York Police Department, 1970; Dougherty, 1964). Nothing else was changed. The result was a decrease in the crime rate of 55% and a 66% increase in the number of crimes for which someone was arrested. He concludes that a substantial increase in manpower, rather than new programs, is the surest way to decrease crime (Rigert, 1968).

The Police Role And Social Change

Advocates of both the enforcement and involvement orientations agreed that the rapid social changes of the last decade have made the task of law enforcement more difficult (Skolnick, 1966b; Watson, 1965; Fleck and Newsom, 1969; Police Yearbook, 1965). Sociologist Jerome Skolnick notes two major ambiguities of the police role (Skolnick, 1966a). The first, and perhaps most central, is the subjective nature of standards for enforcement of much of the law, especially law relating to minor crimes (H. Goldstein, 1963; J. Goldstein, 1960).

The decision as to what constitutes disorder or loitering must depend on the officer's personal concept of "order," as they cannot be usefully defined objectively (how much noise constitutes disturbing the peace?).

The second ambiguity Skolnick notes is the question of which laws to enforce. Clearly it is impossible to enforce all the laws all the time; hence, intentionally or not, some of the laws will not be enforced, or some laws will be enforced only part of the time. Traffic is perhaps the clearest example. Virtually everyone who drives is aware of laws relating to speed and parking. Most people are also aware that they may break some laws (i.e., five miles over the speed limit on an open highway) without much chance of being stopped. When such people are stopped, they tend to attribute it to their bad luck rather than their legal transgression (Gardner, 1966; Skolnick, 1966c; Schmideberg, 1960).

Rapid social change has made of such once academic issues, vital national concerns. How has this come to pass? Donald Bouma (1969) has analyzed one crucial factor: the demise of the useful stereotype (see also Kimble, 1969; Skolnick, 1966c). If much of the operational decision-making in law enforcement is essentially subjective, it is essential that the officer be able to identify quickly and accurately the potential lawbreaker and be able to distinguish him from the law-abiding citizen. The author notes today there is even less certainty that behavior and attitude toward the police will follow predictably from the social standing of groups or individuals. One example of this is the attitude of many middle-class college students toward the police (Harrison and Rieser, n.d.; Coe and Duke, 1963; Falk, 1964).

Social change has been instrumental in limiting police prerogatives in two major ways. On the one hand, court decisions have in recent years had the effect of disallowing certain formerly accepted police criminal practices, especially with regard to confessions and searches (Edwards, 1968; Goldstein, 1968a; Remington, 1964). The International Association of Chiefs of Police has voiced the concern of many law enforcement professionals that the balance between the rights of the individual and the rights of society has swung too far toward the former, resulting in a deleterious effect on police capacity to maintain law and order. Herbert T. Klein (1968) has highlighted a working policeman's frustration with what may be called the "procedural" orientation of many of the nation's highest courts (see also Van Allen, 1968). He emphasizes that the police task is essentially to apprehend criminals and prevent crime—and that present evidence indicates that this battle is not being won. Rising self-awareness and pride among minority groups creates another limit on police discretion (Waskow, 1966; Goldstein, 1968b; Misner, 1967; V. Turner, 1968). It is relevant here that the Report of the National Commission on Civil Disorders, after finding the great majority of riots to have been sparked by incidents between police and ghetto residents, concluded that "A new mood has sprung up among Negroes, particularly among the young, in which self esteem and enhanced racial pride are replacing apathy and submission to the system" (National Advisory Commission, 1968; Bayley, 1969; Stahl, 1966) Frank J. Remington (1964,1965) has pointed out how adherence to officially neutral principles (i.e., the most police in areas with the most crime) can, in practice, give the impression of unequal enforcement (Misner and Hoffman, 1967):

> In some large cities, a law enforcement practice is used which is called aggressive, preventive patrol. Sometimes the objective of this practice is to find and confiscate as many dangerous weapons as possible. This is done by stopping and searching persons on the street or in vehicles. The practice is usually confined to those police precincts or districts which have the highest crime rates. These are commonly districts in which the vast majority of persons are members of minority groups. As a consequence preventive patrol tends to be used only against members of the minority group.

Law, the basis for police legitimacy, has been affected by social change. Two aspects appear to have gained particular attention from professional writers—the intentionally broken law as a tool for furthering some social/political goal, and the consequences for police of enforcing laws during demonstrations not specifically aimed at breaking them (McMillan, 1964; New York University Graduate School of Public Administration, 1963; Towler, 1964). Quinn Tamm (1965) has commented with regard to the first point that respect for law is, in some circles, being replaced by the assumption that selective lawbreaking, if intended to further what is considered a worthy cause is, in itself, a praiseworthy act (Waskow, 1966; Scott, 1962).

The political demonstration not aimed at symbolically breaking a particular law presents a greater problem for the police. While in the former case, arrest is an expected and, in fact, a required part of the demonstration, here those participating are likely to interpret enforcement as an expression of official disapproval of the purpose of the demonstration. The police view has been well stated by former Superintendent of the Chicago Police Department, O. W. Wilson (1964; see also Selzman, 1969; George, 1966):

> We have a duty and a responsibility to maintain law and order. If people throw themselves in front of trucks or climb poles or otherwise engage in obstructionist tactics, in violation of the law, we have to arrest them.

It is of interest here that even such an expert in police administration as Wilson (former Dean of University of Southern California School of Criminology) chooses not to note publicly that, in fact, the police DO have, by virtue of their discretionary powers, the power not to arrest (Wilson, 1968d; Bittner, 1967, Goldstein, 1960). The wise exercise of such an elusive discretionary power may well mean the difference between a harmless demonstration and a destructive riot.

Professionalization

Increasing crime rates and decreasing respect for law enforcement have led many professionals to ask how these trends may be countered. Thomas J. Aaron's (1965a) article is representative of the self-examination that has marked the past decade's literature. Professionalization has generally been accepted as a means of both gaining public respect and improving the effectiveness of law enforcement. The concept, as presented in the literature, has two aspects: individual professionalization concerns the education and job performance of every officer (Aaron, 1965b); departmental professionalization entails organizational changes, the adoption of sophisticated technologies, the improvement of methodologies and the physical plant for police training.

Individual Professionalization

Louis Radelet (1966), a pioneer in cogent thinking in this area, has explained personal professionalization as a balance between the benefits accruing to police—especially higher pay, greater respect, and public support—and a new set of obligations. Developing higher standards of education and professional attitude are the foremost of these obligations.

A discussion of the importance of personal education to law enforcement must distinguish between the concepts of "training" and "education." As Sheriff Peter J. Pitchess (1970) has stated:

> In brief, training involves the absorption of practical skills, relating to the performance of a certain specific function. The heart of the training program is its role in providing the individual with "how to do it" knowledge. Training is essentially problem solving oriented, and it is an absolute necessity for police. Personal education of the police officer supplies something more complex than mere training. It involves a concern with theory or philosophy of goals and procedures. Education requires not just simply answers [sic] to the question "how" something operates, but the more ultimate question, "why."

Better-*educated* police officers are available via higher standards of recruitment and in-service education for officers now on duty. As O. J. Tocchio (1970) has stated, the problem with police recruitment is generally qualitative rather than quantitative. Nationwide, there were over four times as many applicants as there were openings in law enforcement in 1965, and even this figure masks the large number of highly professional departments which took far fewer applicants (the LAPD accepted 2.8% in the same year). Charles R. Taylor has lamented the fact that state-regulated entry standards for the police profession have not gone past high school graduation for the most part, while such callings as barbers and embalmers have (through their own efforts) raised the educational level for entry to several years of postsecondary training or schooling (Taylor, 1969). Charles R. Hildebrand (1969), commenting on the same subject has suggested that one of the major reasons college-educated men avoid police service is that the immediate prospects for service as a patrolman do not appeal to many. He suggests that one way to attract more college men is direct entry into the detective branch. In summation, he asserts, "Lateral entry is perhaps the key to the problem of professionalization. If it were an accomplished fact, salary structures would improve; it would obviate the need for tenure, and law enforcement could successfully recruit college trained personnel."

Along with recruitment, much of the literature on improving educational levels has stressed programs for those already on the force. Paul M. Whisenand's (1966a) evaluation of the Federal Law Enforcement Assistance Act of 1965 points to the growing interest of the federal government in sending working policemen back to school. Frank Day (1965) has echoed this thought. The April 1968 issue of *The Police Chief* noted with pride that 26 officers were completing their

M.S's under the sponsorship of the OLEA grant. In-service education is by no means entirely oriented toward colleges and universities. The Los Angeles County Sheriff's Department is representative of the large number of agencies that hold education courses for maturing officers—in this case, the career development sequence includes Advanced Officer School after several years on the force, Supervisor School on becoming a sergeant, and a middle-management course conducted in conjunction with California State University, Long Beach. A. F. Brandstatter (1968) has predicted that, in the future, more academic centers for research on law enforcement problems (such as the Michigan State Center for Police Community Relations, which he heads) will greatly enhance the prospects for the educated officer.

The idea of *training* (as opposed to education) revolves around the technological explosion that has shaken most sectors of our society since World War II. As Thomas F. Coon (1969) has stated, "Law enforcement does not want to be left at the post, and its hopes for professionalization revolve a good deal around expertise in the areas of technological enforcement." Some of the major areas of expertise now needed by law enforcement are indicated by the following small sample of titles from *Police* magazine:

- "Automatic Fingerprint Search Techniques Employing the Videofile System" (Bradley, 1969).
- "Criminal Justice, Computer Related Technology and the Scientific Method" (Gallati, 1968).
- "Lights! Camera! Action! The Role of TV in Law Enforcement" (Grauman, 1968).
- "From Posse to Computer" (Lamb, 1970).
- "Law Enforcement Technology Welcomes the 'Chopper Copper' " (Coon, 1969).

The literature on training is extensive. It is beyond the scope of this article to pursue it further. We refer the interested reader to bibliographies by Becker and Felkenes (1968) and by the International Police Association (1968) for further information on this subject.

It is widely recognized that, along with improved education and training, individual professionalization entails instilling a professional attitude in the officer—a pride and confidence which Kansas City, Missouri, Police Chief Bernard C. Brannon (1968) has described as a combination of respect for the public and respect for one's abilities as an officer. George Payton (1966) and Caroll Price (1963) have written of the ethical standards implicit in the death of a professional policeman. Several thoughtful writers have interpreted the professional attitude as essentially characterized by detachment and self-control. That is, one who can react in terms of a specific task-oriented frame of reference, rather than as an individual. Albert Reiss (1969) has stated this idea nicely:

> I mean by professionalization not necessarily that one has to have a higher education—I mean that police are trained and highly trained to remove *themselves* from involvement in situations. This does not necessarily mean that one changes attitudes fundamentally—but one teaches them to learn how to deal with their attitudes in situations [of stress.] In short, one has to create a kind of collegial order in which the responsibility is to one's duty and what one does rather than to one's self.

Joseph D. Lohman (1968) brings out a similar consideration when he defines the professional officer as one who "must understand the effects and implications of his skills and techniques—this is in order that he may be able to decide which skills and techniques to apply in a given case. This is the fundamental distinction between a professional person and just another technician." Thus, for example, if the task at hand is dispersal of an unruly group of citizens, a professional attitude requires that the officer have some knowledge of the reactions of the people involved—which general techniques are likely to work best in this specific case. It is precisely this type of situation which is most enflamed by unprofessional action. The numerous commission reports on successive riots have all concluded that the most common immediate cause is some form of police-citizen conflict.

The implication of this concept of a professional attitude for community relations is immense. On the one hand, the officer is being trained to make objective judgments of police problems. On the other hand, like the M.D., there is the need to know when to "step out" of the professional role and show human concern with the problems of clients. It is a delicate balance that is easily upset. Technological and other developments in law enforcement tend to make the officer increasingly separated from those he serves, yet their support—so important to police work—depends in large measure on how well the police can combine compassion with efficiency.

There is an abundance of literature on how the officer can make the most of his personal contacts with the public, although little of it recognizes the dilemma above. From 1965 to 1968, the annual *Police Yearbook* which reports the yearly conference of the International Association of Chiefs of Police, contained major sections on improving the officer/citizen contact. Common courtesy has become a major concern with the FBI Law Enforcement Bulletin (1967) and with Kenneth W. Haagensen (1969). Writers such as Walter A. Lunden (1965) and Robert M. Phillips (1965) note that courtesy should also be considered a form of crime prevention. One is likely to have more respect for law if he has increased respect for those enforcing it.

To equate the professional attitude with courtesy, in our view, is to miss its fundamental significance—namely, a hard-to-achieve blend of detachment and compassion. It appears, for example, that former New York Police Commissioner Murphy (1967) may have been oversimplifying when he asserted, "It's just as easy to take a person into custody by saying 'won't you step this way sir' as it is to handle him roughly and uncivilly. Either way, he gets to the stationhouse."

Departmental Professionalization

Technological advances and the search for greater effectiveness have led to important changes in police organizational structure. As Daniel M. Cowley (1965) points out, the computer, which has become a necessity for most major departments today, requires not only a new skill, but new concepts of organization. At the least, this involves setting up a new department of data processing, which is separate from the records department but takes over much of its functions. The use of helicopters creates the need for a special section staffed with pilots and perhaps maintenance personnel. Looking through any major law enforcement periodical, one is struck by the large number of courses in specialized technical fields offered to the policeman. Robert Mitchel (1966) has summed up the challenge posed by this growing fragmentation. His conclusion is that the organization of the future will not only necessarily have more diversity, but the potential for greatly increased effectiveness as well.

The upgrading of training facilities and training techniques is an important function of the professional department. Much of the more advanced training is now being given in statewide programs such as the Oregon experience reported by Karl Van Asselt (1967). Another example is the seven-week Advanced Police Community Relations Leadership Training Program sponsored by California's POST (Peace Officer Standards and Training Commission) and held at three University of California campuses. Large departments are expanding facilities and using advances such as videotape techniques to explain the problems of law enforcement to students (Bonan, 1967). In a later section, we will explain some of the modern methods for PCR training. Here it is enough to note, as did John P. Kenny (1964) in his study of California's police, that the academies of major departments are becoming regional centers of training, taking students from many surrounding departments for both basic and mid-career instruction. The author was privileged to observe one outstanding example of this trend: the Los Angeles Sheriff's Academy.

The Professional Department and the Professional Policeman

In many areas, the move toward the professional department reinforces that toward the professional policeman. Certainly the improved training offered by a professional department can only increase the patrolman's confidence in himself. New technological developments can help make the policeman's judgment more accepted by the man in the street—especially in areas such as traffic enforcement. Several writers have warned, on the other hand, that professionalization of both the department and the individual may have some unintended results. Arthur Niederhoffer (1967), a long time New York policeman, has pointed out that the great importance given to education almost guarantees that anyone who works very hard on his schooling will get promoted—hence, those who will be least "professional" will be left in closest contact with the public. Other sources note that the more highly educated the officer, the more difficult he is to keep, due to his greater choice of alternate employment.

The same training and specialization which make the individual and the department professional may have the effect of downgrading the patrol function. Walter Arm (1969) has related that every new specialty, in which experts take over from generalists, reduces the sphere of competence of the generalist—i.e., the patrolman. Hence, he may find himself left with only the most mundane and least interesting of tasks. This can lead to lower self-confidence and less public esteem.

Albert Reiss (1967a) has asserted that only when the officer's judgment is taken as authoritative by those with whom he interacts will he be a professional. Some aspects of departmental professionalization, especially centralization of command and the growing tendency to make decisions at the staff level, may not, in Dr. Reiss' view, be leading to a professional patrolman. For PCR, a major important consequence of the move toward professionalization may be the tendency of specialization and efficiency criteria to limit informal, personal contacts with law enforcement officers. It is to counter this trend that many of the present programs in police-community relations have been initiated.

James Q. Wilson (1968e) has hypothesized that there is a qualitative difference between the patrol function and a professional orientation. He is therefore pessimistic about the possibility for change, as he states:

> "The patrolman" is neither a bureaucrat nor a professional, but a member of a craft. As with most crafts, his has no body of generalized, written knowledge, nor a set of detailed prescriptions as to how to behave. It has, in short, neither theory nor rules. Learning in the craft is by apprenticeship—but on the job, and not in the academy. The principal group from which the apprentice wins (or fails to win) respect are his colleagues on the job, not fellow members of a discipline, or attentive supervisors. An attempt to change a craft into a bureaucracy will be perceived by members as a failure of confidence, and a withdrawal of support, and thus be strongly resisted. Efforts to change it into a profession will be seen as irrelevant, and thus largely ignored.

It is perhaps worthy of mention that law enforcement professionals have seldom been as pessimistic as the above, although most recognize problems and challenges along the way.

Contrasting Perceptions Of The Police Role

During the past decade, the literature of police-community relations has increasingly focused on role perception as a key to understanding police-public interaction. By role perception, we mean the pattern of expectations about group conduct. Here we will review the literature concerning (1) the police view of their role, (2) the police view of the public, and (3) the public's expectations about the police.

Police Self-Perception

Jerome Skolnick (1968d) has concluded that the policeman sees his role as a function of danger and authority, with a constant pressure from the department for efficiency. He states: "Danger makes [the patrolman] suspicious, while his duty makes him respond to the danger." This has two consequences for PCR: (1) the development of a feeling of separateness from the rest of the population, which does not share the dangers of police work, and (2) the foregoing of strong social bonds within the police fraternity. Knowing firsthand the difficulties of making immediate, impartial, legally correct decisions gives great understanding and support to officers beset with post-facto evaluations.

A large number of articles dealing with the police self-image emphasize the primacy of the basic law enforcement task. R. E. Anderson (1968), a twenty-year veteran of the New York Police Department and currently a professor of police science, has stated that all the technical improvements in modern police work, "no matter how sophisticated and costly, will be of little or no value unless they are used to enforce the law, in accordance with our traditional concept of justice in our democratic society." He goes on to emphasize the need for an aggressive posture in the war against crime.

The emphasis on crime fighting is directly related to the concept of "real police work." The President's Commission on Law Enforcement has noted that the phrase "conjurs up in the minds of some a dramatic contest between policemen and criminals in which the party with the stronger arm or craftier wit prevails." The commission concludes that "a great majority of the situations in which the policeman intervenes are not (and are not interpreted by the police-man to be) criminal situations." A U.S. Conference of Mayors study of municipal law enforcement, by contrast, reported that over ninety percent of their time was spent in crime-connected duties. The exact definition of crime-connected duty in both cases need not concern us here; of significance, rather, is the apparent tendency on the part of the departments concerned to see themselves as overwhelmingly occupied with the criminal aspect of their work. Indeed, as Michael Banton (1964) has emphasized in his stimulating comparative study of police in the United States and Great Britain, one of the most frustrating aspects of the police task for police is the large number of "unpolice-like" duties they are required to perform (i.e., breaking up family fights, attempting to find lost children, helping out motorists in distress, and the like).

The police perception of their role as primarily concerned with criminals has several potentially negative consequences for their interaction with the public.

1. As Gerhard Falk (1964) has noted, policemen have a ten-dency to assume they arrest only the guilty (indeed, if the officer felt otherwise, he could only rarely be required to act). This assumption, plus experience with dangerous and violent persons, may lead to the conclusion that strong-arm

tactics and a disrespectful attitude toward those arrested is justifiable behavior.

2. There is the danger that the authoritarian attitude most appropriate for criminal situations will be used for service functions as well.
3. The many noncriminal community service functions of the police may be only grudgingly undertaken by officers who feel such duties are not "real police work."

The Police View Of The Public

Police departments see themselves as serving the public by catching criminals. Since this essential function is far more effective with public support, apathy is of great concern to many professionals. As Fred Ferguson, the innovative Chief of Police of Covina, California, has put it:

> To Mr. Average Citizen, the police patrol car, weaving through traffic under siren and red light, is just another common, everyday occurrence [sic] Mr. Citizen notes only that the police are intent on reaching a scene of emergency somewhere in the community. He gives no thought to the helmeted, uniformed man behind the wheel. He doesn't know the officer's name, and would not be likely to recognize him in a meeting on the street. He is not particularly interested in the officer's problems for he has his own to attend to. So, until he needs help or breaks the law, Mr. Citizen will remain detached and aloof from the uniformed men who safeguard the community. [Anderton and Ferguson, n.d.; Ferguson, 1969].

Concern over public apathy is generally coupled with the conviction that if the public were only better informed of police practices and the rationale behind them, better community support for the police would result. For example, the IACP (1965) stated:

> Too few citizens are familiar with what the police can and cannot do, or why they are compelled to follow a certain course of action even if their actions are against the grain of public sentiment. Understanding of the police and their role in our society is indispensible to real justice and effective police service. If each citizen becomes more personally involved and educated to the fact that the law is after all, a public instrument, administered by the police for the benefit of the people as a whole, then the police-public partnership becomes a reality.

As we shall see in later sections of this article, the problem of citizen apathy has evoked many creative responses from law enforcement agencies throughout the nation, ranging from citizen rides in cars to police lectures to school children.

On a different level, the question of the police perception of the public relates to how various members of the public are perceived. Harold Lett (1963) has commented, relative to police-minority relations, that there is a tendency in police work to divide the world into two groups; the in-group and the out-group, the "we" and the "they." He asserts, "While members of the in-group are judged as individuals, the "they" are judged as a single entity, by the lowest common denominator of our experiences with that group." Thus, one black thief makes all blacks thieves, but a white thief is just one white who is a thief.

The crucial question for PCR thus becomes: To what extent do the police allow their personal stereotypes to color their behavior as law enforcement officers? The attitude of one large West Coast department is summed up as follows:

> All people may have prejudices, however, a police officer must learn to distinguish between his right to hold personal opinions as a citizen and his sworn duty as an officer. While his rights to hold his beliefs as a citizen are inviolate, any manifestation of prejudice while acting as a member of the police department cannot be tolerated [Los Angeles Police Department, 1968].

A survey of several midwestern police departments, conducted by Donald Bouma, indicated that the police feel a strong sense of racial differentiation. In one response, over half the officers felt that Negroes would have lower moral standards no matter what their economic condition. The same survey noted that three fourths of the policemen felt that residents of the inner city had become more antagonistic toward the police during the last ten years. Jack L. Kuykendall (1970) has postulated three possible bases for police "negative perceptions" of minority groups. These are:

1. Police contact with these highly visible groups is overwhelmingly with lawbreakers.
2. Extent of personal and social disorganization of the minority culture is determined by the police on the basis of the
   a. prevalence of perceived minority criminal deviance
   b. prevalence of perceived threatening and challenging situations.
3. Police deal with pressure strategies utilized by minorities for effectuating changes in status.

Public Perception Of The Police

There are many different "publics," each with widely differing perceptions of the police. We will consider only three here: the middle class, youth, and minority groups.

T. A. Fleck (and Newsom, 1969), writing in *Police*, has made a useful attempt to summarize the attitude of the middle class toward the police. He cites three basic attitudes:

1. The police are seen as servants, not masters.
2. The primary purpose of the law is to protect individuals.
3. The police are the enforcers of accepted moral standards.

Oliver J. Keller, Jr., and Clyde B. Vedder (1965) have noted the assumption on the part of many that the police should be concerned essentially with lower-class criminals and that any enforcement against members of the middle class (especially of traffic violations) is really time that could be better spent on more serious matters.

The police perception of "young people" and vice versa cannot be considered without asking which young people are we talking about. As Richard Scammon has pointed out (Scammon and Wattenberg, 1970), there are more conservatives under thirty than liberals, and it is only a small proportion of the latter that might be considered "hippies." Nevertheless, in this small minority is reflected, in an extreme form, many of the attitudes held by a significant segment of Americans presently entering society as adults. That these attitudes are concentrated on college campuses, where future leaders are being developed, makes them all the more important.

Our considerations of the police and social change in earlier sections discussed the effects of present-day challenges to formerly accepted conventions. Professor A. C. Germann (1967), in one of the few articles in professional literature seeking to understand the youth subculture, has suggested that their view of police is based on the assumption that police defend current conventions, not only when flouting these conventions involves breaking the law, but all the time, and primarily because the police themselves feel strongly, personally, challenged. The attitudes of three different groups of high school students toward police has been reported by G. L. Kuchel and A. P. Pottavina. They conclude that the differences in attitudes between the lower-working, and upper-class schools are primarily a result of frequency of contact with the police. The working-and upper-class students had much larger totals under "don't know," while the lower class (predominantly black school) showed very low totals for this heading. Substantive results from the survey indicated that the lower-class youth had greater fear of, and less respect for, the police than the other two groups, but the blacks tended to see the police job as better paid and more desirable than did the other two.

The question of minority-group perceptions of police is a very large one and has been the subject of a great deal of emotionally inspired writing on both sides. This subject is important to police-community relations, but its scope precludes a thorough treatment in this review.

Minority groups tend to see the police as discriminatory in their enforcement of many laws. One survey indicated that 66% of a sample of Northern blacks felt that the police were prejudiced against them (interestingly, this is 6% higher than the corresponding figure for Southern blacks; Bouma, 1969). An exhaustive study of a western city, in which the local police department took part, concluded that "there is a widespread feeling in the community that the police, particularly those assigned to our (black) neighborhood, are either highly insensitive toward minority culture or are outright racists" (San Diego Model Cities Program, 1970). The study cited the following factors as contributing to the above view:

1. Consideration of police as symbolic of white injustice.
2. Use of arrest for harassment purposes.
3. Higher arrest rates in the ghetto (i.e., more people arrested but not charged with a crime).
4. Juvenile curfew enforcement used as a means to break up street corner gatherings.

Implications For PCR

These role perceptions give rise to several important questions for PCR:

1. To what extent does the general police emphasis on enforcement and strong desire for "real police work" affect the possibility for meaningful training or programs in PCR?
2. How can the mutually antagonistic perceptions of the ghetto dweller and the policeman be modified? At present it would seem that each is likely to have a self-reinforcing image of the other; that is, the cop sees the need to be tough in the ghetto because he feels least popular support there, while the black's unfavorable image of the police is thereby strengthened.

3. Given the strong identity of the police, is their stated desire for public support and understanding likely to run against a strong dislike for outsiders meddling in police affairs? (Witness the strong police resistance to anything resembling a police review board.)
4. Role perceptions appear to be based more on social and cultural factors than on actual police actions-that is, if one accepts the orientation of the flower children, one will tend to dislike police whether or not one has had contact with them.

It is the authors' contention that a vigorous attempt at bringing closer the police's and the communities' views on the role of the police is crucial to the success of any major police-community relations program.

THE SUPERVISOR AS A PLANNER

A police supervisor's responsibility includes one obligation that is overlooked or minimized in some police departments and frequently ignored in others—long-range planning for growth and development of himself and the department. For accomplishing this purpose, he needs to be consulted when plans are being developed that affect his organization or himself. If inadvertently uninformed, but he hears about such planning, he should make efforts to contact the correct people to provide his input.

As is more frequently the case, first-line supervision is confronted with short range planning such as operational activities. This usually consists of developing new techniques to assist in carrying out the goals of the organization. As in most planning of this nature, the supervisor needs to make several decisions, the first one being a determination of exactly what needs to be accomplished. Once this has been clearly conceptualized, he then must ascertain the best person to perform the job. This decision is often as critical as deciding what is to be done. The supervisor must know his staff intimately in order to decide which one can best carry out the assignment.

After these two decisions, the supervisor must then determine how the task is to be carried out. He should not, however, tackle this phase in isolation. The person who will carry out the mission should be called upon for advice and any other possible assistance. Involvement of the subordinate in the planning will provide a sense of participation, create enthusiasm, and help insure the success of the project.

The supervisor's decision is concerned with the timing of the plan. Once again the supervisor needs to consult with those directly affected subordinates, management, and parallel units.

The supervisor and his personnel are part of a team. He is the most knowledgeable person concerning problems in his area of responsibility—therefore, he may be considered an arm of management. The first-line supervisor and his men are closest to the problem areas and therefore it is the supervisor's responsibility to have an input into agency planning. Once the higher plans are formulated, the supervisor's plans are developed.

What are some of the kinds of planning that the supervisor does? He must frequently become involved in plans for fulfilling training needs and requirements, completing work shift assignments, developing emergency plans for his unit that may affect his function as a supervisor, creating vacation schedules, searching out new methods for performing the organization's mission, and resolving common problems. The supervisor also will want to seek alternate ways to effectively utilize the talents of the personnel in his unit. Thus, the supervisor is bringing into the planning process the individual, which in turn is likely to result in increased price, productivity, and internal motivation.

The actual work of the supervisor in the planning process cannot be defined specifically until his supervisory responsibilities are clearly and adequately defined. For example, in a small department, the responsibilities of the supervisor will be much different than those in a large urban police department even though they are theoretically performing the same job. Also, the various kinds of supervisory jobs such as patrol and personnel, present different kinds of planning opportunities for the supervisor.

With the emphasis today in many police departments on decentralization and accountability, the line supervisor is increasingly in a central position relative to the overall planning process. Consequently, line supervisors need to be given the opportunity to participate. Operational planning responsibilities of the supervisor need to be recognized and given credit in the hierarchy of tasks which he must perform. His role must be acknowledged as an essential ingredient in the total administration of the police department.

The supervisor has been a planner for years. He must be recognized as one who contributes significantly to the accomplishment of the planning goals of the department. As a planner, the supervisor can be an impetus to necessary changes in the department by his thoughtful, patient, and innovative approaches. He indeed can become a stimulus to change.

PLANNING: A STIMULUS FOR CHANGE*

The concept of planning continues to increase in popularity. In fact, there appears to be a growing tendency to accept the notion that many of the problems of police agencies can be solved through use of management techniques which have proved successful in other organizations. As one who accepts the values of planning, I am specifically disturbed by such trends when they are not based upon a healthy skepticism and a reasoned commitment to a particular planning effort. I shall, therefore, examine some negative points before discussing various benefits derivable from a planning effort. Finally, we will look at the planning process itself.

Some Negative Aspects Of Planning

In many ways, police agencies are very different from other organizations. For example, colleges and universities tend to hold that the institution exists to increase the contents of the sets of knowledge, aspirations, values, and mental skills associated with *each* individual involved in the academic process. Thus, we have students undergoing experiences intended to expand their knowledge and we have faculty engaged in research and scholarship to enlarge their own understandings. Even when academic activities are intended to contribute to goals more general than individual growth, these goals tend to be extra-institutional. So we have a physicist working to add to knowledge in his discipline and we have an agronomist seeking methods of overcoming starvation, but such motivations also tend to be highly individualized. These are some of the realities in a number of other professions, but they are not to be found to the same extent in most other public service organizations. Consider industry, for example; the preservation of the integrity and continuity of a company's own purposes are paramount. Individuals may relate to the organization to achieve personal fulfillment, but only in ways

---

*SOURCE: George T. Felkenes, "Police Planning: A Stimulus for Needed Organizational Change," reprinted by special permission of *Police*, copyright © 1972 by Charles C. Thomas, Publisher, Springfield, Illinois, Vol. 16, No. 10, pp. 24-28.

which contribute to organizational goals. Exceptions, when discovered, are usually not tolerated for very long.

I am definitely committed to the police and want to make every effort to increase the workability of their organization. This commitment is well worth the income lost by avoiding more lucrative pursuits. Now, suppose that under the struggle for institutional survival we decide to introduce planning and other management techniques. What we must recognize is that planning brings the tendency to focus attention upon institutional goals. It also introduces many concepts, activities, and uses for data which are strange to the police environment. By what it carries with it, planning is capable of transforming a police department into a completely new organizational configuration from that which previously existed. Planning is based partly on the new and innovative, often some of which have not been adequately tested and analyzed for workability. By precipitously adopting new ideas as part of the planning processes, the wise administrator will always keep in mind that traditional operating methods will change. He must likewise weigh carefully the freedom given by perpetuation of traditionally adequate operations with some uncertainty and temporary restrictions found by adopting the new.

Another way of looking at it is that one purpose of planning itself has side-effects which may create unwanted change. All that can be done is to urge any planner to be constantly critical of what he is doing. In fact, one of the personal frustrations of the planner —namely, an inevitable agency resistance and skepticism—is actually an excellent means of protecting this critical attitude. What may appear to be recalcitrance is often a natural tendency to conserve that which is valued, and the planner should be sensitive enough to ferret out the meaning of such "conservatism."

Another important negative aspect of planning is the tendency to generate a *plan*. This plan is considered a blueprint of the future. It is the *way* the organization will go. Such plans are normally quickly forgotten, except perhaps when resurrected occasionally to demonstrate to outsiders (legislators, civic leaders, and budgetary analysts for example) that the institution *knows* its own purposes and methods of achieving them. Planning should be somewhat predictive, by revealing future possibilities and by getting people to use their imaginations. It would encourage people to think in terms of alternatives. The plans, rather than being a static blueprint, should be a "roadmap" which reveals numerous paths into the future. Planning should be open and dynamic and it should never tend to preclude the spontaneous creativity which is so important to institutional vitality.

Another danger inherent in some planning systems, such as those built upon computer-based information systems, is that a set of relationships is built into the system, often at great expense. When many thousands of dollars are spent in developing such a system it is not easy to let go of. Consequently, there can be a tendency to try to maintain the invariance of the relationships. To illustrate what I mean, take the fictitious overly-simplified example of the formula: "Patrol vehicle = the number of street miles X number of serious crimes in the particular area." In this simple formula you are free to insert a number of street miles and the number of serious crimes in order to determine the required vehicle density. My contention is that street miles may have some vague statistical meaning for traditional policing, but I would not be able to assign any meaningful value under a drastically modified and highly diverse urban setting. Now, imagine that the preceding formula has been highly elaborated. It is still based upon many traditional experiences and assumptions concerning the forms of relationships in a police agency. It has been very expensive to develop. Along comes some innovative thinking, creating new theories which do not fit this elaborate formula. What goes, the formula or the innovation? Ultimately, the formula will go, but probably not without some undesirable resistance.

The final point is that planning is hard work and that it creates new demands for both information and effort. Expansion of personnel and resources to accomplish successful planning may not be possible for many smaller departments, but there is always a price to be paid. The question is: "Will the benefits of planning offset the price?"

Some Benefits Of Planning

Only you can answer the preceding question. I can, however, describe some of the possible benefits of planning one police agency is trying to realize.

In these days of conflict, job pressures, and competition for personnel among various police agencies, it is very easy to lose the silent people. In losing them, we lose their ideas and energy and the opportunity to give them relevance. A planning system can be designed to involve these people and to give agency relevance to their thinking and actions. When you look, you find these people among the students, practitioners, other departments' personnel, and with your own agency. At the same time, the planning effort can channel the energies and enthusiasms of the more aggressive people and groups within the department.

In focusing attention upon change and potential actions (i.e., because of its future-orientation) planning tends to intellectualize conflict. It gets people together to argue and discuss differences before they occur. This, it seems, is far superior to having an evolutionary process create unexpected conflict conditions; and it is also consistent with the traditional organizational commitment to rational process.

Closely coupled to the aforestated benefit is what might be called the integrative function of planning. By this, I mean the bringing together of individuals, groups, efforts, and goals. Planning should tend to counteract the isolation of groups so common among bureaus, divisions and sections in a police department. The detective division, for example, does not communicate with the patrol division. The command, field, and administration personnel view themselves in separate ways. Distinctions are made between operational goals and administrative goals. Such distinctions may be valuable for some purposes, but they should not prevent people from interacting in meaningful ways. I believe that planning can be designed to remove these barriers.

Another important integrative benefit of planning is related to what we might call the community-relations function. An integrative planning system can contribute to increased understanding of both the organization functions and its external environment. Personnel officers, for example, can be encouraged to remain alert to social changes which may affect the operations of the community relation function as well as remaining aware of innovations in normal work techniques in the particular field of expertise. This process of organizational awareness might also be called a process of "searching the field" for new ideas, techniques and innovations. In an integrated planning program, organizational awareness can easily be made one of the steps in the planning activity. For example, given the opportunity to interact in new ways with command and field persons, the personnel officer can become acquainted with some of the realities of agency needs. Patrol leadership decisions also can lead to a greater appreciation of the personnel selection methods. Thus, operations personnel can be given the chance to develop insight into the fundamental administrative goal of preserving the organizational equilibrium by careful utilization of personnel resources.

One of the principal reasons for planning is to introduce conscious intelligence into the change process. This puts the department in the position of being able to pursue change rather than being pursued by it. Anticipating change means that the agency need not merely react to every chance event, but rather that it can establish a creative balance between intelligent choice and evolution.

Once the alternative departmental plans are developed, they can be used to design various support programs such as community relations, capital construction, public relations, and personnel development and recruitment. They can also be used for monitoring program activities, for allocating space and for budgeting. In other words, planning can serve the purposes of "effective management;" but "effective management" may be secondary to the opportunities for leadership which can be created by planning.

In conclusion, some of the goals of planning as I see them from the perspective of an educator viewing a police department are:

1. To bring people together in performance of significant actions and, in general, to develop an integrative force within the agency.
2. To provide a basis for monitoring programs, allocating resources and using information.
3. To provide for experiences and exchange of information which serve to create mutual understanding in the various groups within the organization.
4. To associate decisions with people having the information and expertise to best make them.
5. To seek out and solicit the thinking of people from all groups within the department.
6. To create a method for using mathematical and computer techniques in ways which support, not supplant, the full range of human intelligence and aspirations.
7. To provide guidance for future action without destroying the possibility of rapid departmental evolution.
8. To encourage investigation of the behavioral aspects of administration to assist in satisfying human needs, goals, and desires.

The Planning Process—An Overview

There are many steps in the planning process as used in most police departments. Details are often described in departmental manuals. However, no attempt is made here to cover the details, but rather to set forth a broad general overview of the planning process.

The first general step is to prepare some of the background information needed for the planning. In most cases, budget projections should be developed, personnel figures for the various divisions projected in detail, and space needs projected. I call these numbers "planning parameters" or "optimal desires." It must be emphasized, however, that many agencies will not have the data base, manpower, or computer capability support to make projections as reliable as those generated in the large police departments. In the system, as envisioned by me, the "shaky" data is not critical, as the developing of alternatives is an answer to incomplete or inaccurate assumptions.

The next step is that of orienting the department to the new concepts, language and processes involved in planning. Most people will have difficulty in appreciating the purpose of planning or the importance of making much effort to understand it. One approach would be to conduct a two or three day workshop for all the command staff and chief administrative personnel. This workshop would include several talks and some simulation of the planning process. Although a fair degree of enthusiasm can be generated during such a workshop, one cannot expect to have communicated full and lasting understanding. If an expectation that something is about to happen is created, and the notion that what is about to happen is not undesirable, label the workshop a success.

The third general step is to organize the personnel into working groups. A central planning committee sets the parameters, reviews plans and makes recommendations to the Chief. A very important innovation in the planning process is to create a number of subplanning committees consisting of interest groups within the department, patrol officers, and perhaps unions. These committees conceivably do the actual program planning. A planning office must also be formed to do the staff work involved in coordinating the planning effort and in making calculations and analyses of plans.

The fourth step is to set up a provocative situation for each of the planning committees and to record the reactions in a uniform way. The provocation (or system perturbation) is amply provided by the parameters given to the committees. Each committee is told that they must design a program which does not generate more departmental resources and use more money or space than the central planning committee says they will have in five years. They may also be given other constraints which are non-quantifiable and are issued as statements, such as: "You cannot plan a public relations program," or "You must develop three general training courses to show the relationship of your division to other divisions in the department."

Sometimes I suspect that inadequate data will be an advantage in that it often creates a strong enough reaction for attention to be captured. One important purpose of the planning, however, is to get the committees thinking in the terms of *alternatives*. Consequently, they also should be told that they are free to generate as many alternative programs as they wish. This instruction serves both as a means of getting alternatives and also as a safety valve.

The fifth stage is to analyze the plans to put them together in a comprehensible form. During this state the central planning committee reviews all plans and seeks trustee approval.

The sixth stage, following the approval of the Chief, is to design implementation programs—including seeking funds and the creation of time schedules.

The final stage is to use the plans as part of the budgeting process and to provide for their annual review and modification.

In the final analysis planning involves a major effort. Since the program budget is becoming more popular as a method of management decision making, it must be remembered that police program planning assimilates the budgetary processes. Consequently, by implementing a program planning approach, the former line-item budget is cast into a different mold to permit a more rational decision at the various organizational levels. Basically, the purposes of the program approach (i.e., creating thought stimulation, utilization of intelligence, involvement of outside groups, increased communication and creation of an orientation toward the future), creates a system oriented toward people as an integral part of planning. As most executives in police work realize, planning is done in an environment of probabilities, possibilities, and uncertainties. Precise information is often non-existent and definite answers are unavailable. To overcome those hindrances, there must be a willingness to intelligently guess and explore alternatives. Program planning permits this and reemphasizes that there is no such thing as *The Plan*.

Topics for Discussion

1. Contrast the trait and situational approaches to leadership.
2. Contrast the skills required by the first level supervisor, middle managers, and top level managers.
3. Discuss the human problems issuing from specialization in terms of supervisory problems caused by overzealous staff personnel.
4. Define and distinguish between job enlargement and job enrichment. Which do you prefer? Why?
5. Do promotional examinations have any relationship to the expected job to be performed in your department?
6. How are supervisory personnel selected in your agency? How are they rated in regard to job performance? Is there a rational relationship between the two?
7. In your estimation, what are some of the negative effects that bureaucracies have on the individual. What are the positive effects?

Supervisory Problems

PROBLEM #4—THE SAME OLD STORY

Background. The June City Police Department (JCPD) has seventy-five sworn personnel, sixty of whom hold the rank of patrolman. Of these sixty, fifteen are in special positions termed unclassified positions. These positions are as follows:

Court liaison officer	— 1 position
Training officer	— 1 position
Community relations officer	— 1 position
Detectives	— 6 positions
Traffic officers	— 1 position

Although these positions, with the exception of detectives, are of patrolman status, they are viewed as definite promotions in the JCPD.

About the only time that one of the positions opens for a new appointment is when one of the incumbents is promoted, returns to patrol, or retires. Consequently, when a position does become vacant, fifteen to twenty-five officers apply. The only criteria for an application is that the officer must have been employed at least three years with the JCPD.

Under the former chief, Chief Nez, persons were selected following submission of their names to their supervisor who turned the names over to the chief who then made the appointment.

Sergeant Fair, was not satisfied with the process, so when the new chief, Chief Allmighty, came on board, Fair presented to him (and he approved) the following procedures for selection of persons to fill vacant unclassified positions.

1. Each applicant was to prepare a two page resume and present it to his sergeant who forwarded it to the chief.
2. When all resumes were collected, the chief gave them to a committee of three JCPD sergeants who rank-ordered them and made any appropriate comments about the applicant. At no time were any of the sergeants to discuss the applicants with each other.
3. An oral board was then convened, composed of the assistant chief, the one captain in the department, and the ranking sergeant (there were no lieutenants). The board was given the responsibility of reviewing the sergeant's recommendations.
4. Group orals were then conducted for the top ten applicants.
5. Individual oral interviews were then held with each of the top ten applicants.
6. The oral board, with the compilation of information, rank-ordered the ten applicants.
7. The Chief then interviewed the top five applicants and appointed one.

Problem. The men in the department initially accepted the new procedure and viewed it as a fair and objective way of making appointments. This situation did not last long however, because after the first few appointments, the men began to realize that the selection processes were still subjective with no objective safeguards built in to insure that everyone had an equal chance. The feeling persisted that Chief Allmighty still had absolute control over the appointments.

Issues. The men found that in spite of the guidelines, not all of the JCPD sergeants were even permitted to be placed on the initial selection committee of three JCPD sergeants. Of those who were on the committee, some discussed the applicants openly with others and made their judgments based on what they heard.

The oral board always consisted of the candidate's immediate supervisor. If an applicant had a conflict with any of the oral board members, he could request that individuals removal. This never happened for fear that the applicant would hurt his chances. It was also learned that the oral board did not review the sergeant's recommendations, and Chief Allmighty was making appointments without holding interviews with the top five men.

In short, the men looked at the procedure as the chief's way of going through the motions to make it look fair in order to appease the men. Even if the procedure were to conform to the guideline, nothing prevented favoritism or personality conflicts from playing a significant part in the final outcome.

Alternatives. One alternative available would be to keep the procedure the way it was. What other alternatives are available? Discuss the desirable and undesirable aspects of each alternative.

Actions Recommended. Which alternative would you select? Why? Why were the other alternatives rejected? Assume that the procedure in the JCPD has not been changed. What are the consequences of this decision? What are the future consequences of each of your other alternatives—assuming that each one was adopted? What are the primary supervision problems that are likely to arise under each alternative? Discuss fully.

Problem #5—THE PRESSURE OF EXAMINATIONS

Background. The Uabe Police Department (UPD) has the responsibility for preserving the peace in a city of some 25,000 persons. It has a complement of fifty-five sworn officers from a wide range of ethnic backgrounds.

To be promoted to sergeant, one must first pass the civil service examination for sergeant. Until very recently the Sergeant's Promotional Examination was completely written. The Civil Service Commission recently requested a change of the city charter, later approved by the electorate, whereby the examination is graded as follows: 60 percent for the written part of the examination and 40 percent for the oral portion. The oral board consists of three UPD police lieutenants.

Problem. Patrolman Imahood, a competent and efficient police officer, recently took the sergeant's examination and scored very high on the written part but was disqualified because of a very low score on the oral part.

Officer Imahood complained that two lieutenants on the oral board were not impartial when it came to their evaluations of him. He claimed that Lieutenants Honest and Haphazard exhibited open hostility toward him on several occasions because of his work as president of the Uabe Police Officers' Association. The conflict arose over the proposed establishment of two neighborhood police community relations centers. The Lieutenants strongly favored the idea but Officer Imahood denounced the plan on a local radio station broadcast.

Officer Imahood as president of the association also publically denounced the manner in which Lieutenant Haphazard pushed through the appointment of six Assistant Inspectors (detectives) without the benefit of a Civil Service Examination. Once again Imahood openly condemned this process of "blanketing in" the Assistant Inspectors two days prior to the law being changed requiring an examination for the Assistant Inspector position. The proposed law required that before any officer could receive an increase in salary, he had to pass an examination. Imahood actively and forcefully demanded that this should have been required for the six appointments. He also estimated that some of the six could not have passed a reasonable examination and were actively being shown favoritism by Lieutenant Haphazard.

Issue. Lieutenants Honesty and Haphazard categorically denied the allegations that they were in any way influenced to give low oral ratings by the overt animosity between them and Officer Imahood. Neither of the Lieutenants could substantiate with articulable facts the reasons for the low oral rating. Their contention was that they were not required by the law to give reasons.

Alternatives. As the sergeant directly authorized by the UPD chief to monitor the new testing procedure, what alternatives do you see available to recommend to the chief to solve the above problem? Discuss each alternative in relation to the responsibility that the Civil Service Commission has for implementing the new testing procedures. For example, should you recommend that the chief disregard the oral part of the examination?

Action Recommended. Recently the Police Officer's Association voted to omit the oral part of the examination. Based on this information what action should you as the chief's representative take? Defend your solution in face of the argument that the oral board acted unfairly but the Civil Service Commission could not change the law for the benefit of Officer Imahood. Should you recommend a return to the spoils system in effect prior to the new examination law? What would be the consequences of recommending that the test in the case of Officer Imahood be accepted as final even though there was evidence of considerable animosity by the two lieutenants toward Officer Imahood?

Problem # 6—THE SOFT CAP CONTROVERSY

Background. In the late 1960s Seamy City Police Department began wearing helmets after one of its officers suffered a severe injury from being struck on the head with a piece of pipe. Before this incident, officers had worn the soft military-type dress caps—the late 1960s were a turbulent time with frequent attacks directed at police officers. The helmets proved effective for protecting an officer from serious head injury if he were hit directly on the head, but several officers were injured when an object struck the edge of the helmet. One officer was partly blinded when a bottle shattered (after striking the edge of the helmet) and glass slivers penetrated his eye.

Personal comfort became a problem because it was not possible for tall officers to wear the helmets while sitting in patrol cars. As a result of this problem, an order was promulgated stating that the helmet was to be worn whenever the officer was outside his vehicle. In the two-man patrol cars in Seamy City, storage of the helmets in the vehicle also presented a problem.

For safety purposes the helmets were white with a black band and visor. The distinctive color was also supposed to aid in revealing the police officer among a crowd. Further adversities were soon noted as the high visibility did not save one officer from serious injury when struck by a car. It also came to be realized that the gleaming white helmet stood out as a potential target by someone intent on shooting an officer. The officers were then ordered to purchase a black cloth cover to be worn in possibly dangerous situations.

Problem. Over the past year the officers in the SCPD began to question the utility of the helmets as a safety factor. Many were not wearing their helmet when they were supposed to. Rumblings were heard that the officers wanted to return to wearing the soft caps. Sergeant Rumor heard the complaints and was aware of an informal survey by the patrolmen which revealed that about three-quarters of the men wanted to have the soft caps returned. Sergeant Rumor was increasingly disturbed over the vehemence of the rumors and especially the outspoken remarks of several officers on his shift. He realized then that the department was faced with a unique problem—the officers wanted a change in uniform requirements. Sergeant Rumor was aware that the patrolmen were quite upset about the hard versus soft hat matter especially about the arbitrary manner in which the use of helmets was mandated.

Issues. Sergeant Rumor was faced with the problem of attempting to squelch the dissent which his men had been voicing, or facing the chief of the SCPD who had spoken out strongly in favor of the positive aspects of wearing the helmets. Rumor immediately recognized the difficulty of having the chief change his ideas on uniform regulations as he had to take into consideration the safety of all the officers, particularly those in hazardous situations. Is there a deeper problem than the issue of hard versus soft hats as part of the uniform regulations?

Alternatives. What alternatives are open to Sergeant Rumor? Which ones are clearly not feasible? Which ones offer the best chance of offering a realizable solution to Sergeant Rumor's supervisory problem?

Actions Recommended. What actions should Sergeant Rumor take? Why? If you were the chief of the SCPD what alternative would you adopt? What would be the short and long range consequences of the actions of Sergeant Rumor and the chief? With what particularly difficult supervisory problem was Sergeant Rumor faced?

ANNOTATED BIBLIOGRAPHY

Bristow, Allen P., *Police Supervision Readings*, Springfield, Illinois: Charles C. Thomas, 1971. This book is a collection of articles and papers on those tasks, duties, or requirements performed by the average police supervisor. Most of the articles are written by chiefs of police or former chiefs of police. The book covers subjects ranging from disciplinary problems to performance rating, from disaster supervision to counseling techniques, and from training techniques to morale problems.

Hansen, David A. and Thomas R. Culley, *The Police Leader, A Handbook*, Springfield, Illinois: Charles C. Thomas, 1971. In this book the authors provide the modern police supervisor with some general as well as specific guidelines to assist in creating and maintaining an efficient, smooth running department.

Iannone, N. F., *Supervision of Police Personnel*, Englewood Cliffs, New Jersey: Prentice-Hall Inc., 1970. This text is planned specifically to describe the role of the supervisor within his organization, his prime functions, and the responsibilities of his position. A discussion of his administrative and management functions is included to give the reader a broad view of the guiding principles relating to personnel managment. Elements of leadership, the training function of a supervisor, and evaluation are discussed in detail.

Melnicoe, William B. and Jan Mennig, *Elements of Police Supervision,* Beverly Hills, California: Glencoe Press, 1969. This textbook contains complete coverage of all aspects of police supervision including chapters on the supervisor's role in management, the psychological aspects of supervision, motivation, leadership, morale discipline, communication, counseling and interviewing, complaints and grievances, decision-making and planning, performance appraisal, and the supervisory training function. Ten appendices are included with sample forms, rating scales, and training courses.

Munro, Jim L., *Administrative Behavior and Police Organization,* Cincinnati, Ohio: W. H. Anderson Company, 1974. This book presents various concepts from the behavioral sciences which are helpful in understanding the behavior patterns of the supervisor and the elements necessary for human development. Individual chapters deal with issues arising from group dynamic theory and from communication studies within groups. Leadership and supervision, motivation, morale and productivity also receive attention in separate chapters. This text views administration as a general phenomenon so that both scholars and police administrators may draw upon a wide range of research findings from other areas of administration and use those findings to increase their own insight into the behavior of people in law enforcement agencies.

Pell, Arthur R., *Police Leadership,* Springfield, Illinois: Charles C. Thomas, 1967. This book presents the fundamentals of successful leadership to police supervisors and shows them how to apply these principles in their daily work. The book covers such leadership problems as morale and motivation, discipline, communicating ideas, handling problems, and training men.

Wadman, Robert C., Monroe J. Paxman, and Marion T. Bentley, *Law Enforcement Supervision: A Case Study Approach,* St. Paul, Minnesota: West Publishing Company, 1975. This text contains cases and problems especially selected for the training of law enforcement supervisors; problems for solutions drawn from patrol supervision, police-personnel administration, records utilization, staff development, employee discipline, planning for organizational improvement, and other areas of law enforcement administration. The sections on "General Law Enforcement Supervision" and "Training" are especially helpful to the police supervisor who must deal with the everyday problems of planning and assigning, evaluation of problems, coordinating work with others, acceptance of responsibility, and utilization of personnel and equipment.

Whisenand, Paul M., *Police Supervision: Theory and Practice*, Englewood Cliffs, New Jersey: Prentice Hall. This book focuses on the growing importance of the inclusion of modern behavioral research findings in the theory and practice of police supervision and serves to introduce the most current knowledge in the role of the supervisor in a police organization. It portrays the supervisor as a team leader with basic responsibility for developing the human resources of the law enforcement organization. It examines the various dimensions of the supervisor's role and develops detailed guidelines for implementing a totally modern mode of effective practice. Other features of the book include detailed discussions of organizational communications, the supervisor's vehicle for exerting control, and an examination of supervisory leadership in terms of mutual support, interaction facilitation, goal emphasis, and work facilitation.

NOTES

PART 2 BEHAVIOR PATTERNS OF THE SUPERVISOR

Perceptions Of Role Performance And Organizational Effectiveness

1. See Richard H. Hall, "The Concept of Bureaucracy: An Empirical Assessment," *American Journal of Sociology* (July, 1965), pp. 32–44, and Peter M. Blau, *Bureaucracy in Modern Society* (New York: Random House, 1956).

2. See A. H. Maslow, "A Theory of Human Motivation," *Psychological Review*, 50 (1943), pp. 370–396.

3. See Frederick Herzberg, *Work and the Nature of Man* (Cleveland and New York: World Publishing Co., 1966), pp. 71–91.

4. See Lyman W. Porter and Edward E. Lawler, III, *Managerial Attitudes and Performance* (Homewood, Illinois: Richard D. Irwin, Inc., 1968).

5. See Paul E. Mott, *The Characteristics of Effective Organization* (New York: Harper and Row, 1972), pp. 22–24.

Personality Characteristics Of The Supervisor

Allport, G W., Vernon, P. E. & Lindzey, G. *Study Of Values* (1960).
Gough, H. G. *The Adjective Check List* (1952).

Hathaway, S. R. & McKinley, J. D. *Minnesota Multiphasic Personality*, Revised Edition (1951).

Misner, G. E. The Response Of Police Agencies. *The Annals Of The American Academy Of Political And Social Science*, 382, 109–119 (1969).

Naroll, H. G. & Levitt, E. E. "Formal Assessment Procedures in Police Selection." 12 *Psychological Reports*, 691–694 (1969).

Wilson, O. W. *Police Administration*. (1950).

Personality Traits Versus Administrative Judgment

1. Edwards, Allen L., *Edwards Personal Preference Schedule*, The Psychological Corporation, New York.

2. Baehr, Meland E., Ph.D., *Psychological Assessment of Patrolman Qualifications in Relation to Field Performance*. LEAA Grant No. 046, Law Enforcement Assistance Administration, U.S. Department of Justice, Washington, D.C.

3. *Administrative Judgment Test*, Series O. Personnel Measurement Research and Development Center, Standards Division, Bureau of Programs and Standards, U.S. Civil Service Commission, Washington, D.C.

4. Owens, Robert G., *Personality Correlates of Administrative Judgment*, University of Wisconsin, 1965 (unpublished).

5. *Ibid.*

6. Baehr, *op. cit.*

7. Edwards, *op. cit.*

8. Baehr, *op. cit.*

9. Owens, *op. cit.*

Self Evaluation, Personality And Job Performance

1. Jourard, "Age Trends in Self-Disclosure" *Merrill-Palmer Quarterly of Behavior and Development* (1961) Vol. 7, pp. 191–197; *Personal Adjustment: An Approach Through the Study of a Healthy Personality* (1963); *Self-Disclosure: An Experimental Analysis of the Transparent Self* (1971); and "Cognition, Cathexis, and the 'Dyadic Effect' in Man's Self-Disclosing Behavior" *Merrill-Palmer Quarterly of Behavior and Development* (1960), Vol. 6, pp. 178–186 (co-authored with M. J. Landsman).

2. Carkhuff, *Helping and Human Relations* (1969).

3. Parker, "Self-Disclosing Behavior in Police Work," *The Police Chief* (1971), Vol. 38, No. 7, pp. 44–46.

4. Lasakow, "Police Officers Versus College Students," in Jourard's *Self-Disclosure: An Experimental Analysis of the Transparent Self* (1971), at pp. 55–58.

5. Watson and Sterling, *Police and Their Opinions* (Washington, D.C.: IACP, 1969); Black and Reiss, *Studies of Crime and Law Enforcement in Major Metropolitan Areas* (Washington, D.C.: U.S. Government Printing Office, 1967); and Neiderhoffer, *Behind the Shield: The Police in Urban Society* (1967).

6. McNamara, "Uncertainties in Police Work: The Relevance of Police Recruits' Backgrounds and Training," in Bordua's edited text, *The Police: Six Sociological Essays* (1967), at pp. 137–163; Matarazzo, Allen, Saslow, and

Wiens, "Characteristics of Successful Policemen and Firemen Applicants," *Jour. Applied Psychology* 1964, 48, pp. 123-133, and D. H. Bayley and H. Mendelsohn, *Minorities and the Police: Confrontation in America* (New York: Free Press, 1969).

7. Smith, Locke, and Walker, "Authoritarianism in College and Non-College Oriented Police," *J. Crim L., C & P.S.*, Vol. 58, pp. 128 (1971); McNamara, footnote 6; and Parker, Murray and Reese, "Authoritarianism in Police College Students and the Effectiveness of Interpersonal Training in Reducing Dogmatism," *Journal of Law Enforcement Education and Training* (1971), Vol. 1, No. 1, at p. 20.

8. McNamara, footnote 6.

9. Neiderhoffer, *Behind the Shield,* footnote 5.

10. Tauber, "Danger and the Police: A Theoretical Analysis," *Issues in Criminology* (1967), Vol. 3, at p. 69.

11. See Gough, *Manual for the California Psychological Inventory* (1957).

12. Black and Reiss, *Studies of Crime and Law Enforcement in Major Metropolitan Areas.*

13. See Jourard, "Age Trends in Self-Disclosure" and Lasakow, *Self-Disclosure; An Experimental Analysis of the Transparent Self.*

Arrests, Job Satisfaction And Personal Variables

1. The President's Commission on Law Enforcement and Administration of Justice, *The Challenge of Crime in a Free Society* (Washington, D. C.: United States Government Printing Office, 1967), p. 10.

2. Patricia C. Smith, M. Kendall Lorne, and Charles L. Hulin, *The Measurement of Satisfaction in Work and Retirement* (Chicago: Rand-McNally & Co., 1969).

Weighting Scores In Promotional Examinations And Their Effects On Performance

1. Variability refers to the degree of unlikeness of the scores in a set of scores from each other and from some standard. The greater the degree to which the scores differ, the greater the variability.

2. Although these raw scores are hypothetical, they do reflect the kinds of scores one frequently finds in a real promotional situation.

3. This discrepency is also affected by the correlation between the two factors. However, for the purposes of this paper, a discussion of this issue is unnecessary.

4. For an interesting account of this kind of situation, see "Promotional Testing: A Critical Look at the Civil Service Testing System" by Thomas A. McFarland, *Police,* October, 1971.

5. See pages 60–65 in *Basic Statistical Methods* by Downie and Heath, Harper and Row Publishers, 1959, for further discussion of this procedure.

6. See Table A in *Statistical Analysis in Psychology and Education* by George A. Ferguson, McGraw-Hill Book Company, Inc., 1959.

Planning: A Stimulus For Change

Golembiewski, Robert T., and Gibson, Frank: *Managerial Behavior and Organization Demands.* Chicago, Rand McNally, 1967.

Kenney, John P.: *Police Management Planning.* Springfield, Thomas, 1952.

Novick, David, (ed.): *Program Budgeting: Program Analysis and the Federal Budget* Washington, D.C., U.S. Government Printing Office, 1965.

President's Commission on Law Enforcement and Administration of Justice: *The Challenge of Crime in a Free Society,* Washington. D.C., U. S. Government Printing Office, 1967.

President's Commission on Law Enforcement and Administration of Justice: *Task Force Report: The Police.* Washington D.C., U.S. Government Printing Office, 1967.

Pfiffner, John M., and Sherwood, Frank P.: *Administrative Organization.* Englewood Cliffs, Prentice-Hall, 1960.

U.S. Bureau of the Budget: *Bulletin No. 66–3,* October 12, 1965.

Wildavsky, Aaron B.: *Politics of the Budgetary Process.* New York, Little-John, 1967.

Wilson, O.W.: *Police Planning.* 2nd ed. Springfield, Thomas, 1958.

Wilson, O.W.: *Police Administration.* 2nd ed. New York, McGraw-Hill, 1963.

PART 3

HUMAN
DEVELOPMENT

The Study of this Part Will Enable You to:

1. Discuss the means by which a first-line supervisor represents the humanistic values of an organization.

2. Identify the characteristics of a supervisory style that emphasizes a situational approach to leadership.

3. Present a brief analysis of the need for evaluation of training programs.

4. Discuss the factors that make up a contingency model of police training. Consider fixed and variable factors.

5. Present an analysis of the process of developing supervisory skills.

6. Discuss the factors that motivate people to better performance.

7. Discuss the need for humanism as a reflection of command. Consider such features as character, literature and imagination.

8. Identify the four meta-learnings of laboratory training.

9. Present an analysis of means of creating and maintaining a healthy discipline.

10. Discuss common rating errors in the measurement of employee performance.

Introduction

Specialization is part of our society, be it in business or government. It is also important in police agencies especially since the teachings of O. W. Wilson. His theory of police organization and management is one of defining jobs narrowly and training a specialist to perform them in a "by-the-number" fashion. As a result of this high degree of specialization, human problems arise. Compounding this is the fact that the staff has expertise above and beyond that of the first-line supervisor. The introduction of this staff expertise creates additional problems in human relations, such as: resentment by line personnel in having their responsibility reduced; constant changes being introduced to upset the status quo, implication that the staff are more knowledgable than the line personnel or their supervisor; resentment being developed because staff personnel are frequently younger and better educated; and finally the staff seems to move very rapidly, sometimes by-passing the supervisor, with little regard for human relations.

Once these problems are recognized, the supervisor has two choices; throw up his hands and give up or seek to solve the problem. He can solve the problem through seeking accommodation, compromising, educating, and politicking. The best solution to relieving the difficulty, however, is to seek to alter the behavior of the staff by urging consultation with the supervisor and personnel so they may adapt to the line requirements. The staff must prove its value to the line officers and the first line supervisors who frequently view the staff with apprehension.

A frequent human relations problem crops up which the supervisor must be prepared to handle. In many police agencies the line function is both complex and boring at the same time. Occasionally there is a need to broaden individual jobs by adding new duties. The enlargement is a horizontal broadening. Another problem is created when this occurs. The supervisor must immediately start to find ways of solving the discontent that is likely to follow. This is best done by seeking to alter the job enlargement so as to allow the patrolmen (or other workers) the opportunity to set their own pace in accomplishing the job, assisting in determining the quality of the end result, and encouraging the individual to seek ways to grow in the new job. This approach, called job enrichment, is however, not applicable to all people. Some may prefer low-level jobs and not to be bothered with changes to make the work more palatable. The supervisor must be trained and fully oriented regarding the interrelationship of all jobs as they pertain to his unit so that as questions arise he can relate proper answers and give accurate reasons for changes which occur.

It must be remembered that the bottom or first line supervisor is in an extremely unique position in an organization. He is the only member of the department who has a manager (administrator who represents the department) on one side, and non-managers on the other who represent the humanistic values in the organization. The supervisor is thus caught between conflicting needs and desires. Siding excessively with one side alienates the other. There is a tendency for the supervisors, however, in the classically oriented departments to orient upward. This orientation then contributes to the social problems of employee alienation. With this in mind, one can successfully answer the question, "What makes John such a successful supervisor?" He is successful because he is able to walk the fine line between the opposing components, without alienating either.

A very difficult task for the supervisor in dealing with subordinates is to understand the human needs of each individual. These needs are termed "wants" and can be classified into several broad catagories.

1. The need for security which is translated into the "want" of an adequate seniority system, a no job loss guarantee when technology is introduced, insurance plans, fair leaders, and pension systems.
2. The need for social opportunities such as the "want" for meeting facilities for employees, physical work layout that permits contact with others, conversation on the job,

periodic rest and coffee breaks, and various kinds of recreational programs.

3. The need for psychological peace which translates into "wants" for adequate pay, comfortable conditions in which to work, and a feeling of safety in the work surroundings.
4. The need for ego satisfaction manifests itself in the "wants" for satisfactory and able supervisors and upper level leaders, an opportunity to advance on merit pay which recognizes the status of the job, praise, and credit for the work alone whether routine or exemplary.
5. The need for self-realization translated into the "want" for some participation in management and supervisory decision making, an interesting and challenging job, and self-control rather than oppressive supervision.

The supervisor as a wise person cannot employ statistics, and total scientific methods to carry out his job. Too much scientific planning creates major human problems in any unit. First of all when scientific management principles are used to an excess, the independence of the worker is severely restricted which will likely be counter-productive in fulfilling the goals of the police department. Boredom of his workers is another drawback which the police supervisor faces when he relies excessively on "mechanizing" the job of the patrolman. Employee maturation is likely to suffer by strict adherence to scientific management. The worker is reduced to a semi-automaton who will respond to certain pre-programmed stimuli. Little else in the self-motivation of the worker will occur. He has no need to mature in the job, in his estimation, because his activities are scientifically calculated. His own initiative will be stifled because acting outside of his narrow confines will subject him to disciplinary procedures of various kinds.

Scientific work management also discourages participation in planning which affects each of the workers. The worker simply fits into a work-slot which has a pre-planned work-out. In a police agency, strict adherence to scientific management by a supervisor will likely result in discouraging new ideas for the complete department as well as destroying any patrolman's initiative to find more effective ways of doing his job. Participating with the supervisor in decisions that will affect them, will create the idea among the workers that they are part of the organization which relies on them to assist in achieving its goals.

Scientific management by the supervisor also reduces the worker's perspective—especially in regard to their contribution toward goals. His perspective is solely circumscribed by the tasks he must perform. Dissatisfaction is likely to result in accidents, and create an atmosphere that eventually leads to disciplinary actions, and termination.

Through the years, as was alluded to previously, police work has tended to take on an aura of specialization which often bodes ill and well for the supervisor at the same time. Police circles debate vigorously the optimum distribution of personnel resources, and the mix between patrolmen and specialists is a topic about which few agree. However, one thing is generally agreed upon—all policemen (from the patrolman to the specialist, to the supervisor, to the chief) are expected to know more and more of the vast array of information and techniques which have come to make up the totality of police work. Therefore, each supervisor needs not only to know the basic skills of being a good supervisor, but also have a broad general knowledge of the various specialized skills in the police department. The supervisor, like all police officers, by being held responsible for distinctive abilities and knowledge to meet the demands the public places on them, are forced to become more professional. In fact, the basis for requiring professionalization in modern law enforcement is such as to no longer be distinguishable from the basis for requiring professionalization in law and medicine.

One supervisory approach to directing a group of highly skilled specialists is to encourage participatory management by subordinates. Even though it is frequently argued that specialization and technology call for the classical model of supervision and management, participatory management techniques can be utilized—these may include periodic group meetings to discuss problems like parking, vacation scheduling, unusual work hours, and other similar matters of group concern. One can note that from this short listing, the supervisor still retains the authority to impose rules regarding many of the environmental aspects of the patrolman's work setting such as; all patrolmen will wear the crash helmets when engaging in high speed pursuits, wear a tie when answering home disturbance calls, file the proper forms when equipment repairs are necessary, complete the correct forms prior to being reimbursed for authorized expenses, and similar matters.

The supervisory style, in short, becomes a function of human preferences and needs. The Supervisor will find that very frequently the situation and its environment will dictate the type of supervisory leadership required, be it autocratic or participative. Too often in the police setting, so-called leadership traits (bearing, command presence, maturity, and motivation) have been used to tap new supervisory personnel. While a specific set of traits may result in a person being a leader in one situation, the same set may result in his being a follower in another. The situational approach is not based on a mechanistic listing of traits which point out future leaders. This approach to leadership in police agencies is to be preferred because it consists of identification of job elements which can then be used to match the most effective leadership pattern required.

In a contemporary police department, supervision is not as it was in previous generations. Higher educational standards, greater individual training, desire for more job satisfaction, and the wish to be treated as a thinking human being have necessitated a break from the traditional authoritarian mode of leadership. The new thrust of supervision is based on the idea that the person performs best when he is understood as a complete human being—physically, psychologically, realistically. In the police setting the new supervisor will be successful if he understands and applies this knowledge to his relationship with his workers.

TRAINING: KEY TO HUMAN AND ORGANIZATIONAL DEVELOPMENT

The need to train and educate police personnel is not only clear but is an immediate necessity. This need has been documented time and time again by governmental commissions and police professionals. Training produces change, but for change to be effective, it must be guided by the best that can be offered in the way of research and experience. New experiences and techniques must be the guide for the future of the police. Too often the police setting has been cloistered with its practices totally determined by bureaucratic and political considerations to the exclusion of new and innovative knowledge of police practices. Positive changes in the police obviously cannot come all at once, but they must come quickly.

The training component in the police department to a significant degree determines whether or not the organization will prosper in order to meet the new and ever-changing needs in our modern society or will settle back into the posture of maintaining the status quo, a totally undesirable situation today. The costs of a failure to act in keeping up with modern conditions, are substantial. But the costs of inaction are much greater. Inaction means that the police department would rather continue to avoid (than to confront) the critical social problems facing it. Decisive action by the organization and its leadership can insure that the police themselves are fully prepared to understand and cope with change. One further plan for this action is within the police setting. If the police staffs can be made to realize the necessity for change, a series of positive events would occur. First, those closest to the problem will face the fact that traditional police techniques frequently have not worked. For example, in the field of community and police relations, a better understanding of the public's involvement is required of the police. Once the problem, whatever it is, is recognized, the police organization can commence trying to find a solution. Second, much research and experimentation is necessary. These can be expedited through the encouragement and experience of the existing police organization and its personnel. Third, police leaders would then be more likely to consider and study the applicability of police research. For example, it has been established that individual pride has a positive correlation to increased ʃroductivity. The issue then becomes how this knowledge can be used in the police organization. Fourth, and quite possibly most important, police leaders would begin to see the necessity for changes in the organization and in the behavior of its personnel.

There needs to be a commitment to positive change. This has not been the case in traditional police organizations. An open-mind toward change will give the police the key to increased success in performing their mission.

To bring about such changes in the police organization and its personnel is not simple. New patterns of behavior and thought must be considered on both emotional and intellectual levels. It is at this point that training plays a key role in organizational development.

A well-conceived training plan is the necessary ingredient for helping police staffs consider the overall concept of change as well as the specific changes necessary in a particular police organization. As noted, a training program must be committed to change. It helps the police personnel toward a change in attitude and practices (which in turn serves the primary mission of the police organization) and in providing more effective police services. If the need for change is accepted by the police staff member, he must take on two new responsibilities: (1) learning new habits, attitudes, and beliefs, and (2) unlearning old ones. Both facilitate the positive aspects of the training effort.

In order to deal with training needs, the training officer, in consultation with the police organization staff, must consider changes in organization viewpoints, goals, personnel, and functions. He must fully consider the individual perceptions of jobs by members of the police organization. In the early planning and development of a training program, the training officer needs to help the police leadership determine just what the job-function expectations are. This may be accomplished by holding one or a series of staff meetings in which the various administrators are asked to list the various job-functions of line and other working personnel in the department. Because of his intimate knowledge of these functions, the supervisor should be called upon to submit his perceptions in this highly important phase. It must be pointed out, however, that the job functions of *all* persons should be considered, including the supervisor and top and middle-level personnel. Finally the organization, through the training officer, can develop a set of training priorities and a comprehensive organizational training effort will be accomplished.

It is not the object in this short introduction to discuss the content of a training program. However, a word must be said about one of a program's most important considerations—evaluation. The goal of evaluation is to determine how effectively the training program achieves its objectives: did change take place in the trainees? Is their knowledge increased? Has their behavior changed? Does the organization perform its mission in a more competent and professional manner? Evaluation helps the training officer define and redefine training objectives. Individuals in the organizational training process may have varying degrees of success in achieving desired change. The training officer, with the aid of evaluative materials, can tailor the program to fit the needs of the personnel as they pass through the training program. Evaluation permits a check on the long-range benefits of training by determining whether changed attitudes and behavior have become a permanent part of the individual's rational patterns.

Change can be measured on numerous scales, i.e., attitudinal, knowledge, organizational, and behavioral. Evaluation is both formal and informal. It is composed of questionnaires and checklists as well as questioning and observation to determine if new behavior attitudes and knowledge are being put into practice. Evaluation is, in reality, feedback. It is communication to the training officer which permits him to assess the impact of his efforts. He needs to know: Has desired change occurred? Did the trainees in fact show increased knowledge, greater sensitivity, positive attitudes and behavioral alterations that increased their skills in working in the police organization? Without this measurement, the future development of the organization can never be adequately determined and the training efforts may be for naught.

ROLE OF LAW ENFORCEMENT TRAINING COMMISSIONS*

After many years of underemphasis, police training has now emerged as a means of increasing the competence of police officers and the effectiveness of police organizations. Unfortunately, police training, in and of itself, is no guarantee of these benefits. Too often, training programs are instituted with great expectations and fanfare, only to fail in their final objectives. It is time to look critically at police training programs, because their failure threatens the hopes and expectations of advancing and professionalizing police work. Each such failure makes it that much more difficult for the next program to succeed.

Success in training requires that there be transfer of training content from the learning environment to the police environment. Without such transfer of training, no benefit is derived from the process. Learning fact and theory, without behavioral change, is a meaningless accomplishment. Of course, just any behavioral change does not constitute a success. It may represent a form of negative transfer, in which the training content is misapplied to the police environment, to the detriment of the police department.

The purpose of this paper is to classify the major elements of a police training program and to propose a contingency model as a first step in increasing the effectiveness of training.

The elements which must be considered in designing an effective police training program are:

1. Training Recipient—The police group to be trained.
2. Training Subject—The nature of the material to be learned.
3. Training Source—The person or institution responsible for giving the training.
4. Training Method—The teaching technique.

In order to facilitate conceptualization of training issues, it was necessary to use generalizations in establishing the categories of the contingency model.

*SOURCE: Jay M. Finkelman and Walter Reichman, "Police Training Strategies: A Contingency Model," *Journal of Police Science and Administration*, Vol. 2, No. 4, December, 1974, pp. 423–428. Reprinted by permission of the publisher.

Training Recipient

Trainers often make the mistake of planning a single training program applicable to all levels of police. In fact, there are very great differences among police groups and to treat them all alike is to compromise the potential effectiveness of a training program. For example, sergeants in state police organizations differ in many personal characteristics and job functions from sergeants in local police organizations, and therefore should not be trained alike. In a similar vein, an appointed police chief differs from a civil service police captain and also should not be trained in the same manner. To clarify these differences, three training recipient groups will be considered: state and municipal police, chiefs of police, and local police.

Experience in training programs with state and municipal police, chiefs of police and local police reveal certain distinctions which suggest the utility of differential training approaches.

State and Municipal Police

These groups usually enter a training program with a high degree of formal education and general sophistication. They are likely to accept and identify with the hierarchical structure of the police organization. They cover a wide territory and serve a heterogeneous constituency. They are part of a career-oriented civil service-type structure which is supportive of objective measures of achievement as a basis of promotion. As such they are likely to undergo the greatest amount of formal training in the course of their careers.

Police Chiefs

This group has wide responsibility and authority for law enforcement in a given area and is relatively autonomous in its functioning. The majority of chiefs are affiliated with rural-based departments of small and medium size. They must assume a major leadership and administrative function in running their departments. As such, they must direct, motivate, coordinate, and evaluate the men who serve under their command. In general, they assume their positions with little formal preparation for these functions. Their appointments are usually political and therefore mandate some affiliation with the political structure of the community. Their autonomy may therefore be contingent upon their proficiency and sensitivity in political dealings. Because they are highly visible in their communities and subject to criticism, they must strive to maintain amiable relationships with their constituents. Seniority in age and position makes them less receptive to formal training programs.

Local Police

This group usually possesses the least amount of formal education and manifests the least amount of general sophistication. They live and work predominantly in small and medium-sized rural communities, and, as such, tend to be provincial and poorly paid. Their potentially conflicting roles as neighbors and law enforcement officers impose a unique set of interpersonal demands upon them. They are probably exposed to the least amount of training, although they may require it most. As a function of their background, they tend to be least responsive and most hostile to formal training programs.

Training Subject

Traditionally, the nature of the training material was not a consideration in developing training programs because only specialized police activities (such as traffic regulations, pistol proficiency, arrest procedures, municipal codes, etc.) were taught. With the acceptance of the behavioral and management sciences, training in human relations, motivation, organizational change, etc., became a legitimate aspect of police training programs. Quite obviously, a training strategy that is effective in teaching pistol accuracy may leave something to be desired in teaching race relations. To illustrate these differences, two categories of training will be described: specialized police subjects and psychological subjects.

Training Source

Perhaps the first form of police training was carried out informally by a fellow officer who proved proficient in a necessary skill. It soon became apparent that individuals who were effective performers were not necessarily effective trainers. In addition, training placed heavy time demands upon individuals who were assigned training responsibilities in addition to their regular duties. Together, these difficulties encouraged the designation of training specialists with training as their major activity.

As the discipline of police science grew, and as its interface with other disciplines became necessary, the concept of a police training academy emerged. Modeled after specialized training institutes, it brought together experts in a variety of specialties for the purpose of educating the police.

As the fund of specialized knowledge continued to grow, even the academies could not fully meet the needs of the various police departments. The training deficiencies first became acute in the social sciences, especially in psychology and sociology. There were insufficient practitioners in these professions who were affiliated with the training academies. Certain innovative police departments began searching for training consultants. Thus, the three training sources to be included in the model are: internal department trainers, training academies, and external consultants.

There are advantages and disadvantages for police departments in using each of these training sources. Depending upon the police group, the subject matter and the training technique, each source will have differential utility.

Internal Trainers

The trainer who is a part of the police department has common ground with the men he is training and is acceptable to them. In addition, he has intimate knowledge of police work and knows the operating problems and system restraints under which the trainees must function. On the other hand, while the internal trainer is acceptable as a fellow officer, he must convince the police that he has something to teach them. The internal trainer must spend time and energy overcoming the trainees' perception that he may be no more competent than they. Their uncertainty with respect to his academic credentials will often establish barriers against cooperative problem solving.

Because the internal trainer identifies with the mores, values and norms of his particular police department, he is unlikely to be able to criticize it constructively. He would certainly hesitate in suggesting changes that might reflect adversely upon his career. While the internal trainer might be adept at conveying specialized police techniques, he will not be effective as a change agent.

Training Academies

Training academies are recognized and established institutions. This confers upon them a degree of credibility in the eyes of the police. It is further enhanced by the traditional close association between academy and police. In spite of this alliance most police academies have been successful in maintaining independent standards of academic quality. They thus have the potential for providing instructors who are both technically competent and experienced in dealing with the police. Under these circumstances there is little likelihood that instructors who are popular but unqualified will be retained.

As with any organization, the police academy has self-perpetuation as a major function. It therefore expends resources on nonacademic functions and develops an inertia which minimizes change and reduces flexibility. Thus, courses may not reflect the current needs of police departments but instead represent the result of compromise and accommodation by the academy staff. In order to make training responsive to current needs, police departments often bypass the academy in deference to outside consultants.

External Consultants

The training credentials of a qualified external consultant are usually beyond reproach. He is in a unique position to draw on the data and theories of his discipline in augmenting his training program. This permits the consultant and the trainees to interpret police experiences within a broader perspective.

Because of the typical diversity of the consultant's affiliations, he has the potential for setting up lines of communication between the police and other groups in the community and academic spheres. He brings the police story to other groups and their positions to the police.

Because the consultant does not have a vested interest in the police organization and is not dependent upon them for his sole support, he can be more open, flexible, and amenable to change. He is therefore capable of inducing critical reflection and thereby constitutes an effective change agent.

It is necessary that an effective change agent be capable of conveying respect for the current level of police work, the police profession and the difficulties under which the police must function. However, because the consultant seldom has in-depth knowledge of police functioning, he may find it difficult to convince the group that he understands the restraints under which they operate and the difficulties which they encounter. In these efforts, he runs the risk of providing minimal input so as to avoid alienating the police with seemingly radical ideas and proposals. In an attempt to acquire additional knowledge, he must rely on his students, who are more knowledgeable in this area. But he runs the risk of conveying the impression that the main objective is for him to learn from them, thus exploiting the training relationship.

Training Method

The standard approach to training and learning is for the instructor to lecture and for the student to listen. This time-honored procedure has merit in the efficient presentation of organized material to groups of individuals. On the other hand, it may be appropriate in certain training situations for the learner to actively participate in the training process. This paper will examine the contingencies under which the lecture method of training and the participative method of training will be most effective.

The Contingency Model

The following model is presented as an optimal strategy for aligning the training recipient, training subject, training source, and training method so as to achieve maximal effectiveness of the training program. The first two (recipient and subject) are fixed factors and the second two (source and method) are variable factors. The fixed factors are always determined in advance of the training programs and the variable factors must be carefully chosen for their congruence. Figure 1 presents an optimal contingency model.

Training State and Municipal Police in Specialized Police Subjects:

The most effective and efficient means of training a sophisticated state or municipal police group in specialized material is through lecture in a training academy. The lecture is a direct method for conveying a prescribed body of information. The academy has all the appropriate facilities to support this training.

Training State and Municipal Police In Psychologically Related Subjects:

The optimal strategy for training these groups in this subject matter is a lecture by a professional external consultant. Whenever psychology-related topics are taught, a psychologist experienced in police training can relate the material to police more effectively and directly than any other training source. His knowledge, experience, and interpersonal skills are assets in this process. The lecture method is still deemed suitable for this type of training because of the sensitivity and sophistication of the recipients.

Training Chiefs Of Police In Specialized Police Subjects:

It is advisable that an external consultant conduct a participative training program with these officials. Chiefs usually perceive themselves as requiring a high level of specialized training—such that it cannot be provided by the typical academy or internal trainer. While, in fact, certain academies can provide such training, the chiefs are likely to resent it. This resentment will necessarily reduce the effectiveness of the training. In addition, because the chiefs have considerable experience and authority, they are not likely to accept the process of being "lectured at." They benefit more through mutual interaction with a consultant in which they can discuss the material and its application. Thus, while the participative method may be less efficient in terms of training time, it will be more effective in achieving the training objectives.

Training Chiefs Of Police In Psychologically Related Subjects:

For basically the same reasons specified in conjunction with the training of this group in specialized police subjects, the external consultant using a participative style of training will be most effective. In order for the chiefs to best transfer the training material to their police work in their home communities, it is necessary that they have the opportunity to discuss, concretize, exemplify and criticize its psychological content.

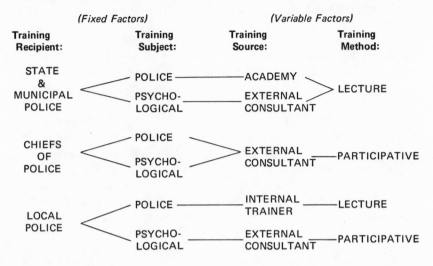

FIGURE 1 CONTINGENCY MODEL OF POLICE TRAINING EFFECTIVENESS

Training Local Police In Specialized Police Subjects:

An experienced trainer from within a local police organization can quickly and effectively convey the specialized information required by local police officers through the lecture method. The training material is usually directly applicable to the subjects' work, and its transfer from classroom to job activity is facilitated by the trust which they are likely to place in a fellow police officer who is intimately familiar with the nature of their work. A well presented lecture is a direct means of teaching the material, and it entails a minimal imposition upon the job schedules of the local police.

The Role Of The External Consultant

The utilization of a skilled external consultant is advocated for all psychology-related training and for one of the specialized police training programs. It is therefore appropriate to conclude a discussion of police training strategies with a consideration of the relationship between the consultant and the police.

An insensitive training consultant who perceives his mission as that of setting the police straight on what he decides they must know will quickly lose credibility and succumb to the image of the pedantic patronizer. On the other hand, a trainer secure in his identity and role, who does not have to demonstrate his personal and professional superiority to the police, can apply his knowledge in a manner that will truly enhance his effectiveness.

When such individuals are discovered, the police administration should do all in its power to make them as effective as possible in relating to the police. That training consultant must be thoroughly familiarized with all relevant aspects of police activities, experiences, and problems.

All too often, police respond to a consultant in a manner which perpetuates his ignorance of the police. Under such circumstances, the predictions of those who are hostile and fearful about the consultant's presence to begin with, will come true. The consultant will not be able to relate his training material to the reality of police work. This is known as the self-fulfilling prophecy, and the police must assume their fair share of responsibility for its occurrence.

Rather than perceive the external training consultant as a "nosy foreigner" who must be shielded from certain aspects of police problems and activities, the police must make every effort to expose and orient the consultant to these activities and problems as soon as possible. It is only in this manner that the consultant and the police can work cooperatively to bring officers of all services and ranks to the desired level of professionalism.

DEVELOPING THE POLICE SUPERVISOR

The police supervisor is "developed" over a period of time. He is not born with the innate ability to lead and supervise people. Throughout his career in the police service, he goes through a process in which a series of supervisory skills are developed and honed to a fine edge. Several of the determinants that go into the making of a supervisor will now be discussed.

Initially, the supervisor is a trainer who, by his own behavior, helps the subordinates in developing their own job-related skills and knowledge. By accomplishing this, the supervisor materially assists in improving the quantity and quality of the output of his unit as well as the entire organization.

The supervisor must be able to engender (through his own behavior) faith, pride, loyalty, and job satisfaction in his employees. Personal confidence, enthusiasm, and job competence assist in keeping the employee's morale at a high level. Leadership is an art in which the supervisor facilitates work in his unit. The supervisor's behavior in such areas as deploying personnel, planning, organizing, coordinating, and the budgeting of his own and overall organization resources, materially assists in facilitating work loads.

The supervisor must learn to develop (to the utmost) personal behavior that serves to promote exchange of information between himself and subordinates, superiors, and horizontal supervisors. Communication is not a one-shot effort. The supervisor must sustain these efforts.

For a supervisor to develop and have the control necessary for the organization to accomplish its goals, he must work on the art of influencing the ways in which his subordinates operate. In the same vein, the supervisor must master behavior that presents to the subordinate the philosophy and goals of the organization. To accomplish this he must both allocate and explain duties required of the subordinate and show how they fit into the organizational scheme.

Community relations, skills, and understanding are important in the development of a supervisor. He must have the ability to develop relationships with the community in order to accomplish his goals and prevent the hostility that can easily develop between the police and the community they serve. A competent supervisor learns behaviors that facilitate the handling of the numerous administrative tasks that are part of his job. Such small administrative matters as insuring that reports are submitted on time, that subordinate requests for leave are handled expeditiously, and that organizational requests for information are fully supplied, go a long way toward maintaining healthy supervisorial relationships.

The supervisor must develop a positive attitude toward safety by preparing set policies and procedure in advance. By doing this he reduces the threat of injury to himself and his subordinates during performance of routine as well as emergency duties. The supervisor is a coordinator since he facilitates, supports, and guides his employees in accomplishing their tasks. The supervisor learns this behavior over a long period of time, not only by coordinating the activities within his unit, but by lateral participation with other closely alligned organizations as well.

Another learned behavior that the supervisor finds indispensable is providing each of his subordinates with feedback concerning that individual's growth and organizational worth. The supervisor's training responsibility ties closely into this behavior. When the supervisor appraises a subordinate of deficiencies in performance, he has the obligation to train him to overcome the deficiencies. By so doing, the supervisor can change a mediocre employee into an outstanding one.

"Developing" a supervisor is incomplete without showing him how to set forth the facility of influencing police personnel to work in a relationship of close, rewarding work harmony. By accomplishing this, the supervisor can generate an enthusiasm that becomes infectious and of great assistance in meeting the department's goals and achieving personal excellence in performance.

On the human side, it is important for any supervisor to develop the ability to promote a feeling of personal worth within each of his subordinates. He does this by stressing the importance of their individual tasks toward the accomplishment of organizational goals. Once again this is a long-term art that must be studied and mastered if the supervisor is to be completely successful.

Briefly, the foregoing discussion leads into a subject-area crucial to the police service—development of a police supervisor. Some of the suggested techniques for such development are learned in a short period of time. However, others will require the ultimate teacher —experience.

MANAGING FOR RESULTS*

The most overworked caricature in the history of law enforcement lampoons is that infamous cartoon depicting a traffic officer secretly positioned behind a signboard, waiting to pounce on an unwary motorist. The 1972 version would have the officer on a freeway ramp—but the trappings are incidental.

Unfortunately, the passing years have not changed the implied message that a traffic cop's work is anchored in stealth, that he operates by trick and device. His purpose? The prevention of accidents, of course, but somehow, that gets lost in the translation. The image of the traffic officer remains that of a man "assigned" to write tickets.

In fact, this image is perilously close to reality. A traffic officer's performance too often has been reduced to an impersonal statistical measure which, at best, offers a mechanistic comparison of his efforts and, at worst, a lever for stimulating him to increased production.

*SOURCE: Walter Pudinski, "Managing For Results," reprinted by special permission of the *Police Chief*, copyright © 1973, by International Association Of Chiefs Of Police, Vol. 40, No. 1, pp. 38–39.

Perhaps a major reason for this gravitation toward "measurement by numbers" has been that those charged with the responsibility for review of a line manager's performance frequently rely upon statistical bases for making objective comparisons. Thus, most administrators have found themselves trapped by a process that holds them accountable for results they obtain through the expenditure of organization funds, but one which uses numerical indices as the primary basis for evaluation of their performance.

Law enforcement administrators have been particularly vulnerable to this review process. How many police administrators have not at one time or another been confronted by fiscal managers with statistical evidence of an increasing crime rate in their city, or of an increase in traffic fatalities? Most evaluations made of the administrator's effectiveness eventually rely upon some quantitative index to support the analysis, thus forcing the chief executive to resort to counterstatistics to support or defend himself. In these circumstances, he becomes virtually preconditioned toward developing good statistical reports designed to convince the auditors, analysts, and others in government that he is doing a good job. He may not be giving the public the service they have a right to expect, but he can point to statistical evidence that proves his department is functioning "efficiently" and is "well managed."

This phenomenon is nowhere demonstrated quite so dramatically as in traffic law enforcement. An almost fanatic attachment to statistical means of evaluating traffic enforcement programs has developed over the years. Some people become obsessed with ratios, indices, death rates, and other concise methods of depicting trends in motor vehicle accidents. Unfortunately, they also apply these means of evaluation to enforcement programs and therefore place more emphasis on the enforcement than what effect, if any, it is having on accidents.

We have created our own statistical prison. We have used statistics so long to support requests for additional funds or manpower that the very people we had to convince soon began using our own methods against us. Once granted additional manpower, we are expected to produce a corresponding increase in arrests. If a decrease fails to materialize, we are hard put to explain, and as often as not try to develop our own figures that seem to rationalize our failure. Everybody becomes obsessed with the numbers game, and the cost and misery resulting from traffic accidents somehow become secondary in importance.

Another factor that cannot be overlooked is the income derived from an aggressive enforcement program, a tax source not willingly relinquished by cities and counties. Although no traffic enforcement program is or should be operated as a revenue source, it may soon become one, and the administrator who permits a reduction in arrests (with an attendant drop in income) may find himself subject to subtle reminders of fiscal responsibility.

No one can argue against the value of an aggressive enforcement effort in terms of accident reduction. All of the principles of selective enforcement are as valid today as they ever were. But, without adequate manpower to fufill its precepts, this factor becomes reality in name only. Without adequate manpower, it sometimes appears that the rationale behind selective enforcement becomes relegated to secondary consideration or is abandoned completely in favor of sheer production. We sometimes forget that the purpose of the application of the principle is to *reduce accidents*.

No one can argue with the need for methods of measuring departmental effectiveness, for this is a responsibility of good management. While a management information system is essential to satisfy the various checks and balances of governmental operations, it should not become the factor which dictates operational processes and procedures that the police administrator should follow to accomplish his department's objectives.

The California Highway Patrol recognized this phenomenon and began a search for alternatives. We felt that the emphasis had to be turned around and that accident reduction should be our primary concern. We were convinced that means other than sheer volume of arrests were available to reduce accidents and that these means should be sought out and implemented. From this fundamental concept grew our involvement in "Management by Results— Participative Management" techniques.

The principle underlying participative management recognizes that there are many qualified people at all levels of any organization. Participative management invites and encourages all members of the organization or unit to participate not only in their own duty functions, but also in management decisions and in developing new procedures or techniques in order that the organization can function more efficiently or better achieve its goals. Participative management recognizes that the greatest amount of untapped talent and ability is probably in the lower ranks of any organization. Traditional police authoritative methods of management tend to waste this potential. Participative management not only makes use of the greatest potential of all employees in an organization, but also provides the greatest possible opportunity for job satisfaction to its member.

The California Highway Patrol concept of participative management could also be described as democratic, or "bottom-up" management. The Patrol views participative management as a method of encouraging subordinates to exercise a degree of authority and responsibility for their own jobs through the process of consultation. Subordinates at all levels are being involved in decisions affecting their own jobs that formerly were made at upper levels in the organization. This decision-making process is implemented by including people at the operational level in all phases of planning, execution, and review.

Upon first exposure to this concept, some experienced managers may mistakenly view participative management as equivalent to "soft" management or, perhaps, "nonmanagement." In actual practice, however, high management standards and establishment of definite work objectives are essential elements of such a program. In the California Highway Patrol, application of the principles of participative management is inseparable from our philosophy of management by results. Under this concept, major managerial and operational emphasis is placed on the *product* rather than on the *process*.

After establishing the overall mission or purpose of the department—and identifying the current state of progress toward accomplishment of that mission—broad departmental goals are established at the executive level. These goals become the basis for subgoals developed by each subordinate organizational level.

Then, each organizational level develops an operational plan for goal accomplishment. The only constraint we place upon operational units is that their planned activities must be in harmony with and supportive of departmental goals; they must be legal; they must conform to broad departmental policies; and they must be effective.

Effectiveness is measured in terms of a proper identification of the problem, the efficient use of available resources, and the degree of success in achieving predetermined goals. Although difficult to measure, such factors as employee morale, motivation and personal development are also considered important yardsticks of an effective operation. For this reason, we encourage a balanced program that includes both operational and personnel development goals.

Upon initial analysis of our operation, we found differing levels of effectiveness, although all of our managers had similar technical resources available to them. We strongly believe the difference in performance could be traced to the fact that the more effective managers capitalized on motivational forces that were mutually supporting. For example, their organizational goals were integrated with employees' personal goals in a manner that resulted in fuller utilization of each individual's potential.

We found that by expanding the employee's scope of responsibility and authority, by permitting him to participate in establishing his own work goals and procedures, we could unleash a largely untapped source of energy and ingenuity. The individual reflects heightened interest as he sees his own ideas and efforts producing results.

By enriching the jobs of their subordinates, supervisors also benefited, finding that their own jobs had become more challenging and personally rewarding. The effect seems to originate with the man on the beat and radiate upward. The Patrol has documented a number of examples where field commanders and their personnel have organized operations so that resources could be concentrated in areas having the greatest potential for results. They have defined their problems, assigned individual and group responsibilities, marshaled their resources, and instituted control procedures designed to keep their programs on course.

The most significant and personally gratifying aspect of participative management is the renewed enthusiasm generated at all levels. The emphasis on product rather than process also created a beneficial side effect—elimination of certain outdated and unneccessary procedural controls. Still another advantage is the increased willingness to experiment and innovate while searching for improved ways to do the job.

Obviously, as with any other major change in managerial philosophy, the participative approach has not met with immediate 100 percent acceptance. Some managers and supervisors feel that expected benefits could be cancelled by undesirable results. Some officers have displayed an apparent reluctance to assume additional responsibility for their own activities.

Neither attitude is surprising, since participative management does represent a significant modification of philosophy. It becomes effective only when it has the firm commitment of top management. It demands reshaped thinking and considerably more patience from the manager. An employee who has seldom been asked for his opinion on how a job should be done does not instantly develop the capability or the willingness to provide a meaningful contribution. Thus, instituting a program of participative management is not only time consuming, but it also requires a continuing expenditure of effort.

This is not to suggest that participative management is a cure-all. It is neither a patent medicine nor a "miracle" drug that will, in itself, revive an organization suffering from a lack of effectiveness. To be successful in adopting the participative approach, top management must honestly accept it as a legitimate technique for accomplishing organizational objectives. If seen merely as a device for manipulating employees to give them a sense of participation, the approach loses its validity; it will be short-lived and could even be counterproductive.

The greatest deterrent to genuine managerial acceptance of the participative concept seems to be fear of losing personal authority and recognition. This attitude obviously must be changed before participative management is instituted on a broad scale. The California Highway Patrol program, to modify attitudes and to produce a receptive atmosphere in which participative management can operate effectively, employs three principal elements: time, education, and continuous follow-up.

We recognize that several years may be required before the process is fully understood, accepted, and implemented. During this period, managers and supervisors will be trained in both theory and practical application. Results of their efforts will be regularly reviewed and, as appropriate, correction, guidance, and commendation will be used to reinforce the results desired. All managers will be encouraged to share their successful application of ideas and programs with their counterparts. In this manner, we will continually develop the capacity to prevent or anticipate problems before they arise.

Properly applied, participative management can reduce the tedium of routine jobs, make them more demanding, and, as a result, more interesting and satisfying to employees at all levels. Participative management provides each person with an opportunity to develop his abilities, to increase his personal contribution to the overall goal, and to achieve a greater degree of job satisfaction.

Based upon our experience to date, we believe that responsibility, achievement, recognition, and growth opportunities are factors which motivate people to better performance. Improved performance by the individual ultimately results in the improved effectiveness of the organization. For this reason, we believe participative management holds real promise for the future of the California Highway Patrol and, in turn, for the people we serve.

HUMANISM IN COMMAND*

The word *humanism* is not in very good odor nowadays because it has become attached to the idea of a secular system of ethics as opposed to one founded on religion. I do not use it in that sense, but in its older and more rational meaning, which has been best expressed by the Victorian writer Walter Pater in his essay on one of the great Italian scholars of the 15th century, Pico della Mirandola:

"For the essence of humanism is that belief of which he seems never to have doubted, that nothing which has ever interested living men and women can wholly lose its vitality—no language they have spoken, nor oracle beside which they have hushed their voices, no dream which has once been entertained by actual human minds, nothing about which they have ever been passionate, or expended time and zeal."

So humanism is the study of mankind in the grand perspective, which is the long history of literature and art, the perspective which enables us to relate ourself to the living past. It may be asked what this has to do with command.

In our increasingly mechanical world, with its obsession with science and technology, with its fallacious belief that everything can be weighed, measured, and reduced to formulae, with its pathetic delusion that human individuality can be authoritatively and finally reduced to type and predictability, one might think that humanism had little place. But it is precisely *because* there is so much mechanism in life today that humanism is needed. It is needed most of all by those who have power over their fellowmen. They need it because it can give them vision, insight, judgment, and intellectual strength, because it can stimulate imagination and creativity.

General Culture

It is only too easy nowadays to become a prisoner of one's day-to-day professional work. It is hard not to do so in professions like the police, where there is always too much business. But if we succumb to the pressure of the here-and-now, we are cutting ourselves off from the larger realities, from the expanse of the ocean over which our own narrow course must lie. Every generation has to chart for itself its

---

*SOURCE: John Phillip Stead, "The Humanism Of Command," reprinted by special permission of the *Police Chief*, copyright © 1974, by International Association Of Chiefs Of Police, Vol. 41, No. 1, pp. 26-28.

course across the great sea of human activity but this it can only do with proper realism if the nature of that heaving and extensive mass is duly appreciated. To know only present and immediate things is to be under their spell and in their power. We need to know more than our own small environment if we are to judge the world wisely.

General de Gaulle had this modern predicament very much in mind when he said: "The real school of command is general culture. . . . There has never been a famous captain who has not had a taste and feeling for the heritage of the human spirit. Behind Alexander's victories one always finds Aristotle."

Aspects Of Command

Charles de Gaulle joins hands in this sentiment with Francis Bacon, who remarked that the best counsellors are the dead. We are foolish indeed if we choose to ignore the fact that in every age men have been confronted by the same great problems of survival and of social order, the same difficulties in arriving at a just and happy life. Francis Bacon attained high office, and gave much thought to the situation of those who seek command. Somewhat ruefully, perhaps, he writes: "It is a strange desire to seek power and to lose liberty, or to seek power over others, and to lose power over a man's self." I hope this will not discourage you: it did not discourage Bacon. But what he is saying is something police officers have always known: that having power over others sets a man apart, imposes limitations on his whole manner of being that are imposed on few other men. And as you rise to the highest posts in the service, this apartness and limitation become more pronounced. This at least is common in most walks of life: the higher you get, the lonelier you become, and a command position cuts one off from many of the contacts that less responsible people can freely enjoy.

I venture to suggest that this isolation can in some measure be relieved by the fellowship which books can offer when men can not. Those of you who know my teaching will not for one moment think that I am saying that books can take the place of actual experience. Nothing can do that. But books can make that personal knowledge, gained amid the practicalities of life, take on new meaning and new relationships as we connect our own small scheme of things with the great world's scheme.

The Commander's Knowledge

There is so much that a chief officer of police needs to know, apart from the technical side of his work. He needs to know the principles as well as the structure and operation of government; he needs to know, as it were, "the state of the nation" in its political, economic, and sociological aspects. He needs a keen insight into his own police area, with its special history and characteristics. These are not matters he can just be "briefed" on—they need study and reflection. It may well be that as men approach the higher levels of their profession, rising from the craft ranks to the direction of the organization, they need to appoint a kind of vigil for themselves, to make, as it were, a rededication of their lives in the light of what lies before them.

In that vigil one thing above all, perhaps, they should seek. That thing is self-knowledge. "Know thyself" is among the most ancient of Greek precepts. It may be salutary for us all at a critical period of our lives to read the *Maxims* of the Duc de la Rochefoucauld. I find a perpetual source of self-reproach in one of the maxims: "It is the habit of mediocre minds to condemn all that is beyond their grasp." La Rochefoucauld was a highly civilized but remorseless realist: "We always discover, in the misfortunes of our dearest friends, something not altogether displeasing." This French nobleman of the 17th century, who had been a soldier and courtier in war and peace, was a great expert on man's capacity for deluding himself. Men in command cannot afford the blindness which vanity and the other passions so often induce. It is a great thing to be aware of one's faults and to see through the rationalizations which we are always unconsciously making in order to justify them. "Self-love"—and what man except a saint does not love himself?—says La Rochefoucauld, "is the greatest flatterer of all," and it can "outwit the shrewdest of men."

I believe that literature helps us enormously in our quest for self-knowledge. As we read biographies and memoirs, novels and stories, books about character and achievement, we quite naturally measure our own doings and our sense of our own potential against the subject of the writing. Every man is a king in his own heart and it is good for him to match his attributes and aims against the salient personages he encounters in his secret and personal relationship with the great ones of literature and history.

Character

Alongside this self-knowledge, literature also imparts knowledge of other people. One of the greatest themes of art is character. Even a superficial reading of the Western masters, that is, the great authors of Europe, the United States, and this country, indicates their preoccupation with the mysteries of human individuality. The lesson is of capital significance to the commander, for it behooves him to learn that human beings are infinitely complex and unique creatures, that within the broad typing of men and women there is an infinitude of personality. It is important to learn to distrust the stereotypes and generalizations to which every generation is prone.

"The proper study of mankind" should teach us to resist the charlatans who come with their seductive simplifications to tell us how we can "reform" our fellowmen, as if individuality were a disease and they alone had the secret of curing it. Respect for personality is a precious gift for the commander. He who respects it in others is likeliest to be respected himself.

It is heartening to recognize that of all the world's writings those of the West are richest in character studies and that none is as much so as Anglo-American literature.

Society

It is rich also in studies of what may be called manners, by which I mean simply its pictures of social behavior, of the ways in which different classes of society live. This is another field in which none of us can ever be completely experienced. Our acquaintance, however socially enterprising we may be, is inevitably limited. But again, wise reading will help us to extend it and thereby to gain sympathies and insights from which we should otherwise be barred and exiled. There is no need to restrict oneself to contemporary authors, valuable as these are—C. P. Snow's *Strangers and Brothers* series being a good example. I have found more insight into French society today in Balzac and Molière than in any living writer and it may well be that Gogol and Dostoevsky have more to teach us about Russia than Pasternak and Solzhenitsyn.

This business of manners leads on to another concept which literature helps us to form—the concept of the traditional way of life of a community, be it local or national, a county or a city or a state. Those whose work it is to guard the community should understand its deeper nature, that general character which is rooted in its history and reflected in its arts. Literature has a great deal to offer in this respect to those who may be called to the aid of a community in moments of crisis and doubt; this we have seen in de Gaulle and Churchill in our own lifetime. It was their sure vision of the spirit of their peoples which made it possible for them to appeal as they did and to work their miracles. That vision had been nourished in each case by the general culture to which de Gaulle referred. It gave them their firm grasp of what was noblest in the tradition of two great nations.

Literature Of Command

I need hardly mention the literature which exists on the subject of command. There is a great deal of it. There are books explicitly about it, such as *The Prince* of Machiavelli, or Lord Wavell's *Soldiers and Soldiering*. There are biographies of the commanders, such as Churchill's *Marlborough* or Liddell-Hart's *Foch*. There are the memoirs of commanders, such as Caesar's *Gallic War* and Lawrence's *Seven Pillars of Wisdom*.

And one should not neglect the novelists. Many young man's notions of command have been quickened by reading C. S. Forester or Rafael Sabatini; and I would not like to omit a reference to a novel about the soldier whom Lord Wavell considered to be the greatest captain of all time, the selfless and supremely able general who served the ungrateful Justinian, *Count Belisarius* by Robert Graves. There is also, of course, an inexhaustible field of reference in the history books.

The poets, too, have their contribution to make, of which I will permit myself a single favorite quotation. Among the earlier poems of Ezra Pound there is one about sword-fighting, and the poet reads off for us the inscription on the blade of one of the swords. It was in Provençal, but he translates it. The sword says to him who wields it: "If thy heart fail thee, trust not in me." The moral is superbly exacting. Perhaps we can paraphrase it: "It does not matter how perfect the organization is, if the man at the top is not of the right quality." It is a message we can pause to ponder in the light of our own experience. If the commander is weak or hidebound or slipshod or self-indulgent or smallminded, the whole concern is spoiled and discouraged. I do not know any line in the whole literature of command that is more pregnant with significance for the commander. Machiavelli had some such idea when he expressed his scorn of those who blame bad luck instead of their own shortcomings.

Communication

All courses at the Police College stress the importance of good communication. They could hardly stress this too much. The world is bedevilled by its Tower of Babel situation in which people shout at but do not understand one another. The commander cannot afford to be misunderstood. To no man is the art of unambiguous and accurate expression more important. But that art of putting over clearly and exactly what is in one's mind is not an easy one. It needs vocabulary. It needs style.

These things do not come by nature; they have to be acquired. We are more likely to acquire them if we have a genuine familiarity with a fair amount of first-class writing, when we have seen and relished the way the masters use words. And we are more likely to acquire something else, too, which is also of capital value—the art of being *interesting*. Good writing and good speaking are never dull. The commander should never be dull, either. He is the last man in the world who should lay himself open to the ridicule of his subordinates and the public by verbal solecisms and lapses in English usage.

Normality

Wide reading has many benefits. It is particularly valuable to those whose daily work is of a specialist kind and to those whose professions are close-knit and close-ranked against the lay world. All professionals tend to take the professional view. The soldier gazes at the valley and the mountains and mentally places batteries and positions troops. The doctor stares at the Venus de Milo and speculates on what disease caused her to lose her arms. The police officer looks resignedly at John Citizen and wonders what offenses he has committed or what help he is seeking.

Wide reading helps to correct this inevitable astigmatism and brings back the sense of proportion as we contemplate the profuse, the infinite variety of life and its fundamental normality. After a walk round Soho, one really ought to read the *Gargantua and Pantagruel* of Rabelais to get the little squallors and minor filthinesses into due proportion.

Imagination

Among the qualities I would hope to find in the potential high commander is imagination. Joseph Conrad said that Imagination, not Invention, is the Master of Life, as it is the Master of Art.

Persons of limited intelligence often dismiss or discount imagination, writing it off as an idle and errant operation of the mind. So it may be, but it is also the driving force of the mind's higher conceptual and creative power.

Imagination drew Columbus across the Atlantic, conceived the Parthenon and from crude bits and masses brought forth the wheel and the arch. Imaginative power is quickened and vitalized by knowing the great imaginative masterpieces of Greek tragedy or Shakespearean drama, the Homeric or Miltonic epic, the novels of Dickens and Tolstoy. Whatever increases the sum of creativity in the world is to be prized. Certainly the commander must be able to use imagination in ordering his organization and defining its aims and courses. It is not enough to refer to the files.

New Departures

I think it probable that we are entering a new age of policing. The police service in this country has built in the past century and a half a powerful social agency, originally moving on interior lines to prevent and detect crime. Its evolution has gone beyond the old perimeter and the police officer has come long since to be regarded as a helper as well as a guardian of law and order.

The cumulative influence of 100,000 men of good will in a society which has some pretty odd values will, I believe, make the people and the state turn more and more to the police for social action—action of a preventive and at the same time adventurous, enterprising, creative kind.

In this new age our professional police officer will need a wide general culture. His commanders above all will need it. And I do not think I need excuse my title any more, for no one knows better than the police officer that the task is essentially a human task. Let me end with a few words from Bernard Shaw's *Major Barbara:*

"Let God's work be done for its own sake: the work He had to create us to do because it cannot be done except by living men and women."

THE SUPERVISOR'S ROLE IN DEVELOPING THE PERSON

The supervisor must have an active role in developing personnel in his unit. However, in reality what is needed for the positive development of the supervisor is not always what actually takes place. The supervisor needs practice in determining training needs. He needs to be skilled in helping his subordinates to the fullest. In carrying out this responsibility, the supervisor needs to be evaluated and rewarded for the job he does.

In developing personnel under his supervision, the supervisor is in constant face-to-face contact. When he counsels, he is training; when he gives orders, it is a form of training; when he discusses performance, he is training; and when he corrects or rewards behavior, he is training. In almost everything he does when in contact with his subordinates, the supervisor is a teacher. These make up his informal supervisory responsibilities in developing the individual.

The supervisor also has formal responsibilities which contribute to the personal development of his subordinates. He is expected to conduct formal roll-call training. Frequently he is given the job of conducting in-service training courses for his personnel. The supervisor who is provided with a lesson plan and necessary training aids is indeed fortunate. Most often he must prepare the training materials himself.

For the supervisor to truly aid in developing his subordinates, he must take time and effort to ascertain what the individual training needs are. In some of the more professional police departments, he is frequently detailed to present a class on a topic within his area of expertise. No matter what task he is given, the role of the supervisor in personnel development is significant.

Most police experts believe that training is one of the most, if not *the* most, important function of the supervisor. And most will agree that there is a direct relationship between the efficiency and effectiveness of his personnel and his own effectiveness as a teacher. It must also be pointed out that the supervisor who is an expert trainer will have fewer supervisory problems.

The supervisor is in a unique position. He stands between those who are charged with policy formulation in the organization and those who must carry it out. To both he has direct responsibilities. To the planner-managers, he must constantly be alert to weaknesses in plans as well as their successful aspects and report these to the appropriate individuals, with any recommendations he may have. His responsibility to his subordinates includes interpreting the plans, explaining their purposes, and training people to carry them out. In fact, the principal supervisory task of the police supervisor is insuring that his subordinates carry out the mission of the organization. He materially assists in this by advising subordinates of ways in which their performance can be improved. He does this by being a teacher.

The training responsibilities of the supervisor are becoming more complex daily. No longer does he merely transmit information to a subordinate and expect a job to be done. He now understands that motivation must be joined with skills to achieve a goal most effectively. The supervisor needs to understand that learning is not just data transfer but is a complex function of individual capacity, motivation, names of the training group, training methods, behavior of the trainer, and the general acceptability of training in the police organization. In today's complex police agency with its more intelligent and better educated officers, the supervisor must understand that job improvement does not automatically follow special training. Improvement is a complex process which depends on such behavioral subjects as the attitude of the trainer, the group, and the total organization. He must realize that if he has highly trained and skilled personnel, they will become frustrated if not utilized properly.

In carrying out his training responsibilities, the supervisor needs to bear in mind training is a continuous process by which his personnel are updated. In other words, training is not a one-time shot.

The articles in this section discuss some of the training complexities in a police organization. Supervisors are responsible for training their personnel and in professional police organizations, are rated on their performance in this subject. Two of the following articles give an insight into the problems involved in performance appraisal and supervisory rating. Translating these into the training evaluation of the supervisor is still more difficult.

SUPERVISOR'S VIEW OF EDUCATION*

Human relations training has been slow in reaching police departments. When it has occurred, this kind of training has tended to be of the "sound and fury" variety—for instance, interchange role plays with ghetto youths, or formless and vague "community dialogue" sessions. Human relations training of this type, though it may have some short-term effect in that it tends to boil long submerged emotions to the surface, generates a lot more heat than light. Emotions are raised, but there is rarely an inkling about what to do with them. In many cases this kind of training raises anxieties to such a level that not only is there a tremendous fall-off effect because it is hard to sustain unfocused emotion, but there is also a "walking on eggs" effect created in the participant who must now go back to the street "sensitized" but with nothing in which to wrap his new sensitivity—no techniques, no plan. The discomfort is often articulated as "okay, now you ought to go out there and train all those people," or in some cases, "okay, now you ought to train all the bosses on this job."

Statements such as these are indicative of the difficulty that human relations laboratory training has had in translating itself into on-the-job policing. There are no easy answers to this problem. At least part of the problem lies in the fact that rarely in these "sound and fury" sessions is there anything to translate. They tend to be "pseudo-labs" in which the chrome of, for instance, psychodrama obscures the pointlessness that it encloses. If the only point of these laboratory experiences is for the police officers to have an "intensive experience," then they seem to be not only unworthy of the effort but also positively detrimental.

A real training laboratory—one with a clear direction and behaviorally stated goals—is not so sorely afflicted with the translation problem. Real laboratories do not simply raise emotions and leave them dangling; they attempt to relate them to behavioral changes on the job.

One of the handiest ways of conceiving an effective, efficient laboratory is to think of it as laboratory training in which one creates situations similar to or analogous to real life situations. These situa-

---

*SOURCE: Byron L. Boer and Bruce C. McIver, "Human Relations Training: Laboratories and Team Policing," *Journal of Police Science and Administration*, Vol. 1, No. 2, June 1973, pp. 162–167. Reprinted with permission of the publisher.

tions are slowed down in the laboratory so that the dynamics and details can be examined rigorously and analytically, and all the irrelevant variables separated so as not to cloud the base dynamic of the situation; in other words, the experience is reduced to its essentials and examined in its purest attainable form.

As a rule of thumb against which to check laboratory training, one could well ask:

- Is this experience analogous to real life?
- Is it slowed down so that the pertinent dynamics are apparent?
- Are the nonessential variables separated?

If the answer to any of these questions is "no," then chances are the laboratory training will not be useful.

There is no guarantee that even viable human relations laboratories actually are job related or translatable into on-the-job policing. Unfortunately, a lot more is known about what does not work than what does. Two points, however, are beginning to emerge from the obscurity surrounding this problem, which can be stated as principles of human relations laboratories: 1) there are great benefits for policing to be derived from the human relations laboratories and 2) those benefits can become available to the policing effort *if the translation of those benefits into policing is imbedded into the training design.* The problem of translation is brought up in a laboratory context, subjected to a rigorous problem-solving format, and treated as a human relations problem. In other words, an integral component of any human relations training design must be a problem solving effort in which *the participants* themselves, not the trainers, translate the training into on-the-job effects. Simply saying, "one must be more sensitive to interaction with people, both civilian and bosses" does not work. Asking "how this laboratory training can be applied to problems on the job" can and will work, if the question is asked right, and a sequence of suggested steps is used in answering the questions presented.

Laboratory training in policing is still in its infancy, but some idea of how men are using that experience on the job is beginning to emerge. Laboratory training seems to get translated into work situations in two basic ways, and it may be helpful to think of these as "levels." Level one is the hard edged use of techniques, which means the direct translation of a technique displayed in the laboratory to some aspect of the work environment. Level two is the meta-learning or functional awareness level where values that are focused on and reinforced in the laboratory become part of the participant's work ethic.

Level One: Hard-edge Use of Techniques. In a number of laboratory training intensives conducted in New York City, particular attention was given to consensus decision making, the dynamics of group decisions, the efficacy of group decisions, how resources are used for making decisions under uncertain conditions, and so on. The specific activities used were of the kind that could be scored on effectiveness. An attempt was made to generate in the laboratory a style of decision making appropriate to the people who would be making similar decisions in the field. For instance, the "NASA Experiment," "Energy International" and "Twelve Angry Men" approaches were used. These approaches are exercises done in small groups with set data and set situations that examine the process of collaborative or consensus decision making.

Toward the end of the laboratory training, the question of how to apply the laboratory training to the job situation was asked. The answer, somewhat surprising to the trainers, was a quite literal translation of the techniques of consensus decision making into a police context. If one wants to generate a description of a perpetrator, then, by laboratory experience, it is necessary to bring the witnesses together in a consensus making group rather than to separate them.

The participants designed an experiment by which the laboratory group could try out its new hypothesis. Early returns suggest that most of the time the group's description is, by score, half again as adequate as any single description and nearly twice as good as the average description. Although there are rules and procedures, as well as legal questions that must be considered in the actual application of the training in the field, in the laboratory an old sacred cow ("always separate your witnesses") was slaughtered *by the participants*.

This is a rather startling example of the hard-edge use of techniques. At this point, however, it should be emphasized that, as persuasive as this demonstration is, and no matter how much "chrome" is used, it is by far the least important of the two levels. It is rare that laboratory training can be translated directly into action. Because the other level, the meta-learning, is more difficult to perceive and talk about, the trainee tends to use the "chrome" and the hard-edge of level one. When the hard edges are not there, the evaluator (usually not a participant) tends to assume that the laboratory had no effect. This is an accusation that laboratory trainers have had to defend since the inception of laboratory training.

Level Two: The Meta-learning, or Functional Awareness. The translation of this kind of learning into the job context is, obviously, much more difficult to assess. However, some examples can illustrate how it works. An investigating officer decides, during the course of his investigation of an armed robbery, to bring the witnesses together in order to arrive at a consensus description of the perpetrator. (Ignore, for a moment, the legal problems of this procedure.) Here the investigating officer has not only made use of a concrete laboratory technique, but has also *recognized his choices* in the situation at hand. Recognition of choices is one of the most important distinctions between the military and professional models of behavior. The recognition that he has choices, that options of behavior are open to him, and that he is obligated not only to take those options seriously, but analytically as well, is called meta-learning, or, if you like, functional awareness. The investigator has the option of choosing the standard operating procedure of separating the witnesses, the new consensus technique learned in the laboratory, or any other mode of behavior that seems appropriate. The important thing is that he thinks analytically about his options. One understands, of course, that policing has always presented the officer with choices, that choosing among options is in the very nature of the incredibly complex job. But policing rules and procedures have steadfastly denied this fact—just by being rules and procedures. Consequently, police officers are not trained to make choices in any systematic, analytical way. Rather, they are trained to pretend choices *do not even exist!* When a police officer recognizes his options and recognizes that he must take his selection seriously, then, in some quasi-conscious way, he has made a role choice as well. Without quite verbalizing it he has elected to define himself in the professional role rather than the military role. In so doing, he has taken on a role very similar to the professional role of group leader. He has, in other words, approached the situation as if it were a laboratory situation.

But meta-learnings are not always so easy to analyze as this hypothetical case. These kinds of learning work themselves out situationally on the job in nuances too delicate to pin down or in development patterns that are too difficult to see at a glance. The professional model is "in the air" in the laboratory; it is part of the ethos, the milieu that a laboratory attempts to generate, and the idea is to keep it "in the air" when on the job.

This kind of learning cannot be planned. Laboratories are set up on the assumption that men *are* professional officers rather than military drones, and a professional model is the presupposition from which all movement in the laboratory begins. On the job, this meta-learning or professional model may work itself out as a dynamic by the recognition of choices and allows for the possibility (not the certainty) of more adequate decisions. It may work itself out as an unfreezing of role expectations or as an acceptance of an analytical cast that allows an attempt to slow down the action of, for example, a family dispute, thus separating the independent variables in order to look at the generalizable dynamics. In New York, the Family Crisis Unit, operating under an analytical laboratory assumption concerning family crisis, developed a very concrete set of action steps to use in a dispute. The result was a drastic reduction of the frequency of injuries to police officers investigating family disputes. Here is a case in which the meta-learning generated hard-edged techniques.

Warren Bennis of the National Training Labs has worked out four "metagoals" or meta-learnings of laboratory training.[1]

- Expanded consciousness and recognition of choices
- A "spirit of inquiry"
- Authenticity in interpersonal relations
- A collaborative conception of the authority relationship

The latter goal, the "collaborative conception of authority" deserves to be further explained. Bennis states:[2]

> . . . most important is the realization that the teaching-learning process of laboratory training is a prototype of the collaborative conception of authority. Putting it differently, we can say that learning is accomplished through the requirements of the situation and a joint collaborative venture between the trainer and the participants.

Translating Bennis' formulation directly into the policing context, one could say " . . . work is accomplished through the requirements of the situation and a joint collaborative venture between the 'boss' and the police officer (or the lieutenant and sergeant and so on through the chain of command)."

When one starts talking about "joint collaborative ventures" and collaborative authority to police officers, they tend to become uneasy. The military model has been *the* model of authority in policing for so long that any suggestion that it may not always be appropriate is met with suspicion. Lately there has been a lot of fresh thinking on the matter in such progressive departments as New York; Cincinnati; Holyoke, Massachusetts; and Syracuse; and language like "team policing," "beat command," and the like have been used. One thing that all of these programs have in common is that they adhere—implicitly or explicitly to a collaborative conception of authority. The training laboratory is the prototype of the collaborative conception of authority, and the coming together of team policing and the training laboratory under the umbrella of collaborative authority has tremendous implications for the future of both team policing *and* training laboratories. The two are too congenial not to operate side by side. Some of the parallels are:

• Both coalesce around goals (the requirements of the situation for the police team, the requirements of behavioral objectives for the laboratory).
• Both use "collaboration" as a model.
• Both deny the paramilitary model of command as the most efficient.
• Both deny unilateral decision making as the most efficient.
• Both affirm consensus as the most efficacious model of decision making.
• Both espouse some sort of concept of "openness" and honesty as a component of desirable group or team behavior.
• The team policing concept stresses the importance of seeing the team leader as trainer, while the training group sees the trainer as leader. Leader and trainer are virtually indistinguishable roles in both the training group and the police team.

The point is that it is becoming more and more apparent that the best way to train effective police teams and effective team leaders is to get them first into a training laboratory, and then get them to plan the construction of their teams—collaboratively.

Police departments tend to be large, complex organizations, especially in the cities, and the collaborative model of authority pioneered by police teams and laboratory methods has a whole spectrum of other applications. So versatile is this model that it finds ready application in such diverse branches of policing as anti-crime units, investigation teams, and emergency service squads. The model seems particularly useful to police academy training staffs. In short, collaborative authority would seem appropriate anywhere within the aegis of the policing function where the task at hand, the requirements of the situation, are complex and not susceptible to programmed action and role learning, and where the number of men involved in that situation is limited to a workable group size.

The transition from the old authoritarian model of authority toward a collaborative model tends to be long, painful, and subject to awkwardness and recidivism. Because of the similarities and because of the quick, intense learning afforded in laboratories, a laboratory experience can speed the process of transition and relieve some of the growing pains. Further, the laboratory can be the scene where a team works out the kind of decision-making model appropriate to its function, and the laboratory can ease the opening of the communications systems necessary to provide the lateral and vertical feedback within the team.

Also from the New York experience, a two-fold expectation from these teams was deduced: one, with a stable geographical assignment, the men in these teams are expected to move toward a better working relationship with the members of the community in those team areas; and two, with an organization stabilized around a single sergeant and a regular group of peers, the team is expected to generate a more efficient working ethos. Whether these expectations will be met remains to be seen, and it is becoming apparent that the question hinges on how well the teams put laboratory training to work to meet these expectations.

At any rate, there is a tendency toward a greater degree of intimacy between the police officer and the community and between the police officer and the supervisor. This greater degree of intimacy brings problems as well as benefits to the men involved, who are, generally speaking, unskilled in the behaviors appropriate to the situation. Inappropriate behaviors are often simply a function of misunderstood motives or an unclear perception of the dynamics involved in a social transaction. In team policing, these transactions run the gamut from family dispute investigations, through riot situations; and these transactions fruitfully can be explored in the human relations laboratory.

If it is true that neighborhood police teams bring a more collaborative law enforcement effort between the community and the police officer, then it would seem that the police officer's relationship with the community would be analogous to his sergeant's relationship with him. And the sergeant's relationship with the police officer is analogous to the trainer's relationship with the training group. It would not be stretching the point, it is believed, to conceive that one of the goals of laboratory training is to make a team police officer capable of a modicum of behavior appropriate to the trainer's professional behavior.

Therefore, although a very strong case can be made for laboratory training—particularly for team policing—there remains much apprehension about it at all ranks. The easiest of these objections to deal with are the purely pragmatic considerations. Early experience in the New York City project indicates the difficulty of integrating laboratory training into the on-going police team operations. Work charts and scheduling problems are the largest hindering factors, along with the chronic manpower shortage. This means that training must be telescoped so that training and normal coverage occur concurrently. One way to accomplish this telescoping is to make arrangements so that the data used in the laboratory is generated in the field. The greatest asset here is a sympathetic planning officer who can be responsible for rotating men on a consistent basis and at the same time deploy his remaining men so that coverage is adequate. Though scheduling and shortage problems can be met with a modicum of success, there remains a great need for the development of a methodology by which the laboratory can telescope even more into its allotted time. One wants the laboratory to do as many things as possible (without overloading the circuits) and simultaneously relate the laboratory training to field operations as closely as possible. The surface has only been scratched here.

A more basic objection that was feared in the early attempt to set up laboratory training was the notion that a police officer, as a personality type, would be resistant to this kind of "groupy" training, seeing it as "instant sociology," "a setup to make him look foolish," "too much like social work, and not job related," and a luxury "police cannot afford" in these days of spiraling crime rates. This notion, it now appears, has no substance. After doing a number of laboratory intensives, it became clear that officers will indeed not only accept, but welcome laboratory training. The evaluations of the program given at the end of each week-long session indicate enthusiastic response to both content and presentation of the laboratories. Further, the evaluations, in almost all cases, state a commitment to "transfer" the learning from the laboratory into the field situation, and a concomitant commitment to promote collaborative models wherever appropriate.

This suggests that there are two variables that tend to produce such a heartening response: one, that laboratory training is such a distinct departure from routine police training that the novelty and excitement of being part of something new had an effect on the evaluations; or two, that men see the applicability of laboratory training and the collaborative model in their own operations and that applicability is its own reward. If the latter is true, then laboratory training can be a successful program. Probably the truth lies somewhere in-between. The point, however, is that acceptance of laboratory training did not become as large a problem as was predicted.

In New York, at least, the door is beginning to open. It would be presumptuous to predict the long-range effect and the future of this kind of training. It is suspected that there will be more laboratory training time allotted all over the country, especially as the techniques and methodologies begin to build toward their potential and a momentum is generated. It seems apparent that the challenge that faces team policing and laboratory training in the near future is to pool the techniques and resources in all of the related training programs, and forge from the collective experience a viable methodology to confront the requirements of laboratory training and the collaborative style of policing and authority that is beginning to emerge in the United States.

DISCIPLINE AND PERFORMANCE APPRAISAL*

The purpose of this paper is to indicate how healthy discipline is created and maintained in a police department, the necessity of its continuance for successful administration, and the influence of adequate periodic performance appraisals on its continuance.

Webster defines discipline as having the following meanings: "Training which corrects, molds, strengthens or perfects. Punishment, chastisement. Control gained by enforcing obedience or order as in a school or army; hence orderly conduct. To develop by instruction and exercise; to train in self-control or obedience to given standards. To chasten or punish."

A well-disciplined police organization is characterized by the ready and willing compliance of its members, individually and collectively, to orders and directives. The full definition implies that there are two methods of winning compliance. One obtains obedience or compliance through threat or application of punishment. It is supported by the assumption that those issuing orders are infallible and the recipient has no right to question them. In most times, places and organizations, this approach was more prominent than the other. It has found application in the home military organizations, labor unions, corporations, and police departments.

Now such a concept is giving way to the training approach. The presence of police training schools of various descriptions, for example, seeks to instill a "discipline" in their students. The correct way of performing a police activity, ethical conduct, integrity—are all examples of discipline. In the case of rules or regulations, agreement with them, although desirable, is not always possible. Therefore, the rules must be made reasonable and equitable, uniformly enforced and the

*SOURCE: Quinn Tamm, "Discipline And Performance Appraisal," reprinted by special permission of the *Police Chief,* copyright © 1962, by International Association Of Chief Of Police, Vol. 29, No. 9. pp. 6–7, 28–29.

need for them must be explained so that even those who fail to agree with them at least understand them and the need for their existence.

Discipline cannot be stifling. One of the most troublesome problems in achieving proper discipline in a police force is striking the proper balance between rapid and willing compliance with orders and directives, while still preserving and encouraging the independent thought and individual initiative so essential to successful police work. The most perfect disciplinary system would assure the individual officer the greatest freedom of thought and action while at all times promoting his feeling of responsibility to the group. If experimentation in search of improved methods is not permitted, then we will not progress. But such experimentation must be within the bounds of ethical conduct and not at the expense of the total group.

Objectives Of Discipline

The overriding objective of effective discipline in a police operation is to promote efficient and satisfactory achievement of police objectives. Training is intended to develop capacity to perform a task. It must also seek to develop an attitude on the part of the worker to perform as close to his capacity as possible.

More immediate objectives of the disciplinary process are as follows:

1. Produce a change in thinking and actions on the part of the individual to bring his efforts into line with departmental standards.
2. Improve the performance of the group as a whole by deterring its members from engaging in derelictions or disapproved practices.
3. Raise and maintain the prestige of the department by going on public notice that compliance is uniformly insisted upon from all members of the force.

Probably the most frequent reason for municipal police agencies failing to achieve the proper degree of subordination is the failure of superior officers to demand it. This usually results from a failure of supervisors and commanders to understand their responsibility for maintaining effective discipline or their unwillingness to assume the responsibility and discharge the concurrent authority. Such a situation points to deficient discipline among the supervisory and command groups.

It also is a practical result of inadequate training for these positions. Since one of the definitions of discipline is "training . . . which perfects," the obvious solution for an absence of discipline among the superior ranks is training. The transition from patrolman to sergeant has been commented upon many times, and because it does exist and because the two jobs are significantly different, it would seem only natural to teach the new sergeant how to do his job. Such training programs in American police forces, by and large, are most notable by their absence.

"The attainment of discipline" should be one of the most important elements of such a training program. Command personnel are also in need of such training. Regularly established in-service training programs for these levels will do much to achieve discipline in the supervisory and command ranks. Without discipline there, it will be absent throughout the organization.

The chief should demand immediate attention to the little problems. While an apparent increase in minor transgressions will arise, there will be a decided effect on the number of major derelictions. When authority winks at minor infractions, it will be challenged and the end result will be contamination of authority upward and downward. Immediate attention is also necessary to achieve the desired results of swift correction. Delays only tend to dilute the effect of corrective action and discipline suffers.

Periodic appraisals of subordinate's inventories also bring into quick focus the supervisor's responsibilities for the maintenance of discipline. Unless the supervisor is required to evaluate his resources—people—at regular intervals and in a systematic manner, he is likely to forget the factors that constitute successful job performance.

The positive approach, or training approach, to discipline will at times fail to achieve the desired results in certain individuals. Then negative force must be applied. Indeed, the chief's prestige and ability to continue a high level of discipline may depend on his success at applying punishment or censure. A major impediment to successful application of this form of discipline exists in the presence of other authorities which share the chief's disciplinary authority. They are usually appellate boards, but at times they have the power to intervene directly in the exercise of the chief's administrative controls. There is a tendency among such boards to confuse violations of employment regulations with violations of criminal law. Violation of the latter can lead to loss of life or liberty, and because of the very serious consequences require the allegation to be substantiated with proof beyond a reasonable doubt. Disciplinary actions contemplate, at the very most, dismissal of a person from a job, and more often considerably less. Neither his person or liberty are placed in jeopardy. Thus, disciplinary actions in employment situations should require only the test of "reasonable" proof, not proof beyond any reasonable doubt.

The chief cannot ignore his responsibility to provide the reasonable proof, however. Improper action must be followed by prompt application of negative or positive discipline as best fits the situation and the individual and the need must be well documented. The severity of the action taken is not as important as is the certainty that action will be forthcoming.

In addition to sufficient accounting of the immediate cause for censure, well conceived and properly executed performance appraisals can often support the action taken and, at the very least, can provide some guides for the appropriate action.

Complete fairness in administering discipline and adequate documentation of cases, plus education of a review board to the effect that nobody has a right to employment in the same sense that he has a right to liberty will go far toward producing an agreement with the board that will balance the public interest on the one hand, and the protection of the individual against arbitrary or capricious penalties on the other. The need for achieving such an agreement is compelling. No chief can long survive a series of disciplinary reversals.

Another major impediment to effective discipline, particularly among police officers, is the singular form of camaraderie and sense of personal loyalties that develop among them. This very commendable and often very vital trait can be destructive when the welfare of the organization becomes the subordinate criticism. Until police officers appreciate the very serious consequences of misdirected loyalty to them as individuals and to the police profession as an institution, overcoming the destructive characteristics of this comradeship will be a very difficult and time-consuming task. They should be compelled to report derelictions of fellow officers, especially those amounting to a violation of law and appropriate channels for submitting such reports should be established.

Performance Appraisals

A performance appraisal is a statement in writing which points out significant features of an employee's work; that which is satisfactory, the areas in need of improvement, and the manner in which improvement can be gained. Regular personnel ratings provide definite services to the supervisor, management, and the employee.

The supervisor is required to focus his attention, at least for a period of time, on his subordinates' activities, by evaluating their strengths and weaknesses. They pinpoint the needs of his men and provide incentive to improve performance. They offer a way by which potentialities of men can be judged and they assist the conscientious supervisor in appraising his techniques. Most importantly, however, they open the door for regular and periodic consultations between superior and subordinate regarding the latter's accomplishments or failures.

Management is aided by such a system in identifying training needs, as guides for assigning personnel, for evaluating the performance of supervisors, to aid in making layoffs or reductions in force, and as a check on the quality of selection methods. They also provide a means of documenting disciplinary actions.

Well conceived and administered rating systems also aid the employee. The values accruing to supervisors and management, intelligently applied, assist the competent employee in obtaining job satisfaction and indicate to the less competent employee ways in which he can improve his performance. Rating systems also let the employee know where he stands with his supervisor and management. The efficient employee gets recognition for his accomplishment and the review of ratings provides opportunity for discussion and counseling between the employee and his supervisor.

Types Of Performance Appraisal

There are a number of approaches to rating programs, each of which may have a place depending upon the ability of the raters, the objectives of the particular rating system, and the general level of competence of the agency's personnel. The names and descriptions of five general kinds of ratings systems are as follows:

1. *Rank Order.* All employees are considered in relation to each other, and each is listed in the order of his competence.

Useful when employees number about 20 or less.

Raters must make precise distinctions between all employees. Ratings are based on overall evaluations. Ratings do not indicate personal strengths or weaknesses.

2. *Forced Distribution.* All employees are considered in relation to each other and each is placed into one of usually three groups which represent levels of competence.

Useful for large employee groups. Raters do not make precise distinctions between all employees. Ratings are based on overall evaluations. Personal strengths and weaknesses are not indicated.

3. *Graphic (Specific Trait Rating).* Each employee is fitted into a level of gradation for each described trait.

Useful for groups of any size. Precise distinctions between employees on each trait are not necessary. Ratings based on individual traits. Ratings indicate strengths and weaknesses. Difficult to compare employee's overall value.

4. *Numerical, or Percentage.* Each employee is fitted into a particular numerical value for each trait.

Useful for groups of any size. Precise distinction between employees on each trait is not necessary. Ratings based on individual traits. Ratings indicate strength and weaknesses. Ratings yield a numerical score which permits comparison between employees. Differing standards of raters and non-uniform understanding of numerical value reduces validity of ratings.

5. *Factor–Point Scoring.* Each employee is rated according to well defined numerically-weighted degrees of traits. Job-related factors are defined. Degrees of factors are defined. Weights are assigned to each factor and degree. Minimum standards are established.

Useful for groups of any size. Ratings are based on individual traits. Ratings indicate strengths and weaknesses. Ratings yield a numerical score which permits comparison between employees. Defined traits and degrees permit a uniformity of understanding.

Elements Of An Effective Rating System

An adequate performance appraisal program must provide the following:

1. It will contemplate a careful analysis (on the part of the rating officer) of the employee's work.

2. It must be flexible because not all jobs can be rated on the basis of the same criteria.
3. The overall program must be constructed to minimize human errors which creep into individual ratings. These are illustrated, rating high on all traits because of one outstanding characteristic, varying standards among different raters, failure to discriminate between individuals being rated, an overly generous attitude on the part of raters and the tendency of raters to improve subsequent ratings because this is assumed to be a reflection of "leadership" abilities.

Such errors can be minimized by the type of rating instrument.

The Ohio State Highway Patrol, for example, has developed a "forced choice" rating system wherein the rater is supposed to choose among several alternatives, the one best describing the subject of his rating. All alternatives seem to be equally desirable or undesirable. The rater is theoretically unaware of the previously determined weights assigned to each of the possible responses. Therefore, he is unaware of how he rated his subordinate. The main objective of such a rating system is to eliminate the influence of any biases the rater may have. The system does have some shortcomings. First, since the rating officer does not know how he is rating an individual, he cannot discuss his evaluation with the ratee. Secondly, the technique requires the services of a professional psychologist.

Errors can also be minimized in the "subjective" rating systems by proper training of the raters.

One of the most important obstacles to overcome in developing a rating system having the desired characteristic of being capable of review with the employee is to recognize frankly that such ratings will be based on judgments of the rater, and hence will be subjective. Subjectivity in evaluating employees is often regarded as a bogeyman. The quality of the resulting judgment, in truth, depends on the ability of the rater to evaluate subordinates. Few will question that supervisors should possess this quality to a highly developed level, but rarely is it tested for in promotional examinations.

A subjective system should also require the following to minimize errors of judgment: (1) written justifications for each factor rating, no matter what the rating is; (2) a review of the rating with the ratee; (3) adequate review of all ratings by the rater's supervisors; (4) adequate performance rating of the rater, including his ability to rate as one of the factors; (5) establishment of appeal machinery so that an employee who feels that he has received an unfair rating can receive a hearing at a higher level.

Continuous Performance Appraisal

It should be noted that a supervisor's responsibility to evaluate the performance of his subordinates is not restricted to filling out a form. Rating is not a once or twice a year proposition. Supervisors consciously or unconsciously rate their subordinates continuously. The formal appraisal merely requires them to make this a conscious effort once or twice a year. But just as ratings provide one means of documenting disciplinary action, so should the rater keep adequate records continuously to refresh his memory when the time comes to fill out the form. He should consciously evaluate the performance of his subordinates at all times and record the observations. He should keep notes of each subordinate's performance as it is observed, particularly noting by time, date and location examples of particularly outstanding or deficient work. These notes should also reflect the employee's performance forms.

Results Of Adequate Discipline

Any enterprise that is difficult to join and easy to leave has a minimal number of personnel problems. This statement has particular application to a police department where integrity and public trust are critical commodities. Supervisors properly indoctrinated in the need for and ways of obtaining a proper level of discipline probably have a better overall concept of all their responsibilities than do those who are less knowledgeable about this important aspect of their jobs. The end result of laxity is a loss of respect on the part of subordinates rather than achievement of approval. The supervisor is different from his subordinates, status-wise, salary-wise, and in authority and responsibility. Therefore, he cannot be "one of the boys."

Returning to the originally stated objective of discipline, "to promote efficient and satisfactory achievement of objectives," we are also stating reasons for an organizational structure, reasons for directives and established procedure, reasons for administration, and reasons for control.

A well developed sense of individual and group discipline is the moving force which gives impetus to these artifacts of enterprise. With low morale, an enterprise will become sluggish, but can continue to exist and function. Without discipline, however, there can be only chaos. A police force will be merely an armed mob. Effective discipline develops morale, and together they provide the environment for successful administration.

RATING SUPERVISOR'S PERFORMANCE*

The measurement of employee performance is one of the most compelling and vexing problems of supervisors and management. The desirability of deploying methods of rating performance is matched only by its difficulty.

Performance appraisal is a systematic evaluation of personnel by their supervisors or others who are familiar with their work performance. As a tool to measure employee capability, it gives management an inventory of each employee's abilities.

It is impossible for a supervisor not to make judgments constantly concerning the effectiveness of any subordinate's performance. Such judgments are ratings, whether formal or informal written or unwritten. So the question becomes simply one of whether the department wants a formal, written system under an established procedure.

There are good arguments against a rating system, mostly pragmatic: raters frequently are biased; some raters are harder to satisfy than others; employee morale can be adversely affected by a poor rating; ratings are not scientific; and raters are unwilling to tell the truth if the truth hurts. On the other hand, every employee wants to know where he stands with his supervisor. Most employees are satisfactory, but they are seldom told so by the supervisor.

Rating systems are inherently subjective since they involve a personal audit by one person of another's conduct or performance. In addition, many of the personal traits supervisors are called upon to evaluate cannot be measured by precise tests.

Objectives Of Rating Performance

There are numerous objectives of rating individual performance, but promotion is probably the most important administrative use of this process. Such rating should differentiate between the performance of the individual on his present job and potentiality for performance on a higher level job. Although outstanding performance in an employee's current position is not conclusive evidence that the employee will do equally outstanding work in a more responsible posi-

---

*SOURCE: Jude T. Walsh, "Performance Ratings For Police Supervisors," reprinted by special permission of the Police Chief, copyright © 1974, by International Association Of Chiefs Of Police, Vol. 41. No. 4. pp. 51–53.

tion, most supervisors would certainly hesitate to recommend for promotion an employee whose performance record is poor. Other objectives of rating performance are:

1. *To provide incentive and to recognize and reward good work.* An employee knows that he will be rated at least once a year and he looks forward to receiving this official recognition of his past performance. This incentive to make a good showing will induce the employee to perform more effectively and efficiently especially if the supervisor maintains a daily, weekly, and monthly performance record throughout the year and informs the employee of his status on a periodic basis, usually each month.

2. *To help supervisors recognize and remedy weaknesses in employee performance.* The daily, weekly, monthly, and yearly performance record maintained by the supervisor assists him in determining the strengths and weaknesses of his subordinates. The supervisor can take corrective measures to remedy these weakesses during the full rating period and not have to wait until the annual rating report to take corrective action.

3. *To provide employee guidance.* The supervisor should assist in counseling employees by keeping the employee informed of what is expected of him and how well he is performing. It should be the goal of every supervisor to use the performance ratings as a means of pointing out to every subordinate where he has succeeded and where he has failed, and then to proceed with suggestions for improving the employee's performance in the future.

4. *To identify employees who should be given specific types of training.* A well-devised and carefully administered rating plan can be a very useful device for those responsible for the direction of in-service and recruit training programs. Using the rating plan, supervisors often discover that the basis for poor performance is the lack of adequate training. After the supervisor has recorded the activities and other performance factors of the employees, he will be able to isolate weaknesses in certain employees that can be overcome by either formal or informal training. The ratings may show a need for training on a department-wide basis as determined by an examination of all rating reports. If the supervisor determines a need for formal training, he can then pass this information on to his superiors.

5. *To record information for management.* The performance ratings are valuable in connection with change in employee status, transfers, and other personnel actions. The higher levels of management can use these reports to determine exceptional subordinates and utilize their expertise. The management can also use the report to determine and check the reasonableness of established departmental standards of performance, and, if necessary, either adjust its goals of performance to an attainable level or raise the standards.
6. *To establish a basis for discharging or demoting incompetent employees.* If an employee is not performing up to the standards set forth by the department, and if counseling, training, and disciplinary action have not achieved the desired effect, the performance rating can be utilized as a basis for demotion or dismissal of the employee. The performance report can show a pattern, along with supporting reports, of an employee's inability to adjust to the desired standards of the department. The supervisor should then rate the employee, on the performance report, in an unacceptable overall rating. The employee will then be given a certain period of time to improve his rating; if at the end of this period he cannot meet the standards, he will be dismissed. This is an acceptable procedure under civil service systems.

Methods Of Rating Performance

There are many rating methods available, such as the rank-order system, paired comparison system, group rating, behavior checklist, etc. Police departments use a variation of the graphic trait scale system. This system calls for rating traits or personal characteristics by placing a check mark at the appropriate place on a line to indicate the various degrees of possession of or proficiency in the trait.

This system has a number of advantages. The form is relatively easy to construct and can be tailored to fit particular jobs. The rating process itself is simple and can be done rather quickly. The system leaves the rater free to have a definite gradation but at the same time he is given descriptive phrases which help him make his judgments concrete. Even unskilled raters quickly understand the system and give a good distribution of marks.

Evidence has found that the best supervisors are usually the best raters. They are more faithful to their rating responsibilities than are poorer supervisors and are less likely to commit the error of leniency by overrating poor performers. Lenient supervisors who rate all their subordinates alike are covertly disrespected. The outstanding employee is penalized while the marginal one is rewarded, simply because the rating officer does not have the personal interest or integrity to prepare a thorough, accurate service rating report, based on objective evidence which he has gathered.

Some of the more common methods utilized to give a valid rating are:

1. Distinguish facts from feelings or impressions.
2. Weigh the performance of the subordinate against a consistent standard.
3. Establish norms of conduct and performance.
4. Base rating on objective data; ignore individual likes and dislikes.
5. Avoid committing the error of rating on vague general impressions.
6. Rate on the basis of individual personal traits.
7. Be systematic and thorough in recording accurate data relating to observations of employees throughout the rating period.
8. Insure the report is valid, that it is an accurate measurement of the ability it purports to measure.
9. Insure the report is reliable, that it measures consistently and reasonably accurate each time it is used.

Perhaps one of the greatest uses, from a supervisory standpoint, to which a personnel evaluation can be put is for the rater to discuss it with the employee. Some supervisors believe that discussion of ratings with personnel accomplishes little and only leads to controversy; readily apparent and undoubtedly, the benefits outweigh the liabilities.

A counseling interview to improve employee performance must be based on factual information, but the success of the interview will depend on how facts are presented and discussed. The interview with the employee calls for tact and forthrightness if it is to have maximum effect. Rating officers invariably have little difficulty in interviewing the high producer. Difficulty is usually encountered in approaching the marginal or substandard employee. Often supervisors find this an unpleasant task, easier to avoid than face; but if the interview is approached objectively, they will be able to make it a constructive training device.

A. THE COUNSELING INTERVIEW

The supervisor should plan and prepare for the interview by taking these steps:

1. Review the employee's job and what it takes to do it, his record, experience, and training.
2. Review your evaluation of his performance and consider why you evaluated his work as you did.
3. Have available specific facts or illustrations from his job performance to substantiate your opinions.
4. Determine what you want to accomplish in the interview and plan your discussion accordingly.
5. Plan to meet in private, anticipate some curiosity, and be prepared to reduce it.

B. MANNER OF INTERVIEW

1. Create the impression that you have time for the interview and that you consider it highly important.
2. Place primary interest upon development and growth of the individual. Make the subordinate feel that the interview is constructive.
3. Be open minded to facts and opinions presented by the employee. Be willing to learn about him.
4. Don't dominate or cross-examine; avoid arguments.

C. THE INTERVIEW

1. Pick the right time, day, and place. Don't conduct the interview too soon after disciplinary action or an argument. Pick a time when you are in a good mood and when you have reason to believe the employee feels likewise.
2. Put the employee at ease and get him talking.
3. Explain the objectives of the interview.
4. Talk about good points first, then cover each point in detail from the rating report.
5. Don't dwell on failures—get the discussion into prevention of future failures or problems. Allow face-saving.
6. Guide the interview, not allowing it to get out of hand or turn into fruitless conversation.
7. Don't talk about him, instead talk about his work or his job.

D. CLOSE THE INTERVIEW

    1. Review the points made in the interview.
    2. Reassure the subordinate of your interest in his progress and indicate a willingness to discuss problems with him again at any time.

E. FOLLOW-UP

The supervisor should follow up the interview with personal observations which provide clues to the effectiveness of the interview.

Common Rating Errors

Invariably when ratings fail to accomplish their true purpose, the fault lies not in the form used, but in the rater. Either the rater has prepared the report merely to fulfill a policy or legal requirement, or because the activity adds just another burden to his already over-worked position, he becomes indifferent to or unconcerned with the probable results of carelessly prepared reports, and completes them in the easiest way possible. The quality of personnel evaluations, then, is largely a matter of attitude. The attitude of the rater. It is, therefore, a truism that the training of the raters is the most important requisite in the administration of a successful evaluation system. Yet even with training, some errors do creep into the rating process. The following are some of the more common errors:

    1. *Error of leniency.* The error of leniency is by far the most common of all errors in the rating of personnel. Leniency occurs when the supervisor rates higher than the realities of employee performance warrant. The effects of this type of rating are: (a) to force ratings so drastically toward the top of the rating scale that they are valueless to management; (b) to create unrealistic employee confidence when improvement in performance is really needed; and (c) to damage morale of the truly outstanding workers, who begin to wonder if it really pays to work diligently when the less proficient employee receives the same rating anyway.

        There are a number of pressures on supervisors which tempt them to be lenient—the wish to avoid unpleasant scenes; the feeling that low ratings reflect poor supervision; the desire to retain the friendship of their employees; and often the belief that other supervisors do not rate fairly, and they do not want to penalize their own employees.

2. *Central tendency error.* In any normal distribution, more people will be rated closer to the mean than to any other point on the scale. A rating near the norm becomes a central tendency error only when it does not reflect a true evaluation of performance. It is most likely to occur when the supervisor does not know a worker very well or when he has difficulty in collecting verifiable facts. The normal rating for either very good or very bad performance is unfair to the employee, his co-workers and management.
3. *Contrast error.* This type of rating error arises from the tendency of some supervisors to rate employees in terms of their own expectations and aspirations. Employees who satisfy the personal needs of the supervisor will generally be rated higher and vice versa.
4. *Halo error.* The tendency of raters to rate in terms of a very general impression rather than on the basis of specific traits is called a halo error. It occurs when the rater thinks in terms of the good or the poor officer and groups all the ratings (categories) for that individual at the high or low end of the scale.
5. *Association error.* This is referred to as the logical error and is similar to the halo type error. The association error is committed when the rater gives similar ratings to traits which seem to be similar. For example, when the rater assumes that if a person has good judgment, he must also have good presence of mind; if he is attentive to duty, he must also have a high degree of initiative.
6. *Overweighting error.* There is a tendency for raters to be unduly influenced by an occurrence, either good or bad, involving the ratee near the end of the rating period. This error often occurs when one or more outstanding occurrences near the end of the rating period are out of proportion to the average performance during the entire period.

Conclusion

Evaluations should be prepared from evidence collected during a particular rating period. Ratings for an established period should not be contaminated by observations carried over from some other period.

Raters must be given a deep appreciation of the great need to make evaluation reports valid and reliable indicators of performance if they are to have maximum value as a tool of supervision and management. If they do not reflect with reasonable accuracy the relative competency of personnel, the effort and expense involved in making and using the ratings is largely wasted.

Topics for Discussion

1. What is meant by humanism in command? How does this concept compare with the command leadership in your agency.

2. Distinguish between human needs and wants. Relate examples of particular wants to these needs.

3. In what way does the supervisor's desire for planning conflict with the needs of the individual and groups within an organization? Why do most supervisors have a desire to plan?

4. In your agency how does your immediate supervisor go about developing his subordinates to become more effective? Is your supervisor reluctant to spend too much time training his workers for fear that one of them may seek his job?

5. How is performance measured in your department? Does it relate adequately to the tasks expected?

6. Does your agency have a career development plan for employees? Is one necessary? Explain.

7. It is often said that a manager need not be a leader. What does this mean? In your department can you identify good managers who are also good leaders? Is the convergence of both in one person a matter of chance?

Supervisory Problems

PROBLEM #7—PROMOTION TIME—RATING PERFORMANCE

Background. A performance rating system to evaluate the promotion potential of sergeants and detectives was implemented in early 1972 for all qualified officers in the police department. Prior to this time promotion potential was based on scores achieved in a written examination plus points awarded for training and general experience. The new test added a new phase and allocated the tests percentages as follows:

Written examinations	40%
Promotional potential evaluations	30%
Training and experience	30%

The promotion potential evaluation was added to permit consideration of sustained performance over a significant length of time and a judgment of how well the applicant will perform if promoted into a higher position. The rating sheet for the new phase was divided into two parts. Part I consisted of personal qualities such as decisiveness, adaptability, appearance, ambition, and eighteen similar traits. Part II consisted of ten items relating to duty performance factors. Each item was assigned point values from "1" to "5."

Before candidates could be considered for this new evaluation phase, they had to first pass the written part of the test. If they passed the written part, two supervisors of the successful individuals, under whom each candidate worked or was supervised, were asked to evaluate and rate each one.

Problem. After a recent examination, twenty persons passed and were rated accordingly, using the new evaluation system. Immediately after the results were made known, four males voiced their objections to the ratings they received. The following points were the essence of their complaints:

1. Ratings were unfair, biased, and subjective.
2. In one instance a sergeant was asked to rate one of the candidates who was also a sergeant.
3. Some of the raters had been the immediate supervisors of potential candidates for only a short period of time and were therefore unable to rate the persons honestly and validly.
4. Three female officers were rated extremely high although they only had the minimum amount of time and experience in the department; consequently, there was the feeling that they were being pushed up the ranks for political purposes.
5. Raters were improperly instructed on how to perform the evaluations. (The local Civil Service Commission did, however, conduct a class for raters three weeks before evaluations were performed.)

Issues. The main area of dispute centered around the unfairness aspects of the evaluation phase because of the subjective nature of the evaluation. It was also claimed that the evaluations were arbitrary and should be eliminated from the promotional examination. Are there any other issues that you as Sergeant Albright, who has been appointed by the chief to monitor the promotional testing program, can see which may have also caused dissatisfaction? Can these areas of dissatisfaction be removed from any promotional examination?

Alternatives. What alternatives are available for Sergeant Albright to consider? What external policies or regulations must be considered for each alternative? Also discuss each alternative in relation to the apparent widespread approval of the new testing procedure by the younger officers in the department and the widespread dissatisfaction of the process by the older officers. As one of the alternatives, consider elimination of any kind of promotional examination.

Action Recommended. Assume that Sergeant Albright recommended to the chief that he attempt to reach some kind of favorable solution with the four men and the attempt was unsuccessful. The matter is now before the Civil Service Commission and the four are represented by the Union of Male Workers (UMW). Sergeant Albright, the department personnel officer and the raters of the four men were asked to be present. Immediately prior to commencement of the hearing, two of the four men withdrew their appeals. One candidate was not present because he was on vacation. He was later given a separate hearing. Officer Legalbegal, the one remaining officer, based his case on a city ordinance which forbade fortune telling. The section defined a fortune teller as "any person who pretends to tell fortunes for money or anything of value by reading cards or palms or by any other means shall be guilty of a crime punishable by. . . ." Legalbegal claimed that in an indirect way his taxes are paying the salary of the raters who are predicting future performances. Therefore the foretelling of the future falls within the prohibition of the ordinance and the promotional procedure violates the law.

Assume that the appeals of both officers were denied. What are the future consequences of the denial especially in light of the initially made five objections?

Disregarding the action taken above, do you believe there is merit in changing the promotion testing processes? Give reasons for your decision.

PROBLEM #8—MISUSE OF A WEAPON

Background. The Naughty City Police Department (NCPD) made a decision to increase its efforts to apprehend wanted suspects and ordered all officers to aggressively enforce the decision. Sergeant Nightengale did not like the order but said nothing. When the order was issued, a competition was organized between the shifts to reward the one shift which made the most apprehensions within a monthly period. Based on this the NCPD officers began to exert all of their efforts to fulfill quotas set by the sergeant in command of each shift.

The competition was fierce and even included weekly training sessions on the use of various weapons and the legal and departmental rules relating to the use of deadly force. The apprehension movement caught fire with all departmental officers who pressed for rewards for outstanding service.

The competition spread throughout the county. As a consequence, large numbers of wanted persons were arrested in a very short period of time. The movement was going well, but on one afternoon a tragedy occurred. A wanted man sitting on a park bench was shot and killed by Patrolman Quickflex who informed the man he was under arrest. When the victim started to stand up, he apparently brushed against Quickflex who thought he was about to be assaulted and fired in self defense. The victim was unarmed and was wanted for stealing some apples, a misdemeanor.

Problem. When Officer Quickflex kneeled over to check the victim he saw that the man was also a diabetic (by the wrist chain he was wearing) and that he was unarmed. He also noted that the victim had a clubbed foot. Immediately after the shooting, two other officers arrived. Several witnesses said they observed the incident and did not understand why the man was shot.

Chief Nonothing, after getting the information, rushed to the scene with two captains and the mayor. An ambulance also arrived shortly. After the slain man had been taken to the local morgue, the chief told Sergeant Nightengale to make a statement to the press because the chief did not wish to, at that time. He told the Sergeant that he wanted to have time to find a plausable reason for the slaying. Since nothing was coming from the police, the press developed as good a story as possible based on the skimpy information available. Many inaccuracies were in the newspaper articles published after the incident.

As a result of various news media stories, neighbors of the dead man were angry at the police. They wanted to do something to help his family as well as find out the truth.

Issues. Patrolman Quickflex was a young officer who was a hard worker. He was very eager to take part in the competition between the shifts to see which one could apprehend the most wanted persons. He was adequately trained in the use of his gun and thoroughly knew the various rules governing the use of deadly weapons. Sergeant Nightengale never hesitated to assign him to a detail to make arrests of any kind. In fact Sergeant Nightengale sent Quickflex to work the park where the shooting occured because of a recent increase in the number of assaults in the park. Because the crime was a misdemeanor, deadly force could not be used to apprehend the person.

The day after the incident, Sergeant Nightengale was called into the chief's office and was ordered to tell the reporters assembled that the dead man was in fact a felon and was exceedingly dangerous. As a matter of fact this was untrue and the Sergeant, while not absolutely sure, doubted the chief but still did as he was told.

An internal investigation was conducted of the shooting by Sergeant Hawkeye who concluded that the evidence verified that the shooting was unlawful; therefore, Quickflex had misused his weapon. This would be revealed in a coroner's hearing which was to take place in a few days.

Because the police department hesitated to publicize the truth, about 700-800 persons who lived in the dead man's community gathered in a park across from the police station and circulated among themselves and passersby a "white paper" accusing Officer Quickflex of committing a murder. More demonstrations were planned in the future to dramatize the killing.

Alternatives. Under the pressure of the above circumstances what should Sergeant Nightengale do? Of the several alternatives available, discuss the weak and strong points of each. What actions are available to Chief Nonothing? To the mayor? Are the alternatives available to the chief or mayor different from those available to Nightengale? Why?

Action Recommended. Which of the alternatives do you recommend for:

Sergeant Nightengale? Why?

Chief Nonothing? Why?

The mayor? Why?

What are the consequences of the initial indecision and the subsequent falsity recommended by the chief? Assuming the chief can weather the storm, what immediate actions should be recommended to prevent a reoccurrence? As a first line supervisor, what are your reactions to the entire factual situation?

PROBLEM #9—DID THE SUPERVISOR WAIT TOO LONG?

Background. Down Town is a city of about 15,000. It is the largest incorporated city in the county. The main trade in the immediate locale includes sport fishing, textile mills, and canning factories. It has one of the largest seafood canneries in the world.

The Down Town Police Department (DTPD) until a few years ago had a poor reputation, being criticized for its non-progressive attitude and lack of training. It employed little community support. During the past several years new leadership has been brought into the department. It has made significant efforts to change its image to become more trusted and respected by the citizens. Because of the success of its efforts the DTPD has been able to almost double the size of its department from 17 to 33. It is organized into patrol, investigation, and services divisions. The chain of command in the patrol division is the chief, lieutenant, three sergeants, and eighteen patrolmen. A city ordinance states that the chief or his assistant (lieutenant) can suspend officers, but to terminate an officer, the responsibility rests with the mayor.

Problem. One patrol officer has caused an internal morale problem and has several complaints from the community because of his abrasive personality and his approach in dealing with citizens in the community. He has been on the force for about eighteen months, is a graduate of a regional police training academy, and has the A.A. degree with above average grades. Because of his seniority, the officer, Patrolman Jones has been called upon to assist in the training of new officers.

On one particular occasion, the mayor was absent from the city, the chief was attending a meeting of the IACP and the lieutenant was on sick leave, leaving the sergeant as the shift commander. Sergeant Tough, on the evening in question had Patrolman Jones riding with a recruit for training. They were backed up by another probationary officer.

Patrolman Jones, while on patrol with the trainee, received a call to look into a gathering of young people in a city park. Upon arrival Jones found the young people lying on the ground in sleeping bags. They were asked to leave but did not do so quickly enough to satisfy Jones, who lined them up and asked for identification which he proceeded to check via his radio. No records were found. He then searched the youths without finding any contraband. Later two of the youths went to the DTPD and complained to Sergeant Tough that they were harassed and had not received their identification back.

Immediately after the incident in the park, Jones made a statement to the trainee accompanying him, that he kept the identification hoping that the two youths would become abusive and disorderly so he could arrest them. The trainee told Sergeant Tough about Jones' statement thereby affirming the complaints of the two young people.

The next day Jones was confronted with the facts by Sergeant Tough. He denied the allegation.

Issues. What issues did the above incident create, such as knowingly lying to the supervisor, Sergeant Tough?

Alternatives. What alternatives are available to Sergeant Tough? The lieutenant? The chief? The city manager?

Actions Recommended. What actions would you take if you were Sergeant Tough? What would be the consequences of your actions? Is this actually a supervisor's problem? Discuss.

ANNOTATED BIBLIOGRAPHY

Bopp, William J., *Police Personnel Administration* (Boston, Massachusetts: Holbrook Press, Inc., 1974). This text identifies the elements of public personnel administration and places them in a police context. It features a major section on labor relations in law enforcement, including implications for police management. The book's sections on "Manpower Development" and "Internal Affairs" are especially relevant to the two sections of this book concerning "Behavior Patterns of the Supervisor" and "Human Development." These two sections deal with problem-areas that the supervisor must be aware of such as training, personnel evaluation, leadership, communication, group dynamics and interpersonal behavior.

Clark, Donald E. and Samuel G. Chapman, *A Forward Step: Educational Backgrounds for Police* (Springfield, Illinois: Charles C. Thomas 1966). This book is about standards and why a college education should be adopted as a minimum requirement for policemen. The book presents the reasoning which prompted the Multnomah County Sheriff's Police Department to ask for the elevation of its minimum preservice entry educational standard. The book also presents material used to support the request for elevated standards, summarizes press reaction to legislative support, and police education in England and Wales.

Clark, Robert S., "The Police Administrator in a World of Research," *Police Chief*, Vol. 42, No. 12, December, 1975, pp. 50-52. In this article the author stresses the need for the modern police administrator to learn the language of science and to acquire the technical agility to separate findings from conclusions and recommendations. The author maintains it would take far longer to train the academic researcher in the nebulous reaches of criminal justice experience than for an experienced police professional to learn to understand the language and concepts of science.

Gilson, John W., John P. Hagedorm, and Roger F. Crosby, "Regionalized Personnel Development for Criminal Justice Employees," *Journal of Criminal Justice*, Vol. 2, Fall, 1974, pp. 243-248. This article discusses the Dayton/Montgomery County, Ohio Criminal Justice Center's first attempt at systematic personnel development for an entire criminal justice system on a regional level. Through its work in training and education, communications, career pathing and development, and system change, the Center has promoted the idea of an improved, symbiotic relationship among the major branches of the criminal justice system, and has acted as a catalyst for needed systematic change.

Pfiffner, John M. and Marshall Fels, *The Supervision of Personnel*, 3rd Ed. (Englewood Cliffs, New Jersey: Prentice-Hall, Inc., 1964). A basic text that all supervisors should study, its main theme is the need for human relations and human development in the management of men. The authors contend that productivity and healthy employee relationships go hand-in-hand. It views the superior-subordinate relationship as the very center of organizational life and much that happens around it is directly affected by its state of equilibrium. The sections of the book on "Training for Development" and the "Supervisor as a Developer" are especially pertinent for the police supervisor who wants to develop a better understanding of his role in relation to the men under and above him, and the organization he works for.

Soderquist, Larry D., "Upgrading the Service," *Police Chief*, Vol. 36 No. 8 (August, 1969), pp. 53-76. This article's basic thesis is that the police service needs to be upgraded. This upgrading can and should be effectuated by increasing the educational requirements for appointment to the police service. This article presents a view on the direction law enforcement education and training should pursue and holds that training is the key to human and organizational development.

Toch, Hans, J. Douglas Grant, and Raymond T. Galvin, *Agents of Change: A Study in Police Reform* (New York: John Wiley and Sons, 1975). This book presents a strategy and rationale for developing human behavior. The basic theme is that individuals can be reformed in their daily roles and can in turn cause positive changes in their groups and communities. The volume is based on work done in the Oakland Police Department between 1969 and 1971 under a training grant.

In the first stage of the book the authors work directly with a core of seven police officers who have records of participation in violent street incidents. Through revealing discussions these "problem policemen" themselves develop specific recommendations that can be implemented in changing police procedures and departmental structures.

NOTES

PART 3 HUMAN DEVELOPMENT

Supervisors View of Education

1. Bennis, "Goals and Meta-Goals of Laboratory Training," in Golembiewski and Blumberg (ed.), *Sensitivity Training and the Laboratory Approach* (1970).
2. *Supra* 1, p. 23.

PART 4

THE FUTURE
FOR
SUPERVISORS

The Study of this Part Will Enable You to:

1. Propose some of the new techniques of managing for supervisors.
2. Examine the nature of change and analyze the supervisor's role as a change agent.
3. Discuss the differences between planned and unplanned change.
4. Investigate some of the commonly found strategies and techniques for implementing change.
5. Analyze organizational development as it relates to the supervisor and illustrate its relationship to planned change.
6. Begin a discussion of managing by objectives.
7. Look at some of the problems of managing by objectives.
8. Examine goal formation from a practical basis.
9. Introduce some of the supervisory problems associated with increased education found among the police ranks.
10. Examine some of the new information and training required of the supervisor to perform his job efficiently.

Introduction

In preceeding parts of this book the discussion has centered around the central theme that a supervisor must possess a positive view of his worker's potential for commitment to the police department, and that only by proper leadership and wise supervision can their full potential be brought out. It has been seen that the supervisor has a formidable task in providing the worker with the opportunity for a challenging job, greater participation in decisions that affect him, and an opportunity for more self-determination in his job.

The supervisor of today is challenged by the needs of tomorrow. "Managing by Objectives" is a technique that is being viewed with more and more favor in all criminal justice agencies and police departments in particular. In terms of worker motivation, the system is of critical benefit to the supervisor. Where Management by Objectives Programs are used, their greatest effectiveness is derived by enlisting support of subordinates in the setting of objectives. When subordinates participate, there is the tendency toward greater motivational force because the objectives have been "established" by the subordinates and are, therefore, within their control. The MBO programs, in essence, are moving toward a joint establishment of performance goals which concurrently result in some sacrifice of the motivational force previously mentioned in order to obtain more coordination and contribution to needed organizational objectives.

Several important components are necessary in an MBO program even when it is only implemented by the first level-supervisor, in his unit. First of all, the supervisor encourages the subordinate to discuss his accomplishments in relation to previously set goals. Once this is accomplished the supervisor takes the lead in formulating goals for the next period, whatever it may be, with the full participation of workers in his unit. A system of measurement for reaching the goals must be devised, once again with the joint cooperation of the supervisor and subordinate. The last step is then for the subordinate to discuss his plans in relation to his present job and the newly established objectives in order to determine whether there are ways of improving or altering his performance to assist in reaching the objectives.

Managing by objectives is a tool that can be used by the patrolman as well as the chief of the department. For example the patrolman may set an individual objective of personally contacting five more citizens during his work-day. The first level supervisor may set as an objective a ten percent reduction in burglaries in his supervisory area. The chief may set a departmental objective of an overall five percent reduction of all serious crimes in the city.

New supervisory techniques will include a more democratic method of reaching decisions on matters affecting the individual worker. This is very important in relation to the concept of employee participation as it relates to the increasing trend toward police unionization. The concept of having group and individual participation in management decisions has some basic features affecting the drive for unionization. First, the final decision is more likely to be accepted by those affected. Second, the group undoubtedly has a keen interest in the quality of the decision because they have an interest in and knowledge about the problems covered by the decision. It must also be pointed out that the group envisioned might not be a labor union group, since unions frequently oppose participatory decisions because they tend to ally the employee with management. A corresponding reduction in the unionizing drive will likely result. If the union is to be viewed as a protector and protagonist, their increased alignment with management is detrimental to union security. The union needs and wants a participation program organized in a formal fashion and conducted through union devised processes such as collective bargaining and formal grievance procedures.

The supervisor is a key person in the concept of participative management. The supervisor must recognize that time may be sometimes taken from other tasks because the meeting of the group is the basic technique of implementing the program. Participative management requires considerable time for both the supervisor and subordinate to learn how to share in decision-making.

Development of an adequate communication system in the unit is becoming more and more important to the modern supervisor. All organizations require a communications system so the various parts and other components of the organization can be coordinated motivated, and directed toward common goals. If there are no patterns, either formal or informal, then only noise and confusion are created. Without formal patterns, people will informally structure their communications to effect problem solution and develop predictability in the organization. The communications systems in large complex organizations are intricate and sophisticatedly planned so that the decision makers are provided with the necessary information to solve problems. The lower level supervisor, while not concerned with developing a large complex communications system, must nevertheless have an effective way to secure and disseminate information of concern to the well-being of the unit as a whole and the workers individually.

The supervisor needs to keep in mind that he must be concerned with the discovery of subordinate feelings and reactions to orders and events. He must be attuned to the need for feedback regarding the orders—not so much to assume absolute compliance, but to secure information so he can correct or alter orders which may be unworkable, unduly burdensome, or which do not significantly contribute to achieving organizational goals.

The feedback in the communications process is indispensible to the supervisor because he never knows if communication has actually been effected unless he receives some specific response from the intended receiver. It takes two to communicate. If one speaks and no one listens, there is no communication. Feedback is necessary, therefore to ascertain the degree of understanding effected, and if a gap in communication exists, the supervisor should repeat the message to again effect the communication.

The police supervisor, in the future, will be faced with new challenges in the control of his unit. The subordinates, whether new recruits, just out of the police academy, or more experienced officers, are likely to be better trained, more highly educated, and have more of a sense of fairness in their dealings with the public than they have in the past. Blind obedience to orders will not be accepted. Rather than following a system of imposed controls on his subordinates, the supervisor will likely trust the subordinates to exercise self-control to a greater degree than has previously been the case. The supervisor will likely have fewer points where he exercises control. The supervisor in the future will quite likely jointly establish and enforce standards for subordinates. In this same view, the subordinate conceivably will be permitted to establish and enforce standards concerning his own work on the assumption that he is capable and committed to the goals and objectives of the organization.

In controlling the unit, the supervisor will have to develop an effective control system which must be geared to objectives of the unit. He must have learned from the past, in order to control the future. The control system that he utilizes needs to be adapted to the organizational structure to assist in ascertaining the responsibility (or lack thereof) by the individual worker. The future will also indicate a need for a more effective alignment of the rewards offered with the objectives emphasized by the controls. In addition, the cost of collecting information for control should not exceed its value. The information which is received by the supervisor must be timely so that he can use it before it is too late to effect the necessary control.

More and more emphasis will be placed on the supervisor to be an agent of change. As a general rule, changes on a significant scale issue from major forces external to the organization, i.e. demands for police responsiveness to the minority communities, upheavals in the constitutional rights of the public, inventions of new technologies, and so on. Such forces result in formation of a crisis for the police department as well as sub-units within the organization, which in-turn stimulate the necessity for change. The second phase frequently involves the use of outsiders to assist in department reevaluation and reorganization. Necessary information is then collected about the organization. A redistribution of functions and power are often characteristic of the successful changes. The supervisor, to be successful must continue the application of innovation.

The supervisor, before seeking changes, must carefully weigh the benefits versus the kinds of resistance to be encountered from his subordinates. What choices are open to the supervisor when significant resistance develops? One approach may be to make only changes which are recognized as being absolutely required. The supervisor should also seek to reduce the disturbance of formal and informal relationships while providing as much advance knowledge and information as possible about the change. Encouragement of subordinate participation in the change design and implementation serves to reduce anxiety and distrust. Subordinates should be given the opportunity for negotiation and other discussion pertaining to the possibility of future changes.

The role of the supervisor will continue to evolve because of new refinements of past supervisory theory and techniques. One thing, however, will remain constant—the need for a wise, understanding, and compassionate incumbent in the job. How he approaches his work to a vast degree determines the path that the department will take—whether it will be filled with problems and conflict or be a smooth operation. Certainly within his own unit, its success or failure will depend on his understanding of the dynamics of human nature, productivity, and motivation. As a leader his subordinates look to him for wise counsel. He does not fail.

THE POLICE SUPERVISOR AS A CHANGE AGENT

For our purposes, change agents are those individuals in our society who have the role of bringing about constructive change in individuals, social organizations, and social institutions. When one reflects on the job of the police officer, it is immediately discovered that one of the officer's job requirements is to influence people. For some patrolmen the influence is only a minor part of the job, but for others, bringing about change in people is a major ingredient in his professional role. For example, juvenile officers, community-police relations officers, patrolmen, to name a few, devote a large part of their time to the change enterprise—these professionals can certainly be called change agents. They use theories about and have an orientation toward the change process which guides their actions in almost every aspect of their work.

The change orientation of an officer is reflected in several factors present in the change agent himself. First, the philosophy that the officer has about change, his attitudes and value assumptions, determine to a great extent his success as a change agent. His philosophy significantly affects the manner in which changes are brought about. Second, the method or techniques of intervention used to produce change can have a positive or negative effect on the outcome of intervention. Third, the change agent must evaluate the feedback he receives to assess the effectiveness of the technique of intervention in bringing about the desired change. The effectiveness of the change agent is determined by the interplay of these three factors.

The change agent's philosophies and practices differ because of his varying concerns. The first is the concern for conformity to the change goal. For example, if a juvenile officer picks up a juvenile and desires to release him from custody after a counseling session, his goal is to return the youth to society without any stigma. The officer can believe that his philosophy and practice of returning the child to his normal social setting is best accomplished by showing the person the danger of his wrongful activities and instructing him on the proper method to conform to societal mores. The officer's concern for conformity is based on the idea that it may not be possible to change a person's attitude, but one can change behavior. By making it clear what is expected from the juvenile (changee) and what will happen if the changee fails to conform, the change agent (juvenile officer) can expect conformity. The change agent now has the clear responsibility to transmit the necessary information to the juvenile and then "follow-up" to see that the juvenile conforms and knows that the officer means business.

The second concern related to the change agent's philosophies and practice is one for the changee's commitment to the new standards placed upon him. Counselling sessions and follow-up activities by the change officer ascertain and reinforce the degree of commitment by the changee.

From this brief discussion, one can place the supervisor immediately in a position where he becomes an influencer—a change agent. In the contemporary police organization, funds are provided by federal agencies to facilitate change. Pressures from the community with regard to police operations create needs for change. Within his own organization, the supervisor is subjected to pressures by subordinates, superiors, and other supervisors to effect desired or directed change. Few supervisors are unaware of the hostility that large segments of any community hold toward the police. The supervisor has a direct interest in bettering this undesirable situation. The problem, however, is a two-way street. There may be little he can do to directly influence the public, but there is much he can accomplish within his own unit, for example, to influence the attitudes and behavior of his subordinates toward improving relations with minority groups. Setting an example or making a personal change such as refusing to use racial slurs in front of his subordinates can be an influence. Requiring simple courtesy from his subordinates when they deal with community members is an influence. Practiced individually or in combinations, such examples for subordinates have an indirect influence on the way the community views the police.

Understandably, the superior needs primarily to create many more favorable attitudes toward the change process among his subordinates. Without a change in attitudes, it is difficult to get acceptance of change or innovations that are so rapidly being adopted by progressive police executives.

In his position as an influencer, the supervisor sometimes must take corrective action when his subordinates appear to hinder or deviate from the goals of the department seeking to effect departmental change. The supervisor must identify sources of resistance to change and then attempt to provide the individual with information that might reduce the opposition. The supervisor also has the obligation to suggest a different design to the change program that may be more effective. By such measures he may be able to demonstrate to all concerned, that the change program is indeed worthwhile. Fortunately, suggestions sometimes come from the personnel, and may create (in the rank and file) a greater sense of dedication and input into the overall management of the organization.

In summary, the supervisor (by virtue of his position) needs to become a manager of change. He needs to know more about the processes of change, the type of behavior that change agents use, and the techniques for dealing with resistance to change. The following articles address these problems. A new dimension, mental health of police sergeants, indicates the kinds of new realizations that have been identified in contemporary police departments.

CHANGES IN ROLE CONCEPTS*

Understanding the forces behind the change of law enforcement policy and personnel is an increasingly vital concern of today's police administrator. The needs, expectations and demands of the public change with such disturbing rapidity that traditional social institutions seem to be constantly floundering, fighting hard just to keep up with the times. These pressures are felt directly by police departments and by the individual police officers within them. This research deals with one aspect of change in the police environment.

We all know that a man changes after exposure to the routines of police work. Obviously, the seasoned police officer is not the same man he was when he entered recruit training. Nor are his interests, his perceptions of others, or his fears what they once were. Furthermore, the changes a man experiences are not always for the better in

---

*SOURCE: Editorial, "Changes In Role Concept For Police Officers," reprinted by special permission of the *Police Chief*, copyright © 1972, by International Association of Chiefs of Police, Vol. 39, No. 7, pp. 14 and 81.

terms of occupational behavior and personal adjustment. It may be clear enough that change has occurred, but it is very difficult to know precisely what has happened or, ideally, what has caused it.

Almost all police administrators and trainers have wondered about changes which are taking place in their men. Some have thought about the changes which they themselves have experienced. IACP has now published the results of an extensive study covering the first 24 months in the occupational lives of a group of police recruits. The report of this research has something to say to all police and about all police.

Beginning in 1968 this research was undertaken to provide some objective evidence about the nature of personal change in the beginning police patrolman. The research was supported by a grant from the Center for Studies of Crime and Delinquency, National Institutes of Mental Health. The resulting report written by James W. Sterling, Assistant Director of IACP's Professional Standards Division, is called *Changes in Role Concepts of Police Officers.*

Although the work is indeed a formal study in the style of the behavioral science (including extensive documentation and an appendix of original test materials used to obtain the data), the book was prepared specifically for use by police officers. The author was guided by the premise that it was more important for the police to understand themselves than it was for social scientists to understand the police. This means that an effort was made to minimize scientific jargon and esoteric terminology in order to make the findings more comprehensible to the ordinary reader.

Changes in Role Concepts of Police Officers is the result of a longitudinal study of 113 young men in four different cities, who were tested and observed at three key points in their early police career: at the start of recruit training, at the completion of training, and after 18 months of experience on the job as patrolmen. The changes reflected in the subjects' responses to certain questions from one point in time to another were used to determine subtle shifts of role-related attitudes resulting from occupational socialization. The data is presented within the context of role theory and some introductory explanations are given about this theory and its application to the police recruit.

At the outset, the recruits who served as subjects in this research were about 24 years of age and came from stable middle-class families, many with long-standing roots in the community. Two-thirds of the recruits were married. An equal proportion had been in military service. Although all were high school graduates, only one-third of them had attended college. The majority of them were previously employed in lower middle-class jobs which paid less than their initial police salaries. Two-thirds of them already had experienced the effects of shift work on their life styles. The great majority of these men had been employed in jobs which dealt primarily with *data* and *things*. Few had any occupational experience in dealing with *people* nor did they have an interest in jobs which were primarily people-oriented. From the start, almost all of the men were highly satisfied with their new occupational role and they remained so throughout the study.

As one takes on a new role, certain aspects of personality are modified in accord with the demands and expectations of the new role. Because of this, some assessment of personality change was undertaken. The Edwards Personal Preference Schedule was used to measure change in personality needs over the time span of this study. By the completion of 18 months' experience as patrolmen, the subjects evidenced higher need scores in autonomy and aggression and lower scores in abasement, deference and affiliation. From this it was inferred that the subjects' general orientation toward people became more assertive and aggressive after police experience than at the time they originally entered law enforcement. Although this personality pattern is functionally consistent with the crime controlling, law enforcing component of police work, it is inconsistent with the public service aspects of the job.

Sharply etched in the data is the conflict between the officers' need to be authoritarian and impersonal in dealing with criminal matters while remaining capable of friendly and sensitive responses to people involved in non-criminal situations. This basic role conflict represents the underlying problem found throughout this research. In addition to this and other forms of role conflict, the occupational adjustment of these subjects was aggravated by increasingly unfavorable perceptions of various groups of people, the development of pragmatic and conservative attitudes, and the changing perceptions of role-related danger. Overall, the subjects were pictured as taking on a complex vocational role which was beset by ambiguities, conflicts and strains. The expansion of recruit training programs so as to allow a greater emphasis on the behavioral sciences was seen as a way of helping police officers cope with the occupational problems they inevitably confront.

A recognition of the need of the individual police officer for increased self-understanding is a theme that runs throughout the study. Self-awareness is seen as a fundamental prerequisite to understanding and responding to the needs of others. The study suggests that an increased emphasis on self-understanding during the formal police training program could provide valuable support for the man after he undertakes patrol duties. Particularly during his routine contacts with the noncriminal public, such background knowledge could be very helpful. To the degree that self-understanding contributes to self-acceptance, the exposure to new forms of training in the behavioral sciences should insulate the man from much of the strain and conflict found in one of the most psychologically divisive jobs that anyone can have.

The problems posed in this study regarding the initial socialization of the police recruit are pictured as complex and difficult to deal with. Consequently, a considerable number of ideas for new training strategies are presented. All things considered, there is hope that the problems related to changing role concepts can be dealt with positively. However, one should not underestimate the difficulty of the task confronting the police trainer. He must prepare men in the process of personal change to enact a changing role. Moreover, he can only influence the men directly during a relatively brief segment of time.

The virtue of a thing is that condition which enables it to perform ably its proper function. Thus, the virtue of a knife is its sharpness. Similarly, the virtue of a police trainer is his ability to affect men so they can stand the test of time. Such is the value of self-understanding.

IMPLEMENTING CHANGE THROUGH PERSONNEL PARTICIPATION*

Planning is a dominant characteristic of effective police management. The term "police management" is similar to management in the business world. It is necessary that law enforcement administrators realize that their problems are not unique, as was believed in the past, but parallel those found in other profit, non-profit and service organizations. Police administrators are finding that concepts developed through efforts of the business world in solving their problems are applicable in correcting situations in law enforcement.

The purpose of any plan or change is to provide for the rational direction of activities toward established goals and objectives. Basic

*SOURCE: William T. Gentel, "Implementing Change Through Personnel Participation," reprinted by special permission of the *Police Chief,* copyright © 1971, by International Association of Chiefs of Police, Vol. 38, No. 3, pp. 36-41.

administrative or management texts will point out that the *foundation* of any organizational structure evolves around the technique of planning, organizing, directing, controlling, coordinating and staffing. However, the first, planning, has become instrumental not only in solving problems and situations, but as an administrative tool for achieving the necessary professionalism required for effective law enforcement.

It has become clear to many chiefs of police that those who do not anticipate and prepare for the future usually discover a crisis when the future becomes the present. Therefore, a sequence of periodic planning when special problems are identified has become a necessary administrative practice. Obviously, as with any endeavor and particularly in planning, it is essential that a procedure be developed which will, as an end result, bring about a productive change.

As we examine general planning procedures, we find that, first, it is necessary to identify or recognize the fact that a change is required. This change may lie in the area of an existing departmental policy or an operational procedure applicable to only one segment of the total operation; usually, however, an insignificant change may have far-reaching ramifications which in essence affect the entire department.

Once the chief of police realizes that a change is called for, he then compiles all available information about the existing operation. Correct analysis of this data will direct him toward possible alternative changes, as well as providing structured direction which may either rectify the existing problem or create a new and innovative operation. When the path of change has been properly selected, the chief of police faces the task of implementation. Implementation involves more than the mere initiation of the proposed change, and will be considered in another segment of this article. Upon implementation, it is imperative that a follow-up program be initiated. This follow-up phase represents an administrative tool to evaluate the adaptability and success of the plan and identify its weaknesses.

If any one point in the administrative process were to be selected at which failure is most prevalent, or where the chief of police is likely to face the most resistance, it would be during the phase of implementation. Perhaps no other undertaking is as critical or as frustrating to a chief of police as when a plan, after being developed in detail, fails because of faulty implementation.

Implementation is often the weak link! A plan cannot function effectively if the environment for it has not been properly prepared in advance. Environment encompasses both the physical plant, and the personnel affected. Implementation is not merely ordering or placing a plan into effect, but is the process by which the chief of police gains the support and acceptance of those involved in order to facilitate a more productive change.

Once the chief of police recognizes the fact that implementation represents the weak link in carrying out changes effectively, he must familiarize himself with an administrative process which will be instrumental in achieving effective implementation. Perhaps no other process is as effective as *personnel participation.* Participation of those affected by decisions about their own welfare and working circumstances enhances compliance and commitment, and reduces misunderstanding and resistance. Participation can bring about high morale, better understanding and acceptance, and thus a more productive role of those involved. *Acceptance from those involved is essential!* Participation usually increases the interest of the department's personnel, and it helps to ensure that the change is relevant to problems as they appear in the daily operations of the organization.

Participation minimizes various other problems of implementation. One of the most predominant is resistance to change. Sources of resistance are complex because they relate not only to the individual's attitude toward the department and supervisory personnel, but are formulated around psychological characteristics of the individual's personality. If the department's command configuration fails to communicate, an atmosphere of suspicion and secrecy is created, thus leading to rumors and apprehension on the part of personnel.

Lack of understanding is another weakness which often breeds a reluctance to cooperate. The chief of police must furnish adequate background information relating to the circumstances which necessitate the proposed change in a clear, concise manner so as to alleviate misunderstanding on the part of subordinate personnel. If this process is not followed throughout the entire department, it will result in an ineffective change, because personnel cannot be expected to competently perform tasks they do not understand. This not only results in a reluctance to cooperate, but instills frustrations in lower echelon personnel which may impair primary law enforcement functions. However, utilization of the participation concept demonstrates a chief administrator's willingness to communicate and thereby helps reduce misunderstanding. This process also enables him to utilize the vast knowledge and experience possessed by subordinate personnel.

A well-structured chain of command will allow communications to flow upward, downward and laterally within the organization. Frequently in the past this has presented somewhat of a difficulty; in most cases there has been little concern regarding any kind of feedback. Even if there is feedback, the chief of police must consider the effect of *filtering*. This is especially true if the change pertains to a diversity that someone doesn't like. When querying command and lower echelon personnel the chief of police may well be told what the subordinates believe he wants to hear or only what they believe he should be told.

It should be obvious to a chief of police when examining the pulse of the department relative to a proposed change, that he will receive more competent direction for structured change if he encourages personnel "to tell it like it is."

Unfortunately, participation does not always run smoothly and neither are the participants always eager to accept the change even if allowed to participate. Nevertheless, the chief of police has the responsibility of creating a democratic organization which allows its members to be more than automatons—and this may be accomplished through participation. But, first he must consider who is to be involved in the participation? Do they desire to be involved? How will they react after the participation? How should this participation proceed? Should participants be consulted singly or as a group? These are questions the chief of police should consider.

Once the chief of police has identified and isolated the problem and carried out primary planning functions prior to implementation, he is prepared to begin a comprehensive dialogue involving participation.

With these correlative facts at hand, the chief of police is now in a position to present a clear and concise explanation of what is going to be tried, why it is necessary, and why he believes it will improve the service.

To introduce these proposed changes down through the chain of command and allow for active and effective participation he must utilize all levels of command personnel and the communication system, both formal and informal, which exist in the organization.

In analyzing the above theory, one may assume that the chief of police is dealing with an involved complex venture. Actually this process represents a simple and direct method relating to effective administrative practices. The following narrative demonstrates this hypothesis.

To initiate the participation process the chief administrator will call a meeting of his division commanders. These commanders represent the various divisions within the organization and constitute the administrator's immediate span of control. At this time, he will discuss the problem that has been identified and which he would like them to consider. This does not infer that the chief of police has called these commanders together merely to *tell* them that he has something to discuss, because this could imply that a decision has been made and a change is about to take place. At the first meeting, the chief is only explaining various facets of the problem he has identified. He indicates that he would like them to examine the feasibility of a proposed change. He advises the commanders to take the idea with them, study it carefully, discuss it among themselves, and on a specified date return for another meeting at which time a more concrete development of the change will be formulated, incorporating such changes as they recommend.

The chief should indicate at the first meeting that the proposed change and facts surrounding it are to be considered *confidential* since, after consideration, part or perhaps the entire change may prove undesirable. It is necessary that he point out from the beginning that each step, as it takes place, is just an exercise in "thinking out loud." From its conception there is nothing during the participation process which should indicate that the proposed change is actually going to be implemented—it is merely being thought about and examined for possible development. One of the reasons for following this policy is that if information pertaining to the proposed change reaches the general public or press, and the chief is queried for a policy statement relating to it, he is in a position to inform these individuals that this represents *only a proposal*. He may then explain that it is being discussed on a department-wide basis in order to ascertain the necessary facts and alternatives related to the proposed change, as well as the attitudes and opinions of those involved. The polling of department personnel through participation also eliminates embarrassing situations in which individual citizens know more, from reading newspaper accounts of department changes, than operating personnel on the street. It is somewhat embarrassing for an officer on the street to be approached by a citizen and asked about a particular change that is supposedly taking place and which he read about in the paper, when the officer, because of lack of communication, has no prior knowledge of the change or the facts surrounding it.

In scheduling a second meeting it is imperative at the onset that the chief establish a definite time schedule which will enable him to properly program the operation and additionally assure that the division commanders fulfill their responsibilities. The chief should appoint one of the division commanders to act as moderator. This further assures orderly development of the proposed change and compliance with the schedule.

At the second meeting, the chief accepts the various comments presented by the division commanders and additional recommendations and ideas are developed. After this meeting, the chief reviews these comments and recommendations and incorporates valid innovations into the proposed change. This process should allow the chief to develop or select various alternatives, any of which could adequately serve the purpose of the proposed change. At this point in the planning process, he has the responsibility to ascertain whether what has been structured justifies further consideration. If so, a third meeting is scheduled.

It should be emphasized that this process may necessitate a number of meetings, depending upon the complexity of the proposed change and the participants exchange of ideas to develop the plan.

At the third meeting, upon the chief's decision to pursue the change, the best alternatives which have been developed will be selected and assigned priority. The division commanders are now instructed to conduct meetings of their supervisory subordinates. In most cases, this will involve lieutenants and sergeants. The process now requires that each of the division commanders conduct meetings with their respective supervisory subordinates in the same manner as those attended by the chief and the division commanders. After the division supervisory personnel have had an opportunity to discuss and review the alternatives, recommendations are channeled upward through the chain of command to the respective unit supervisors. This would usually involve a lieutenant; however, the individual responsible may be of any rank, depending on the organizational structure in which the operation is taking place.

When this channeling process is concluded, a joint meeting is attended by division commanders and the unit supervisors. This meeting or whatever number are required, should develop firm structured alternative proposals at this level. After this has been accomplished, another meeting takes place between division commanders and the chief of police, again incorporating and developing valid recommendations received through division supervisory personnel.

The next phase of the procedure requires that the division commanders instruct their subordinate supervisors to meet with lower echelon personnel throughout the department and discuss again on the same plane the facts and alternatives relating to the proposed change. This exchange may be accomplished either through divisional meetings involving staff and line personnel or individual shift-change meetings conducted within the respective units. Of the two methods, the more fruitful in relation to constructive participation should occur at the shift-change meeting. Shift-change meetings, which are conducted in a more secure environment, are more productive and allow officers to express their opinions and contribute constructive criticism. It is imperative that presentation at all levels be consistent with the alternatives channeled down the chain of command. If supervisory personnel allow personal interpretation to affect segments of the proposed change, the various levels will not receive the same opportunity and exposure during the participation process. Upon completion of the lower echelon participation, the final recommendations are channeled up through the chain of command to the chief, and valid recommendations are incorporated into a final draft of the proposed change.

At this point, all levels of personnel within the organization have been exposed to the proposed change, and given an opportunity to participate in its development, thus reducing misunderstanding and resistance.

It should be stressed that the success of participation at this stage is dependent upon the channeling of *unfiltered* information and recommendations throughout the chain of command. The final evaluation and responsibility for adopting and implementation of the proposed change lies with the chief of police. No matter what the contention of those involved, whether it is affirmative or negative toward the proposed change, the final decision and responsibility rests with the chief administrator. It should, however, be obvious that whatever his final decision, the chief of police can create a more democratic organization, lessen resistance, and develop greater rapport and understanding through the participation process.

After achieving department-wide participation and selecting the most thoroughly developed plan, the chief is now confronted with various other preparations necessary prior to implementation. First, a department-wide indoctrination should take place. All personnel should be informed of the plan which has been accepted and exposed to a comprehensive explanation in printed form which is distributed to individual department members. The advantage of using a written communication is that less misunderstanding is apt to be encountered. The pre-implementation instruction should present the initial reason for the change, the date of implementation, as well as the responsibilities of individual personnel affected by the change.

Secondly, an analysis should be made to ascertain if the change incorporates responsibilities which require additional individual or departmental training at the in-service level. Many chiefs of police fail to recognize the unfortunate fact that, due to specialization, not all members of the department are adequately prepared to responsibly perform assignments which may encompass new and innovative change. An example of this would be a department integrating the patrol and traffic divisions into a single uniform division. Obviously, there are personnel in each of the respective divisions who are not adequately prepared to effectively accept the responsibility of the other. It may have been some time since a traffic investigator has had the responsibility of investigating a burglary or armed robbery. On the other hand, a patrol officer who frequently investigates these types of crimes may investigate only one or two traffic accidents each year. In most cases, this certainly would not involve fatality accidents, which are usually handled by specialized traffic investigators. These and various other situations confront personnel who are expected, on a specified date, to completely carry out operational changes which are to be implemented.

Thirdly, if the change requires the use of new or specialized equipment, e.g., electronic sirens, riot control devices or communications equipment, pre-implementation instruction is necessary.

No administrator should expect department personnel to respond to change without adequate preparation. Such preparation not only enhances the ability of the individual officer but enables him to effectively perform primary police functions with a greater competency.

As in any other endeavor, there are exceptions to the rule. It must be recognized that the participation process should not be used in all instances when change is necessary. Most changes incurred will be the sole responsibility of the chief administrator; therefore, his ability to adequately select proper areas of participation will facilitate the process. Furthermore, there may be circumstances when emergency situations require immediate change; e.g., legislative enactment, unexpected disasters or ineffective operational procedure that imminently endangers primary police functions.

In conclusion, one should realize that the participation process is not a complex venture requiring highly trained personnel, but a direct administrative tool available to those chief administrators interested enough to allow participation and willing to concede the fact that subordinates are prepared and eager to contribute their time, effort and ingenuity to improve their department. If there is the possibility that timely initiation of this process can improve morale, eliminate misunderstanding, enhance communication throughout the department, and increase service to the community, the chief of police should exercise his prerogative as an effective administrator and encourage departmental involvement.

ANTICIPATING POTENTIAL PROBLEMS OF
SUPERVISORS—MENTAL HEALTH*

From April, 1970 to April, 1971, a mental health pilot project was implemented in two geographic divisions of the Los Angeles Police Department. There were two main elements in the program. First, sergeants were trained in the early warning signs of emotional upset. Brief crisis intervention and counseling techniques were taught and referral resources were discussed. The rationale was that a wider range of emotionally based problems of policemen could be handled at the field level, on early contact, by sergeants who are the department's close contact line supervisors, thus maximizing the prevention of more serious outcomes. The second element in the project was the assignment of a psychiatric consultant to each of the two divisions to act as backup to the sergeants and as a mental health resource to the division commanding officer and his staff.

The main objectives of this project were: to utilize the concept of primary prevention in minimizing the likelihood of major emotional crises in patrol policemen and to broaden the base of human relations competence in the division supervisory staff by the availability of training and the expertise of professional mental health consultants. This could result in an increase in the functioning level of the line policeman by assisting him to recognize that stress factors affect his emotional reactions. It would also apprise him of the channels available to aid him in this regard.

Initially, the sergeants in the two divisions selected were given a 12-hour training program which included material in four main areas:

1. Emotional development, stress and personality.
2. Early warning signs of emotional upset.
3. Crisis intervention techniques.
4. Referral criteria, counseling limits, referral resources.

Subsequent to the initial training phase, the psychiatric consultant was available at each division for a minimum of two hours weekly for group discussion and various kinds of consultation. This ranged from individual case discussions to police community problems.

---

*SOURCE: Martin Reiser, Robert Sokol, and Susan Saxe, "An Early Warning Mental Health Program for Police Sergeants," reprinted by special permission of the *Police Chief*, copyright © 1972, by International Association of Chiefs of Police, Vol. 39, No. 6, pp. 38-39.

Before assuming their consulting role, the two psychiatrists underwent an orientation program to familiarize themselves with policemen, police work and the consultant role requirements. It was felt critically necessary that the consultant not only be knowledgeable regarding police functions but also sympathetic to the goals of police work.[1]

In order to coordinate the overall program and to insure achievement of its long-range goals, regular monthly meetings were held with the program coordinators, the psychiatric consultants, the two divisional commanding officers and the police administrators in charge of the project. It was predicted that the success or failure of the program would hinge largely on two central issues. First, that the personality and relationship-building ability of the consultant be positive; second, that the administrators and divisional commanders be involved and supportive of the project in order to reduce initial resistance and obtain a less biased evaluation of the program.

The original evaluation format included the use of a control division, the administration of before-and-after measures of attitude change and of supervisory efficiency. In addition, rating scales were designed to measure the effectiveness of the initial sergeants' training and the overall usefulness of the program at the six-month and one-year points of the pilot project.[2] We soon found, however, that widespread transfers of sergeants from the experimental and control divisions rendered the before-and-after measures useless. The evaluation finally relied upon the ratings of the training and of the overall value of the program.

The six-month evaluation using the rating scales revealed that with respect to the overall value of the initial training sessions, 81 percent of the sergeants involved rated the 12 hours of classes *Excellent or Very Good*, the two highest categories. In addition, 69 percent of the sergeants indicated that some attitude changes resulted from the training. Those areas of the training portion felt most helpful were the Early Warning Signs of Emotional Disturbance, Using an Adult Approach, and Counseling Techniques.

At this point in the program, several operational problems were apparent. The first was the difficulty in coordinating with the cooperating agency (Los Angeles County Department of Mental Health) to make two psychiatric consultants available quickly. Second, changes in assignment of commanding officers of both divisions and the resignation of one of the initial consultants disturbed the continuity of the program. A third difficulty was the widespread transfer (from the two experimental divisions) of many of the sergeants who had received the training. They were replaced by sergeants who had not had the initial training for this program. A fourth problem was the small amount of time the consultants were able to spend in the divisions. Two hours weekly were not sufficient for the consultant to adequately develop relationships with the sergeants on all three watches. Additionally, it minimized the amount of reinforcement training the consultants could provide the sergeants in group discussion. A fifth problem was that of a personality conflict between a psychiatric consultant and division staff members which resulted in interference with program identification and cohesiveness. This problem was resolved by replacing that consultant with one more able to generate positive regard among the division staff. A sixth difficulty was that the consultants sometimes confused their treatment and consultation roles. This also caused some uncertainty and raised questions about the sergeant's role definition among the police supervisors. These problems were confronted and discussed at the regular monthly program staff meetings. Eventually this led to either a resolution of the problem or to a considerable diminishing of its interference quality. At the six-month point, feedback from the commanding officers of both divisions, the psychiatric consultants and the sergeants was all largely positive.

The overall ratings from the final evaluation of the pilot project continued to be mainly positive. The commanding officer of both divisions gave the program the second highest rating on a five-point scale *(Somewhat Valuable)*. On all dimensions both captains also recommended further implementation of this type of program. The two psychiatric consultants rated the program either at the highest or next to the highest rank on a five-point scale *(Very Valuable or Somewhat Valuable)*. The consultants felt the greatest needs were maintaining continuity of consultative contact and periodic reinforcement of training for the sergeants.

The ratings of all the sergeant supervisors who participated in the program, including those who transferred in after the initial training had been completed, were fairly consistent. Twelve percent of all sergeants rated the program at the top rank *(Very Valuable)*; 61 percent rated the program at the second highest rank *(Somewhat Valuable)*; 6 percent of all the sergeants rated the program at the third rank *(Undecided)*; 21 percent of the sergeants rated the program *Of Little Value*; and none of the sergeants rated it *Worthless*.

In rating *Usefulness* of the project, the sergeants found it *Useful to the Supervisor, Not Too Useful for Use in the Community*, and *Useful With Fellow Officers*.

Final evaluation comments from the supervisors in regard to the training portion of the project indicate they preferred fewer lectures and more discussion of individual cases. More initial training time and periodic reinforcement were felt to be necessary. Sergeants also indicated a need for more frequent and regular meetings with the consultants. There was also a consensus among them that the consultants must understand police work and its attendant problems. As predicted in the initial project outline, the personality of the individual divisional consultant was a crucial factor in making or breaking the program. This requires that more careful attention be given to the screening and selection of psychological consultants.

A summary of the various ratings and feedback from all involved personnel—administrators, program coordinators, consultants, divisional commanders, and sergeant-supervisors—indicates that this pilot project was considered a success despite the multiplicity of problems mentioned above. Perhaps the strongest indicator of positive regard for the program is the fact that preliminary administrative approval has been given to apply for a federal grant in order to expand this program to all geographic divisions of the police department. If this attempt should prove successful, additional reports will be forthcoming.

DISCIPLINE: DOES INCREASED EDUCATION REQUIRE NEW SUPERVISORY TECHNIQUES?

Most professional police administrators agree that the minimum educational standards for a police officer is generally held to be a bachelor's degree. There is, however, some legitimate concern as to whether there *is* a need in fact to have police officers attain the college degree. The pros and cons of this argument are irrelevant for the first line supervisor who is finding a greater number of college educated persons coming into the police service at the patrolman level. As a consequence, the supervisor's style may be altered to fit the new personality types of younger officers.

The despotic and extremely authoritarian supervisor will be faced with a serious dilemma. He can continue his supervisorial style and perhaps force highly qualified, idealistic young officers to leave the department or he can alter his own behavior in hopes of improving the operations of his unit. The highly educated patrolman will quite likely resent supervisors who maintain discipline and productivity through the fear of punishment, tolerating no back talk or discussion, and demanding complete and immediate obedience to each and every order. The day of the "top-sergeant" syndrome in police supervisors is numbered, as the kinds of people he must supervise increases.

The new role of the supervisor is one of a trainer and developer of men. Thus, a clinical relationship is required, in which the object is to get the job done in a collegial setting. The supervisor's role is one of analysis in order to coordinate the diverse skills, attitudes, and personalities of those working in his unit.

The new recruits are more likely to have a questioning attitude. Before requiring a job to be done, the supervisor will probably be required to explain the reasons for the order and the desired outcome. This requirement quite likely will raise his supervisory skill by requiring him to evaluate carefully the manner in which he issues orders. If he is faced with the possibility of questioning by his own subordinates, he is more likely to weigh carefully any alternatives available to him.

The supervisor, in leading a new breed of police officer, will still have to contend with disciplinary problems. However, they are likely to be different in complexity and type. As mentioned in a previous part, motivation of highly skilled persons is somewhat easier than among the non-skilled. However, the job must be kept challenging, therefore the supervisor will have to use his ingenuity to create enthusiasm, interest, and desire among his subordinates. Because the new police officer will be inquisitive, he will constantly be seeking new ways to accomplish a task and in general, challenging the traditional. The supervisor must cope with this new behavior by being receptive to new ideas and change, otherwise disciplinary problems may arise solely because he is unwilling even to listen or to communicate his reasons for acting in a certain way, whether it is best or not.

In dealing with the college educated officer, the supervisor will likely be required to exhibit new supervisory techniques and thereby avoid possible conflict involving disciplinary problems. The supervisor must first seek to establish uninhibited two-way communication in a completely clinical approach to supervision. There must be mutual interaction between the men and their supervisor, thereby minimizing tension. As discussed above, the "first sergeant" method of supervision is counterproductive. A listening, guiding kind of supervisory behavior in place of reprimand, produces better results.

As problems develop, the supervisor can best solve them through individual and group consultation. Strict reliance on reprimands after rule or behavior transgressions will tend to create a worse disciplinary problem than if prompt corrective interviews occur. The supervisor of the future must endeavor to develop an approach to insure the upgrading of his workers in a calculated manner. He must not be so rigid as to forget that mistakes are a part of learning. In addition to accepting these many responsibilities, the supervisor must be willing to absorb some criticism from *his* supervisors while still pointing out that the growth of the person and department will be the end result of a reasonable amount of flexibility in both command and supervisorial levels.

The new emerging role of the police supervisor does not at all lessen his exercise of firm control where needed, but it does require the learning of new social skills and knowledge. These will at times be in conflict with the traditional aspects of police supervision and disciplinary measures. The anguish of those who grew up under benevolent despotism may become evident through their highly vocal criticisms. For the supervisor the pains of change will be fierce, but the highly educated persons sought for police work today necessitate change. New supervisory methods do not cut the effectiveness of the police response to society; rather they decrease potential disciplinary problems, thereby improving effectiveness.

POLICE AND HIGHER EDUCATION*

Law enforcement has been considered so important that during the past decade it received no less than three inquiries from Presidential Commissions: (1) the 1961 President's Commission on Civil Rights and Law Enforcement, (2) the 1967 President's Commission on Law Enforcement and Administration of Justice, (3) the 1968 President's Commission on the Causes and Prevention of Violence. A consensus on the status and future of law enforcement was succinctly summed up in the following statement by the President's Crime Commission:

> Widespread improvements in the strength and caliber of police manpower, supported by a radical revision of personal practices, are the

*SOURCE: "The Police and Higher Education: The Challenge of the Times," by Lee P. Brown is reprinted from *Criminology* Vol. 12, No. 1, May 1974, pp. 114-124 by permission of the publisher, Sage Publication, Inc.

basic essentials for achieving more effective and fairer law enforcement. Educational requirements should be raised to college levels and training programs improved. Recruitment and promotion should be modernized to reflect education, personality, and assessment of performance [President's Commission on Law Enforcement and Administration of Justice, 1967: 106].

To that end, the commission recommended that "the ultimate aim of all police departments should be that all personnel with general enforcement powers have baccalaureate degrees" (President's Commission on Law Enforcement and Administration of Justice, 1976: 109).

This recognition of the need for higher educational standards for the police is not new; to the contrary, as early as 1931, the Wickersham Commission made similar recommendations. Nor have the need and recognition disappeared. This is evident by the work of the National Advisory Commission on Criminal Justice Standards and Goals and its Advisory Task Force on Education, Training, and Manpower Development. This commission has, for the first time, established quantifiable standards and goals for law enforcement. Having a special task force to cover the topic of education, training, and manpower development is significant because if we are to take seriously the whole concept of improving an inadequate system for criminal justice administration—if we are seriously dedicated to eliminating the inequities in the existing process—we must place paramount emphasis on the education, training, and manpower development of the people who operate the system. It is imperative that we look beyond the formal organizational structure and deal with the realities of the informal structure—specifically the human aspect of the system. The caliber of police service rendered to any given community is dependent upon the competency of the policemen. It is not possible to separate the performance of a police agency from the abilities of its personnel. Laws, rules, and regulations, are not self-executing. No function of a police agency has meaning except as it is planned, directed, and carried out by people. If police service is performed well, with fairness and equality for all, communities may have peace and tranquility; if performed poorly, we have only to look back in history for the results (see National Municipal Commission, 1962).

Police work is a complex task. For that reason, it is imperative that those involved in the policing function possess a high degree of intelligence, tact, common sense, emotional stability, impartiality, honesty, and education (President's Commission on Law Enforcement and Administration of Justice, 1967: 125). Yet, while commission after commission and expert after expert have articulated this need, "communities have not yet demanded that officers possess these qualities, and personnel standards for the police service remains low" (President's Commission on Law Enforcement and Administration of Justice, 1967: 125). We must, as stated by Bittner (1970: 83), "abolish permanently the idea that is all too prevalent in our society that if one does not want to take the trouble of becoming something worthwhile, he can always become a cop."

Improvements in the caliber and educational level of police personnel are imperative if we fully recognize the fact that we are indeed undergoing a social revolution in this country. It is this social revolution which is presenting new and serious problems for the police. Joseph Lohman (1966), late Dean of the School of Criminology, University of California at Berkeley, discussed this social revolution in the following terms:

> The contemporary American revolution involves three factors: the explosive rate of population increase; the doctrine of civil rights; and ideological force which has no precedent in recent history; the impact of technology which is producing a shape of things for which we have not bargained and which is profoundly affecting many individuals. These tremendous changes are more than facts in themselves—they are the condition for the creating of a new pattern of human relations in this country.

As the relationships generated by this contemporary social revolution become even more complex, the black and white absolutes in which the police have traditionally dealt are becoming totally inadequate. We are constantly being confronted with a bewildering array of new problems for which the traditional views are hardly a match. In order to function in a society characterized by massive socioeconomic problems; examples being poverty, unemployment, mental illness, family conflicts, discriminatory practices, just to name a few; we need a *new policeman*—one who understands the complexities of human life—one who is able to understand the legacy of discrimination in this country and reflect positively upon the demands for "freedom, justice, and equality"; one who is able to understand the philosophy of dissent; one who understands that he has a legal and moral obligation to be responsive to the people—all the people and not merely the prevailing power structure in his community; one that understands and is able to conduct himself in the manner dictated by the legislature and the courts. To build this *new police*, we must develop on the local level a police force which is just as professional, if not more so, as law enforcement agencies at the federal level.

To do contrary is to invite dishonesty, unequal enforcement, and community chaos. If one were to just reflect upon Toffler's *Future Shock*, it would be difficult to understand how we can continue to take a twenty-year-old, with only a high school education or less, provide him with a few hours of training and then release him in the community and expect him to cope with complicated and demanding societal problems when the problems themselves defy solution.

> It is nonsense to state or to assume that the enforcement of the law is so simple that it can be done best by those unencumbered by a study of the liberal arts. The man who goes into our streets in hopes of regulating, directing, or controlling human behavior must be armed with more than a gun and the ability to perform mechanical movements in response to a situation. Such men as these engage in the difficult, complex, and important business of human behavior. Their intellectual armament—so long restricted to the minimum—must be no less than their physical prowess and protection [President's Commission on Law Enforcement and Administration of Justice, 1967: 126].

If the police are to be effective in this urbanized, existential society which is characterized by conflicting values and interests and differential means and opportunities, they must be able to function in a role that transcends that of the layman and outside the personal biases and prejudices of the individual. There is the need, in other words, to develop within the policeman a real sense of professionalism. Police service, similar to law and medicine, is a profession of high "calling." The importance of police service to any given community clearly distinguishes it from "just another occupation." Police service requires a high degree of knowledge and technical skill. The most important knowledge is an understanding of self, society, and the individual differences that make up a community. The most important skill is the ability to effectively relate to people under both normal and abnormal circumstances. The time has surely passed when a man is assumed to possess this fundamental knowledge and basic skill just because he dons a uniform, straps on a gun, and flashes a badge. Education, training, and manpower development are certainly the cornerstone of modern police work. And these are never-ending functions. The policeman must never be allowed to forget the role he plays as a symbol of society's authority. He must constantly examine his personal attitudes, feelings, and sentiments as they relate to his public duty and obligation. He must be wholeheartedly dedicated to achieving true impartiality and neutrality—being guided not by a powerful few, but by what is morally right and by his legal obligations. This acquisition of knowledge and skills, this dedication to service will not occur through osmosis. Rather, "this is an educational problem in its own right, and it is equal in importance to the acquisition of new information as to the technicalities of crime detection" (Lohman, 1967).

It is an axiom that the effectiveness of a police department is directly related to the support it receives from the community. The respect, and thereby cooperation, a citizen gives to its police is dependent upon the degree to which police service is impartially administered. This is particularly true of minority groups who have little reason to respect and cooperate with the police if they do not receive equal protection from the police. The fair and impartial enforcement of the law builds respect not only for the police, but also for the government in general. If the police cannot by deeds and actions demand that respect, they will not be successful in dealing with the many conflicts that arise between groups and individuals who belong to different groups. There is a natural tendency for those who are part of a system to label those who are at odds with that system as being alienated or estranged. With the emergence of increased polarization—blacks and whites, young and old—more and more groups of people are being labeled as alienated and estranged from both the conventional norms of society and the social institutions. In examining this phenomenon, it is essential to keep in mind that we are being confronted with a crisis in our traditional institutions. This crisis situation is explored in the anthology put together by Skolnick and Currie (1970) entitled *Crisis in American Institutions*. Based upon the realities of that work, and with respect to law enforcement, what is referred to as declining respect for the police may very well be a crisis of the police institution. Police service itself might very well be referred to as alienated and estranged from the people rather than the reverse. In examining this possibility, the words of Socrates, the Greek philosopher, should be kept in mind: "He who first gave names and gave them according to *his* concept of the things which they signified, if his conception was erroneous, shall we not be deceived by him?"

Over a generation ago, William James pointed out that there are basically two orders of knowledge. First, there is the formal *knowledge about persons and things*. Second, there is that equally important knowledge which arises through *acquaintance with persons and things*. Reflecting upon that observation, Lohman commented that it is a unique condition of crime and criminal justice that much of the existing criminal justice educational programs are a reflection of these two orders of knowledge. A substantial portion of police science, or criminal justice programs, if you prefer, is a product of experience of police officers in attempting to control crime. This kind of knowledge, though necessary, is not completely adequate. Correspondingly, if the criminal justice programs offered by colleges and universities are to have an impact upon the police, there must be a change in the colleges' and universities' programs themselves. Although our primary goal must be to change the police institution, the first condition for bringing about those changes through education is to change the college and university criminal justice educational programs. Otherwise, there will be an absence of relevant and effective knowledge and little or no communication.

Based upon the James observation, colleges that presume to offer education for police service must have an acquaintance with the police function, as well as formal knowledge about it. Presently, this is not reflected in much of the traditional subject matter of many of our so-called criminal justice programs. Taught by the retired or ex-law enforcement official, too many of the existing criminal justice programs are merely a perpetuation of what has already been recognized as a failing system. What the police need is not so much classes in the details of police administration, but rather, classes dealing with the fundamentals of public administration illustrated by case material from the police establishment. The colleges and universities currently have in their programs of behavioral and physical science the subject matters which the police require. The police do not need any new special courses which are uniquely distinguished from the liberal arts tradition; rather, they need some materials sensitively communicated and illustrated to illuminate the real problems which confront the police. The college need is for instructors competent in the humanities, and the behavioral and the physical sciences who can, in their course work, make constructive application of the concepts and generalizations of their knowledge to the field of criminal justice (Lohman, 1967).

Clearly, this is not the case today. Through financial support supplied by the Law Enforcement Assistance Administration, we have seen a rapid growth in the number of colleges and universities offering criminal justice programs. A report distributed by the International Association of Chiefs of Police shows that the number of community colleges offering such programs has increased from 152 in 1966-1967 to 505 in 1972-1973. Similarly, the number of four-year institutions offering programs has increased from 39 in 1966-1967 to 211 in 1972-1973 (International Association of Chiefs of Police, 1972).

Addressing himself to the status of community college programs, Saunders accurately pointed out that such programs "are an educational no-man's land, without recognized standards for course offerings or their content, quality of instruction, or awarding of credit" (Saunders, 1970: 101-102). The President's Commission on Law Enforcement and Administration of Justice (1967: 127) reached a similar conclusion when it reported:

> The Commission's examination of these programs disclosed that many of them are highly vocational in nature and are primarily intended to provide technical skills necessary in performing police work. College credit is given, for example, for such courses as traffic control, defensive tactics and patrol procedures. Although there is a need for vocational training, it is not and cannot be a substitute for a liberal arts education.

Baccalaureate criminal justice programs also suffer from their inability to provide a curriculum that provides students with a strong liberal arts education. To the contrary, they reflect an "academic dryness or lack of nourishment. Course offerings change little and chew over and over the standard fare with comparatively infrequent introduction of the new" (Brown, 1965: 9).

It is realistic to assume that the emergence of new criminal justice educational programs will increase rather than decrease. This is particularly true if police agencies appeal to educational institutions to assist them in implementing the standards of the National Advisory Commission on Criminal Justice Standards and Goals (1973) that call for:

1. Every police agency should immediately require as a condition of initial employment the completion of at least one year of education (thirty semester units) at an accredited college or university. Otherwise qualified police applicants who do not satisfy this condition but who have earned a high school diploma or its equivalent should be employed under a contract requiring they complete the educational requirement within three years of initial employment.
2. Every police agency should, no later than 1975, require as a condition of initial employment the completion of at least two years of education (sixty semester units) at an accredited college or university.
3. Every police agency should, no later than 1978, require as a condition of initial employment the completion of at least three years of education (ninety semester units) at an accredited college or university.
4. Every police agency should, no later than 1982, require as a condition of initial employment the completion of at least four years of education (one hundred twenty semester

units or a baccalaureate degree) at an accredited college or university.

Police officials should rightfully be acknowledged as the experts in police work. Criminal justice educators, on the other hand, must be acknowledged as the experts on criminal justice education. Taken in that context, the responsibility is on criminal justice educators to develop an individual for a career in police service. This point was alluded to by Kreml (1966: 34) when he wrote, "A well-trained man is a man competent in his profession, his occupation, his job. A well-educated man is a man competent in his values, his standards, his criterion."

The challenge of criminal justice educational programs is to produce the well-educated man.

More important, college and university programs must be prepared to pave the way for innovations and changes in the police system. The mere placing of new faces with the same knowledge in leadership positions within the police establishment will not produce changes. Therefore, colleges and universities have a moral obligation to produce change agents—change agents that understand bureaucratic procedures and the reluctance to deviate from the status quo; change agents dedicated to and capable of challenging all of the existing assumptions held by the police and, where necessary, implementing radical changes. This is the challenge of higher education.

Criminal justice educational programs can best meet their challenge by developing a curriculum that will "provide students who are interested in the general area of law enforcement with a liberal arts education with an emphasis on social science disciplines" (Lejins, 1970: 28). Professional programs of the "how-to-do-it" type do not meet the needs of modern policing. The key to being a good policeman in modern society is to understand people, self, and society. This can best be accomplished by developing criminal justice curricula that are strongly oriented in the behavioral sciences (see Tenney, 1971). They should have their goal "to provide an officer with a broad knowledge of human behavior, social problems, and the democratic process" (American Bar Association, 1972: 217).

Effective collegiate impact on the police system cannot be made by offering courses which are best described as gadgets and gimmicks. Colleges and universities must assume the role of being the advocates for changing the police system. By doing otherwise, colleges and universities do a disservice not only to the police but also society. It must be clearly understood that unequal application of the law does not just happen. Rather, it is directly related to the power structure of our society. College criminal justice educational programs must be operated with this consideration in mind.

In conclusion, change in the American police system will not occur unless there are substantial efforts made to upgrade police personnel. The American people are demanding better, fairer, and more efficient application of the law. Educational institutions have a tremendous role to play in this endeavor. Likewise, police personnel must commit themselves to responding to this demand. The continuing education process for police personnel is one means of keeping in tune with the rapid changes that are occurring in our dynamic society.

CHANGING NATURE OF POLICE ORGANIZATIONS: A NEW SUPERVISORIAL CHALLENGE

During the past two decades there have been drastic changes in the police service. The beat cop was replaced by highly mechanized, mobile police in the 1950's. Largely because of this step, the officer became a stranger to the community he served. His estrangement subjected the police to charges of being too impersonal during the civil confrontations in the 1960's. In the current decade, the police realize they cannot operate in isolation from the community, courts, prosecutors, and corrections agencies. There needs to be a team effort between the community and the police in order to fight the onslaught of crime in America. Even the best police agency will falter unless its community supports it. Conversely, citizen support will be ineffective where the police are incompetent and inefficient. Cooperation by both is mandatory.

Only when the *need* for change is acknowledged, can it be accomplished—not before. Both the community and the police are encouraging new ideas and are receptive to new approaches to performing police services.

Vast changes are continually being made in police service delivery systems. Police methods are changing. Compact computers and teleprinters in police automobiles, helicopter patrols, and highly sophisticated mobile crime laboratories are now very common. Communication centers, not dreamed of twenty years ago, are commonplace. Automated data records and data retrieval systems have made it possible to maintain a more thorough police administration system permiting more consistent opportunities for supervision and management. These and various other examples of organizational change have resulted in new supervisional stresses. How well he copes with the tensions has a direct bearing on how well the police organization carries out its mission.

The supervisor who operates in a progressive, innovative police department will probably note the trend toward decentralization in organizational processes and decision making. The supervisor is likely to be given the opportunity to participate increasingly in making decisions that affect him and his subordinates. He should then take steps to increase the participation of his subordinates in this decision making. The supervisor in more decentralized and democratic police organizations will find himself making greater use of persuasion and negotiation in dealing with his workers. The supervisor will note that these two techniques are more effective than authority, in up-dating organizations.

In progressive police organizations, the supervisor will find himself in a position to utilize subordinates in positions where they can perform competently. He will undoubtedly be consulting with everyone in the unit before making important decisions, and he will enjoy a teacher-student, rather than a master-slave relationship with his subordinates.

The supervisor must take certain steps to prepare himself and his personnel for organizational change. First of all, he needs to neutralize subordinate resistance and establish support for change by using such techniques as rewards and threats, rationality and indoctrination, cooperation and replacement, and camouflage and diversionary tactics.

Second, he should devise methods of showing subordinates the organization is becoming consumer oriented. To accomplish this, the supervisor needs to institute certain measures; opening communication in his unit, supporting tolerance, reducing unit rigidity, reducing reliance on formal authority, and emphasizing decentralization of authority.

The supervisor must be aware that changing police organizations and consequent changing supervisory methods will undoubtedly be ruffled when moving from the traditional bureaucracy to the new. There will probably be frustration for the individuals involved, and subordinates will likely demand they not be subjected to threatening changes. They will demand stronger rules for personal security and may attempt to disrupt the new organizational process in order to emphasize their dissatisfaction with their new responsibilities. Lastly, the subordinates will insist that their morale is being lowered (this is often a sham to embarrass the supervisor). However, the author believes that the supervisor who understands and believes in the concept of organizational change will also believe that the above techniques pay off in developing a more effective, community oriented police department where each police officer can achieve a higher level of work satisfaction and professionalism.

ARE CURRENT PROMOTIONAL EXAMINATIONS VALID?*

The examinations given by public agencies are coming under closer scrutiny. The federal government is examining them for cultural bias, since there are employees who feel they were not given the best opportunity on these tests to prove themselves qualified for promotion. It is difficult to test for leadership, judgment, and supervisory ability, so our organization generally chose an oral board with members who had these qualities, hoping they would be able to identify the same qualities in the candidates.

There are few areas in the public service where promotional examinations have as much long-term consequence as they have had in the police and fire service. Their promotional examinations generally are open only to members of the department (except for the top ranks), and employees often spend their entire career in a single department. Ultimately, the quality of the selection procedures used influences the quality of the services provided by the department.

Employees in the uniformed service complain, with much justification, that existing examination procedures do not give them a fair chance to demonstrate their leadership or the human skills which are needed at supervisory levels. In effect, the examination process has not been able to address itself to the expanding roles of the police officer and fireman or to identify the command qualities needed for supervisory ranks. To some extent limitations in the testing procedures have been recognized at lower levels and some attempts at improvement made for lower levels of jobs. An attempt has been made to "test" for the desired traits in rookie patrolmen through

---

*SOURCE: A. N. Pauloionis, "The Value of Promotional Examinations for the Police and Fire Ranks," *Public Personnel Management*, Vol. 2, May-June 1973, pp. 179-181, reprinted by permission of the International Personnel Management Association, 1313 East 60th Street Chicago, Illinois 60637.

psychological examinations. It is common to have candidates for fire engineer pass a qualifying driving examination. Command officers, however, are still rated on the basis of how they answer questions in an oral interview.

Obviously, we can say that the man who passed the driving test will be able to perform similar tasks on the job. It is less certain that the candidate who made a high score in the interview will make a good supervisor or command officer. Even if he does, other candidates cannot be reassured that the successful candidate was chosen strictly for his leadership qualities and not for some other trait such as verbal fluency.

There is great value in using practical examinations as part of the promotional examination so that the candidate can demonstrate his ability to perform some of the tasks he would have if he were promoted. Why not have the candidate interview suspects, handle irate citizens, take command at the scene of a hypothetical (but realistic) fire? Is this not what they will be doing, with greater efficiency, when they are promoted?

Will the candidates make charges that this test situation is unreal or creates undue "pressure"? On the contrary, it is our experience that practical examinations which include tests for these higher skills are well received by all candidates. These examinations give them a chance to be tested for job-related traits and abilities and actually help them to demonstrate their leadership, judgment, and intelligence in a way they were unable to before. In effect, this type of examination recognizes the full scope of their jobs, not just the lesser tasks that are easily tested.

Outline for a Practical Examination

The practical examination is meant to supplement, not replace existing procedures. One way of weighting the parts of a total examination would be to have one-third written (could be qualifying), one-third oral, and one-third practical. Such a weighting would include phases of the examination process the candidates are used to, but also give the candidate the best overall opportunity to demonstrate his qualifications.

The primary goal of such an examination is to give each candidate the best possible opportunity to demonstrate his job-related skills and talents, rather than to serve unrelated goals which sometimes take precedence, such as the elimination of candidates or the creation of a list of eligibles of dubious validity. The examination plan should be tailored to meet the individual needs of each department, and the personnel specialist preparing the examination should work closely with the department training officer to ensure that the procedures are technically accurate and in accordance with departmental procedures.

To prepare an effective practical examination, these key elements should be included:

1. *Orient the Candidates* in sufficient detail regarding the situation that the elements of the test situation not physically present are easily imagined. Tell the candidate what assumptions can be made regarding the situation, how it differs from the same situation as he would encounter it on the job, what the limitations of his authority are, and what simulations represent.

His orientation should include a written narrative of the background of the situation (build the scene) and a familiarization with the physical scene to acquaint the candidate with any substitutions being made. The candidate must be basically as familiar with the scene as he would be with any he would encounter on his beat or at the scene of a fire. Of course not all the places where calls for service may occur are physically familiar to public service officers, and officers may be dispatched to new territories in emergencies. But as long as the mock situation is clearly defined, there is no undue ambiguity inherent in the simulated situation. For example, explain to the candidate for fire captain that he has two men to give orders to and that all the equipment found on a fire engine are laid out on the ground for his use.

2. *Create a Decision-Making Situation* so the candidate has to perform an act which can not only be evaluated for conformance to sound practices and policies, but where lack of action would constitute an improper action. To be effective, this confrontation should require the candidate to make a quick decision. This can be achieved by the use of an obviously changing situation or by the presence of a superior officer who gives follow-up commands to the candidate. If a superior officer is to be used, the candidate should be instructed to expect and take commands from the superior officer in accordance with departmental procedure.

A variety of situations can be created, limited only by the imagination of the test constructors, so long as the situations are realistic and do not place the candidate in physical danger. A candidate for police sergeant can be examined on the way he supervises two rookies (one of whom loses his temper) in a confrontation with potential rioters who are using abusive language. A candidate for fire captain can be ordered to engage a fire on the roof of a multistory building. He can then be rated on his reaction, first to an unexpected cry for help from a victim, then by a subsequent order to abandon the building.

If the promotion is to a supervisory class, the test definitely should include a command situation. It could also include more mundane situations, such as the assignment of routine tasks like clerical or maintenance work to an unwilling subordinate.

3. *Orient the Raters* who should be chosen with care to include officers of higher ranks, including, if not entirely composed of, outside raters. They should be given written guidelines and score sheets and be briefed on what would be the appropriate and acceptable actions to be taken by candidates according to departmental policy and regulations.

Benefits of Practical Examinations

This type of examination system creates a heightened awareness of training. During the intervals between examinations the men now are thinking more in terms of "How would I handle this situation if it came up in the exam?" They will be thinking in terms of how to react to situations (application of theory) rather than how to answer multiple choice questions (theory). Since the situations that come up during the examination are some which logically may come up in the line of duty, the department has a better trained and better motivated force.

Also, since sound practical examinations are well received by candidates because the logic for testing for job-related tasks is self-evident, there are fewer appeals, and any that arise are easier to defend than those about the standard written-oral combination. Practical examinations take more thought and preparation, but provide more than a corresponding reward in examination validity, employee satisfaction with the testing process, and, ultimately, a better quality of service to the public.

Topics for Discussion

1. How have changing attitudes and other cultural factors affected the job outlook of supervisors in your agency? Do you think there is a different job perception of supervisors who have held the position for a number of years than the younger, newly appointed supervisor? Explain your answer.
2. Who should be involved in the change effect in the police department? In your discussion, consider the effect that higher level administrators have on changes thought to be necessary by first line supervisors.
3. What are the objects of seeking change? What new behaviors are desired and why do the persons not want changes to be made?
4. What effect will the infusion of large numbers of college graduates have in a police department, relative to disciplinary problems and procedures for handling them?
5. What is meant by participatory management? How will the supervisor effect this form of group decision making?
6. If significant resistance to change on the part of subordinates is encountered, what supervisory approaches can be taken? Discuss each in the context of supervisory problems in your agency.
7. Of what importance is feedback in the communication process?
8. Discuss the need for developing an organizational communication system.

Supervisory Problems

PROBLEM # 10—THE CASE OF THE ILLEGAL COFFEE FUND

Background. Corporal Mensrea was in charge of the Records Bureau in the Snipe Police Department (SPD). He had one secretary to assist him, Miss Bygolly. The Records Bureau was in charge of departmental records, purchasing, and financial matters in the department. The SPD had a complement of sixty-six sworn police officers.

Problem. One afternoon, Chief Eagleeye was in the Records Bureau when he noted an insurance agent at the counter buying an accident report copy. Miss Bygolly made the copy, accepted a check from the agent, went to her desk, wrote out a receipt, and gave it and the copy to the individual who then left. A few minutes later a civilian came in asking for an accident report copy. Miss Bygolly made the copy and collected $2.00 in cash for the report. She then went to Corporal Mensrea's desk, took a receipt book from his desk, and gave the citizen a receipt from it.

The chief returned to his office and called in Corporal Mensrea's supervisor, Sergeant Iampure. He was told what the chief had observed, was admonished, and advised to look into the situation immediately.

Sergeant Iampure summoned Miss Bygolly to his office. She at first denied using two receipt books, but when confronted with the Sergeant's evidence, broke down and confessed to using two receipt books. She had been doing this a number of times and volunteered the statement that Corporal Mensrea was completely aware of what she was doing. In fact she gave the Corporal the money which she recorded in the receipt book in his desk. She denied ever using the money for her own personal use. Sergeant Iampure took a written statement and presented it to Chief Eagleeye who discharged Miss Bygolly on the spot.

The sergeant then returned to his office, called in Corporal Mensrea and confronted him with the evidence. He denied any knowledge of the two receipt books, but when confronted with the secretary's statement, admitted that it was true. According to him the money was not used for personal matters but rather for coffee for the records room, and the rest of the headquarters. Some of the money was used for small supply items used around the office. Mensrea stated that the desk sets on Iampure's and the chief's desks were paid for by the fund. While he was unsure of the amount of money spent from the fund, he said it could not have been over a hundred dollars. Sergeant Iampure then took a statement from the corporal and gave it to the chief. Iampure recommended that Mensrea be suspended immediately pending a more detailed investigation. This suggestion was accepted by the chief.

After a subsequent investigation during which the receipt books were seized and audited, it was found that $120.00 was recorded in the book found in Corporal Mensrea's desk. After counting the money on hand and adding the items purchased, it was ascertained that the Corporal had in fact not used the money for personal matters.

Issue. As Sergeant Iampure, what do you believe are the main supervisory issues involved in this situation? Is there a larger management problem revealed? What is it? Can the issues which Iampure isolates be solved completely by him?

Alternatives. What alternatives are available to Sergeant Iampure.

1. Take no action and reinstate the corporal
2. Oral or written reprimand
3. Additional alternatives which are available

Discuss each alternative fully. Also, since Miss Bygolly has been fired, what is to be done about her? She has threatened to reveal the entire incident and institute legal action to get her job back if the corporal is treated differently from her. She was merely acting under his guidance.

Actions Recommended. Which of the alternatives do you recommend? Why? Also state your reasons for rejecting the remaining. Assume that Corporal Mensrea was demoted. He immediately stated he would appeal to the city personnel board and make the incident public. The chief, after consultation with the city manager then discharged Mensrea outright. In your opinion, what would be the consequences of the latter action? Consider that Mensrea had twelve years in the department, was well liked, and that the morale in the department was already poor.

What are the consequences of the chief's actions on the difficulty with Miss Bygolly?

In handling this entire incident would it have been advisable to go slowly in recommending outright discharge of personnel until all ramifications of action can be assessed based on collection of all the facts? Discuss.

PROBLEM #11—IS THE PROBLEM A LACK OF EXPERIENCE?

Background. This incident occured in the city jail in Coosa City, which has a population of about 300,000 persons. Prior to 1965, the city had no jail; rather all arrestees were taken immediately to the county jail which was directly across the street from the Coosa City Police Department (CCPD). Since 1965 Coosa City has had its own police department jail. The majority of the jail personnel had less than ten years experience in police or jail work. Only one person has over twelve years of police service. The jail organization has continued to grow rapidly both in physical size and numbers of personnel.

Officer Shifty, thirty-nine years old, married and the father of four children, had been assigned to the Jail Division for seven years, the total length of his service with the CCPD. He was as competent and knowledgeable as other jail personnel and had received good ratings by the Jail Division Commander, Sergeant Lockup.

An inmate in the jail had been properly tried, convicted and sentenced to three years on probation with three months to be served in jail. Prior to bailing on the charge, the inmate served two days in jail. The two days were not credited toward the three months. With good behavior and several other credits under state law, the inmate was due to be released on December 26. On December 22, Sergeant Lockup was asked by the inmate to be released two days prior to his scheduled release date of December 26, so that he could spend Christmas with his family. Lockup checked his jail record and found that the inmate had been granted all of the allowable days reduction in his jail term. The request was denied because there was no legal means available to permit early release.

On December 26, Sergeant Lockup was reviewing previous releases from the jail and found that the inmate in question had been released from custody on December 24. He then checked the jail record of the inmate and noted that in addition to the jail credits already mentioned above, the inmate had been given two extra days credit for the time served awaiting bail. No initials were on the record showing who made the entry. The jail watch corporal on duty when the inmate was released was called in by Sergeant Lockup. Both checked the record again and found that the court commitment did not grant the two extra days served before the bail as part of the inmates total jail time. Both agreed that the inmate was released early.

Officer Shifty was next called in and freely and immediately admitted that he altered the card. He likewise admitted that he knew the inmate had not been given the two days credit for the time served. Shifty stated that he had come to know the inmate and his family quite well. When asked by the inmate for help in securing an early release, Shifty said he felt compassion for him and gave him the two days so that he could be with his wife and children for Christmas.

Problem. Sergeant Lockup now was sure that Officer Shifty changed the records of the jail inmate without proper authority or direction. The change in the record resulted in release of the prisoner two days early in violation of the court order.

Issues. As viewed by Officer Shifty, two more days in jail certainly would not have furthered the course of justice. The inmate and his family would benefit more from the early release than the benefit derived by the state by keeping him in jail. Shifty also thought that compassion dictated early release because no one would be hurt by a simple act of kindness. He was also of the opinion that since he might come in contact with the inmate in the future, there was a possibility of helpful information being provided on future cases.

Alternatives. Officer Shifty could have been given an oral or written reprimand by Sergeant Lockup. What other alternatives are available to Lockup? Should Lockup seek action outside the department against Shifty? If so, what kind? What mitigating factors may Lockup take into consideration?

Actions Recommended. Which of the alternatives would you as Sergeant Lockup choose? Why? Suppose Shifty was given a severe oral reprimand with the understanding that any other action of this type would result in an immediate suspension and referral of the case to higher authorities for formal disposition. If Lockup took this approach, one of his reasons would be that Shifty had a long and favorable record in the CCPD and was too well-trained and valuable to lose. What would be some additional considerations that would justify Lockup's severe oral-reprimand?

What are the consequences of the action taken from personnel and supervisory points of view? Would a strong or moderate supervisory response by Lockup have a more positive effect in preserving the already good morale in the CCPD jail division?

PROBLEM #12—POLYGRAPH USAGE—A SUPERVISORS PROBLEM

Background. The Purity Police Department (PPD) has a complement of ninety-five sworn officers and eighteen civilians. All of the employees are under the state merit system and, as such, may appeal personnel decisions (relating to them) to the Purity Personnel Board. If the grievant is not satisfied he can then appeal to the Purity City Council for an open or closed hearing depending upon the wishes of the individual. Three Sergeants, High, Low, and Blank, comprised the internal investigations unit in the PPD.

Problem. Six months ago a sizable amount of heroin was seized during a drug raid. A few days after the seizure, the heroin was discovered to be missing from the PPD evidence room where it had been stored. Two days later the loss of the evidence was admitted in court. Subsequently, all charges were dismissed, the persons arrested were released, and the news media wrote highly derogatory news stories about the PPD.

Chief Likeme appointed Lieutenant Covert to investigate the incident, but he was soon relieved due to his involvement in the drug raid but mostly because several high ranking officers had mentioned his possible implication in the loss. Sergeant Forthright, one of the best supervisors in the department, was given (by Chief Likeme) the job of investigating the loss. Forthright, with the chief's approval, immediately requested aid from the State Attorney General. One investigator and one polygraph specialist were assigned to assist in the investigation. During the investigation, several police personnel were asked to take a lie detector test administered by the state agent. At a later time two of the persons were asked to retake the test because of small discrepancies in their stories. One agreed but Detective Lieutenant Wiseacre refused. He was summoned to Chief Likeme's office and was *ordered* to retake the test. He still refused and the chief reluctantly suspended him from duty until the Purity Personnel Board could resolve the matter.

Lieutenant Wiseacre had fifteen years service on the PPD and had the reputation (among the men in the department), of being a stubborn man with a strong ego problem. Only a few of the detectives were able to get along with him, although he had the reputation of being honest. Wiseacre believed that he could not be *required* to take even one polygraph test, let alone two, but had taken the first in deference to the chief's call for the investigation. Wiseacre assumed he had the right to refuse and asserted his rights, in refusing the second polygraph test. Wiseacre was the last person known to have had control of the missing heroin.

Issues. Chief Likeme and Wiseacre had had a close personal relationship prior to this incident. The chief considered it to be his duty however, to get to the bottom of the whole affair. Because of the professional clash, the situation deteriorated into one of "personalities" between the two. Chief Likeme and Sergeant Forthright surmised that the disagreement would cause a morale problem in the department if the investigation were not actively pressed.

An important factor in the investigation was that the evidence by the investigators and Sergeant Forthright, although circumstantial, pointed the guilt directly toward Lieutenant Wiseacre. The circumstantial evidence plus the poor results from the polygraph caused the investigators to look more closely at the lieutenant as a prime suspect. The refusal to take the second test convinced them that he was the guilty party; or if he was not, then he knew who was. While attempting to remain impartial, they found it hard to believe a person who refused to take the second lie detector test.

Lieutenant Wiseacre stated that his refusal was a matter of principle. He was of the opinion that he was being framed by other members of the department who were jealous of his close relationship with Chief Likeme.

The Chief concluded that the refusal by Wiseacre was an admission of guilt. But what bothered him most was the fact that Wiseacre could put him in such a position because of their past close personal relationship. The personal blow was compounded because Chief Likeme was grooming Wiseacre for bigger and better things. Refusing the polygraph test amounted to a personal slap in the face.

Alternatives. As Sergeant Forthright, do you believe the chief's initial suspension was justified? Give your reasons. What other alternatives could you have recommended other than suspension? Support each by giving your reasons. What would be the likely consequences of each alternative if it were accepted?

Assume that after a thirty day suspension Lieutenant Wiseacre returned to duty and was then transferred to the early morning patrol shift for three months. After that he was transferred to the records room on the same shift. Other undesirable and menial tasks were in store. (What appears to be happening? Is this a sound alternative for you to recommend?)

What other alternatives can you consider? Do not forget that Lieutenant Wiseacre still has an appeal pending before the Purity Personnel Board. Consider each alternative in light of an acceptance or rejection of Lieutenant Wiseacre's appeal.

Action Recommended. Which alternative do you recommend? Why? Should the polygraph continue to be used in internal investigations? What will be the effect of the recommended action on the morale of the department? On supervision at the line level? How will the recommendation be accepted by the city council? Discuss fully.

ANNOTATED BIBLIOGRAPHY

Coppock, J. Laverne, "Evolution in Police Management," *Police Chief*, May, 1972, pp. 18–19. In this article, a chief of police urges the incorporation of the newer behavioral concepts of organizations into the police organization. He perceives the police supervisor as a change agent and shows by his first hand experience that the best way to implement change is through personnel participation.

Hanna, Donald G. and William D. Gentel, *A Guide to Primary Police Management Concepts.* (Springfield, Illinois: Charles C. Thomas, 1971). This text was written for the purpose of identifying the basic weaknesses in police management and to recommend practical guidelines which may be followed or modified by the police administrator in the performance of his management responsibilities. Such issues as the planning and decision-making process, training, education, and personnel confrontations are discussed in detail as they relate to the police supervisor.

Kenney, John P., "Team Policing Organization: A Theoretical Model," *Police*, August, 1972. This article depicts a new conceptual model for a police organization which is a drastic breach with tradition. Team policing is presented as an "ideal" to be strived for which can reduce the rigidity and the tension building features of current approaches to organizations. It provides a supervisor with the means of involving the "new breed" of police officer who brings to the department, talents and potential capabilities superior to his predecessor. Management personnel assume responsibility for broad policy making, planning of operational activities, dealing with substantive issues regarding personnel, operations, budget, unusual situations and community relations. Operational personnel become concerned with routine day to day operations and implementation of broad policy guidelines laid down by the management team.

Lynch, Ronald G. *The Police Manager*, Boston, Massachusetts: Holbrook Press, Inc., 1975. This text seeks to provide a specific step-by-step procedure for police managers to become more effective in executing their assigned duties and responsibilities. The book is basically a practical application of the principles of business management to Police Administration.

The book includes sections on leadership behavior styles, management by objectives, decision making, and demands on the manager's time as they relate to the police organization. The last section concentrates on problems that a modern police manager will encounter when implementing change within the police organization of the future.

Nursey, James, "Management by Objectives: Applicability in Law Enforcement," *Police Chief*, April, 1975, pp. 36–37. A police sergeant maintains that police managers and supervisors must recognize that law enforcement personnel, not unlike employees of organizations in the private sector, need to be motivated, periodically evaluated, and satisfied if organizational goals are to be met. Management by objectives provides a means of meeting these requisites to organizational success.

Pursley, Robert D., "Traditional Police Organization: A Portent of Failure?" *Police*, October, 1971, pp. 29–31. In this article the author maintains that the traditional police organization will fail in all but the smaller departments because of its inability to contend with two major factors: (1) society and its power to redefine aspects of the police role, and (2) rising level of expectation and self-concept among the younger and better educated police officers. The author stresses that police agencies of the future must deemphasize the military standards and trappings and reorganize around a social service model of total integration within the department.

Shanahan, Donald T., *Patrol Administration, Management by Objectives*, Boston, Massachusetts: Holbrook Press, 1975. This text focuses on the need for a management by objectives approach in the area of patrol administration. The book attempts to point out the several areas where job enrichment can be realistically innovated in the patrol function so that officers will be motivated to develop within patrol rather than transferring out of the unit in the police organization. Special emphasis is placed on newly developed and innovative programs such as team policing, joint citizen-police committees, and lateral entry into the operational field. The main theme is that the police manager has an enormous spectrum of ideas available for creativity and innovativeness that are now ready to be operationalized.

Steinberg, J. Leonard and Donald W. McEvoy, *Police and the Behavioral Sciences*, Springfield, Illinois: Charles C. Thomas, 1974. This book is a collection of readings from the behavioral sciences with their major emphasis centered on human relations training for police officers. In addition, this compilation includes reports of programs in areas of recruitment, selection, and organizational development.

Whisenand, Paul M. and R. Fred Ferguson, *The Managing of Police Organizations*, Englewood Cliffs, New Jersey: Prentice-Hall, Inc., 1973. This book is a multi-dimensional approach to the theory and practice of managing a police organization on the city and county level. It draws heavily from behavioral research findings and existing innovative management styles. In regard to future trends in supervision it stresses the participative style of managing human resources, the changing nature of police organizations, and the police manager as a change agent.

Special sections deal with role conflict within the organizational frame-work in a third-party role as intervener in internal conflict; the concepts of authority and power, and the need for new leadership styles among police managers.

PART 4 THE FUTURE FOR SUPERVISORS

Anticipating Potential Problems of Supervisors—Mental Health

1. Reiser, Martin: The Police Psychologist as Consultant, *Police*, 1971, 15 58–60.
2. Sokol, Robert J. and Reiser, Martin: *A Primary Prevention Proposal Utilizing Early Warning Training and Divisional Mental Health Consultants*. Los Angeles Police Department, 1970 (Mimeo).

Police and Higher Education

American Bar Association (1972) "Standards relating to the urban police function." New York. (unpublished)

Bittner, E. (1970 *The Functions of the Police In Modern Society*. Washington, D.C.: National Institute of Mental Health.

Brown, W. P. (1965) "The police and the academic world." *Police Chief* 32 (May).

International Association of Chiefs of Police (1972) *Directory of Law Enforcement and Criminal Justice Education*, Washington D.C.

Lejins, P. O. (1970) *Introducing a Law Enforcement Curriculum at a State University*, Washington, D.C.: Law Enforcement Assistance Administration.

Kreml, F. (1966) "The role of colleges and universities in police management," *Police Year Book*. Washington, D.C.: International Association of Chiefs of Police.

Lohman, J.D. (1967) "The police and higher education: the current challenge to the colleges." (mimeo)

– – –(1966) "Current decline in respect for law and order." (mimeo)

National Advisory Commission on Criminal Justice Standards and Goals (1973) *Task Report on Police.*

National Municipal Commission (1962) *Government for Tomorrow's Cities: A Report*, New York: McGraw-Hill.

President's Commission on Law Enforcement and Administration of Justice (1967) *The Challenge of Crime in a Free Society*, Washington, D.C.: Government Printing Office.

Saunders, C. B. (1970) *Upgrading the American Police: Education and Training for Better Law Enforcement*, Washington, D.C.: Brooking Institution.

Skolnick, J. H. and C. Currie (eds.) (1970) *Crisis in American Institutions*. Boston: Little, Brown.

Tenney, C. W. (1971) *Higher Education Programs in Law Enforcement and Criminal Justice*. Washington, D.C.: Law Enforcement Assistance Administration.

INDEX